Aggressive Nationalism

AGGRESSIVE NATIONALISM

MCCULLOCH V. MARYLAND AND THE FOUNDATION OF FEDERAL AUTHORITY IN THE YOUNG REPUBLIC

RICHARD E. ELLIS

OXFORD
UNIVERSITY PRESS

2007

OXFORD

UNIVERSITY PRESS

Oxford University Press, Inc., publishes works that further
Oxford University's objective of excellence
in research, scholarship, and education.

Oxford   New York

Auckland   Cape Town   Dar es Salaam   Hong Kong   Karachi
Kuala Lumpur   Madrid   Melbourne   Mexico City   Nairobi
New Delhi   Shanghai   Taipei   Toronto

With offices in

Argentina   Austria   Brazil   Chile   Czech Republic   France   Greece
Guatemala   Hungary   Italy   Japan   Poland   Portugal   Singapore
South Korea   Switzerland   Thailand   Turkey   Ukraine   Vietnam

Published by Oxford University Press, Inc.
198 Madison Avenue, New York, New York 10016

www.oup.com

Oxford is a registered trademark of Oxford University Press

Library of Congress Cataloging-in-Publication Data
Ellis, Richard E.
Aggressive nationalism : McCulloch v. Maryland and the foundation of
federal authority in the young republic / By Richard E. Ellis.
p.   cm.
Includes bibliographical references.
ISBN 978-0-19-532356-6
1. McCulloch, James W.—Trials, litigation, etc. 2. Maryland—Trials,
litigation, etc. 3. Bank of the United States (Baltimore, Md.)—Trials,
litigation, etc. 4. Banks and banking, Central—Law and legislation—
United States—History. 5. Exclusive and concurrent legislative powers—
United States—History. 6. State rights—History. I. Title.
KF228.M318E45 2007
346.73'0821223—dc22   2006100984

1 3 5 7 9 8 6 4 2

Printed in the United States of America
on acid-free paper

FOR MY CHILDREN, WHO HAVE MADE ME
A TRULY BLESSED PERSON:
ISOBEL AND JON ELLIS
DANIEL ELLIS
REBEKAH ELLIS AND MIKE ANTONAS
DEBORAH ELLIS

ACKNOWLEDGMENTS

During the research and writing of this book I have incurred many obligations which I am pleased to recognize. Research for the book, which is part of a much larger project on the transition from Jeffersonian to Jacksonian democracy, was made possible by grants from the John Simon Guggenheim Foundation, the National Endowment for the Humanities, and the American Council of Learned Societies. I also received support from the Thomas Lockwood Chair in American History at the University of Buffalo. I owe a particular debt to the late Gerald Gunther of the Stanford University Law School who encouraged me to take on this project and helped point me in a number of fruitful directions. I have also received various favors from Alfred Konefsky, Rob Steinfeld, and Don McGuire. Lynn Mather of the Baldy Center for Law and Social Policy of the University of Buffalo arranged a book manuscript workshop where Mark Graber of the University of Maryland and Martin Flaherty of the Fordham University School of Law made a number of helpful observations. Of great value also were the comments of the anonymous readers of the manuscript for Oxford University Press that were both encouraging and useful. James Cook, my editor at Oxford, was enthusiastic about the manuscript from the beginning and has been a pleasure to work with. Finally, I am enormously grateful to Mike Antonas, a high-powered engineer in his own right, who diligently typed and computerized the manuscript.

Finally, there are my grandchildren, Zachary Antonas, Joseph Ellis, Alexander Antonas, David Ellis, Zoe Antonas, Michael Ellis, and Sarah Moses, who I hope someday will enjoy seeing their names in print. Although they contributed nothing directly to the manuscript, they have immeasurably enriched my life.

CONTENTS

AGGRESSIVE NATIONALISM

INTRODUCTION

During the struggle over the ratification of the U.S. Constitution in 1787–1788, James Madison responded to Antifederalist criticism that it created a consolidated national government by pointing out in the *Federalist*, No. 39, the numerous powers retained by the state governments. He concluded by famously observing that "the proposed Constitution . . . is in strictness neither a national nor a federal Constitution, but a composition of both."[1] Madison was, of course, right. Yet at no point does either he or the Constitution itself precisely explain how power is to be shared by the different governments. As a consequence, what has been termed *intergovernmental relations* has been a recurring and controversial issue since the adoption of the Constitution in 1788. The most serious efforts to resolve this question have come in decisions handed down by the U.S. Supreme Court. And of those decisions none has proved to be more significant than *McCulloch v. Maryland* (1819), which most scholars consider to be one of the most important decisions ever handed down by the U.S. Supreme Court.

Unquestionably, much of the praise for the decision, if extravagant, is merited. For it is brilliantly argued, far reaching in its implications, and unusually eloquent. Among other things, it provides an enduring nationalist interpretation of the origins and nature of the Constitution and the union and a broad definition of the necessary and proper clause (Article I, section 8), which has laid the foundation for the living Constitution, and with it the means for an almost infinite increase in the powers of the federal government. It also contains an explicit narrowing of the meaning of the Tenth Amendment, the bulwark of states' rights thought. Major excerpts from Chief Justice John Marshall's decision in *McCulloch v. Maryland* are included in every casebook on constitutional law, and its findings—the constitutionality of the Bank of the United States and the prohibition it imposed on the states against taxing it and its branches—are described in just about every textbook on American history.

It is surprising, therefore, that no in-depth study of *McCulloch v. Maryland* has been published before now. What treatments exist of the origins of the case and the constitutional issues involved in it are to be found in various general histories of the U.S. Supreme Court and in biographies of John Marshall.[2] Unfortunately, these analyses of the case tend to be done almost exclusively from the vantage point of Chief Justice John Marshall's decision. No attempt is made to examine the case from the point of view of the losing side, which is to be regretted because it dealt with relevant and important issues, many of which are crucial to understanding the case.[3] Indeed, the chief justice chose not to consider many of these arguments in his decision, probably because they would have seriously undercut his own argument. In fact, what Marshall mainly did in his famous decision was to reiterate the arguments of the attorneys for the Second Bank of the United States (2BUS). Modern-day constitutional scholars who have treated the case have also tended to ignore a number of astute treatments by financial and banking historians of the early nineteenth century, which shed useful light on the economic issues of the time, for *McCulloch v. Maryland* is, after all, a case that was profoundly influenced by the banking problems that existed in the early nineteenth century.[4]

Three arguments in particular against the 2BUS were ignored by Marshall. The first had to do with the essentially privately controlled and profit-making characteristics of the bank. Private investors owned 80 percent of its stock and elected a similar percentage of its board of directors. The bank made a profit by lending money at interest, by various investments, and by charging fees for its financial services to everyone except the federal government, which it was prohibited from doing by the provisions of its charter. It almost immediately turned out to be a very profitable institution, which led to a sharp increase in the value of its stock and the payment of high dividends. Although it performed a number of important financial services for the federal government, it hardly qualified, in many people's minds, to be considered an instrument of the federal government, which is the way Chief Justice Marshall characterized it in his *McCulloch* decision by claiming it was analogous to the mint, the post office, the custom house, and the federal courts.

A second issue had to do with the relationship of the 2BUS and its branches to the state governments. The charter granted to the 2BUS by Congress in 1816 gave it the right to establish branches wherever it saw fit. Many states viewed this as an assault upon their sovereignty and believed a state's permission should be required in order to establish and maintain a branch within its boundaries. Many states also feared that the establishment of branches by the 2BUS would adversely affect the revenue stream they obtained by taxing and regulating their own locally chartered banks by taking business away from them and by being a more profitable investment for local capitalists as a consequence of not being subject to state taxes. Beyond this, some feared that other national corporations, particularly lottery and insurance companies, might also be established that could operate within a state and yet be beyond its control.

Finally, there was the question of state taxation of the branches of the 2BUS. The only taxes explicitly prohibited to the states by the U.S. Constitution were import and export duties. In *McCulloch v. Maryland,* Marshall argued that "the power to tax is the power to destroy." To be sure, the purpose of the taxes levied by Kentucky and Ohio was to drive the branches of the 2BUS out of their states. But the tax levied in other states, particularly Maryland, which was of central importance because it was the tax being ruled on by the U.S. Supreme Court, was clearly for revenue purposes and was no higher than the taxes it levied on its own chartered banks. This raised some very difficult issues, about which there was much uncertainty and confusion, even among supporters of the 2BUS. What, in effect, Marshall did in his famous decision was to use a case that came up from Maryland to rule on developments in Kentucky and Ohio, even though the issues involved were significantly different. Consequently, he totally avoided discussing the differences between a tax levied for revenue purposes and one that was meant to make it impossible for a branch to continue doing business in a state.

These were all significant and potent issues, and it is no wonder, in light of Chief Justice Marshall's unwillingness to deal with them, that many people at the time found his decision to be unsatisfactory. In particular, it was the cause of considerable dissatisfaction in Ohio, where proponents of the state's tax believed that the state had a right to be heard on its own behalf. They finally achieved this in the case of *Osborn et al. v. the Bank of the United States* (1824), which was essentially a rehearing of *McCulloch v. Maryland* except that, once again, Marshall found a way to finesse the many key federal-state issues that were involved.

A close examination of *McCulloch v. Maryland* also sheds new light on the role that Maryland played in the case, a development that is usually quickly passed over by scholars. For in addition to levying its tax for the purpose of raising revenue, it is clear that Maryland was not in any sense opposed to the 2BUS or its branch in Baltimore for either constitutional or policy reasons. Rather, *McCulloch v. Maryland* was an arranged case in which the state played the role of facilitator in order to get a case dealing with the question of state taxation of the branches of the 2BUS before the U.S. Supreme Court as quickly as possible. After the decision was handed down, the state quietly accepted it and totally withdrew from the fray.

Virginia's reaction to the decision in *McCulloch v. Maryland* has received much more attention from scholars, and for good reason. The debate that took place in the newspapers involved one of the rare instances where a member of the U.S. Supreme Court, in this case Chief Justice Marshall, writing anonymously, defended his decision against two formidable critics: William Brockenbrough and Spencer Roane. Moreover, the issues debated were the origins and nature of the union and the meaning of the necessary and proper clause, but significantly, the debate only barely touched on the 2BUS and its branches. What is not generally recognized is how atypical this debate was, for most Virginians, including Spencer Roane, who was considered Marshall's chief nemesis, had not opposed the creation of the 2BUS, and Virginia never levied a tax on it. Instead, the debate was for the most part a continuation of the great debate that had taken place in Virginia over the adoption of the U.S. Constitution in 1787–1788 and that continued to rage in the Old Dominion's politics for the next forty years, which was the baseline for most of Marshall's constitutional thought.

Developments in Ohio were much more typical of the kinds of issues raised by the states against the 2BUS and its branches. The spectacular forced removal of the tax by the state under the "crowbar law" has attracted substantial attention from scholars, who generally explain this development in political and economic terms. Yet Ohio quickly moderated its stance, returned the money, and defended its right to tax the branches of the 2BUS in legal and constitutional terms. Under the strong leadership of Charles Hammond, it launched so formidable and penetrating an attack on Marshall's *McCulloch* decision that the U.S. Supreme Court was forced to rehear the case in *Osborn et al. v. the Bank of the United States* (1824).

Chief Justice Marshall's role in all of these developments deserves careful scrutiny. The hearing of feigned cases on controversial constitutional issues in the early republic was nothing unusual. But Marshall's involvement appears to have gone way beyond this. There is circumstantial evidence to strongly indicate that he played a key role in helping the 2BUS at a time when it was under assault not only by various states but also by Congress. His cooperation was necessary to get the Supreme Court to hear the case as quickly as it did. He may also have indirectly influenced the content of the argument made on behalf of the 2BUS by its lawyers, which among other things allowed the chief justice to engage in the *obiter dicta* that constituted the extensive first part of his decision. Marshall also delivered his famous decision in just three days after the closing of oral arguments. The timing of this was important because the High Court's ruling came down only a day before the

Pennsylvania legislature was to begin debating the levying of a tax on the 2BUS in Philadelphia and its branch in Pittsburgh. Pennsylvania was a large and important state, and its taxation of the 2BUS would have immeasurably strengthened the course of action already taken by Kentucky and Ohio. As it turned out, Pennsylvania chose not to challenge the decision handed down in *McCulloch v. Maryland* and instead proposed an amendment to the U.S. Constitution, which would have limited the creation of a national bank to the District of Columbia, where it would not interfere with the states. It also prohibited the creation of branches in the states unless they granted their permission. In the end, the proposed amendment went nowhere. Finally, when things were going badly for the 2BUS in the *Osborn* case, Marshall unexpectedly ruled that the case should be continued to the next term, because a similar case would be heard then. This effectively removed Hammond from the case, because he had a very sick wife in Ohio. The other case turned out to be *The Bank of the United States v. the Planters' Bank of Georgia* (1824). When Marshall finally handed down his decision in the two cases, he made no attempt to link them up. If anything, the decision he handed down in the Georgia case contradicted in an important way his decisions in *McCulloch* and *Osborn*.

A word of explanation about my use of the term *aggressive nationalism* in the title of this volume is in order. The context in which *McCulloch v. Maryland* was decided was a series of innovative, major social and economic changes that swept over the United States during the beginning of the nineteenth century, especially in the years after 1815. These changes were numerous and converging. They included a growth in population and the rapid economic development, albeit in different ways, of almost all of the areas east of the Mississippi River. Louisiana became a state in 1812, Indiana in 1816, Mississippi in 1817, Illinois in 1818, Alabama in 1819, and Missouri and Maine in 1820. It was also a period when the older, established, urban areas like New York, Philadelphia, Baltimore, Charleston, and New Orleans underwent rapid population and economic growth. At the same time, a number of boom towns emerged: Pittsburgh, Lexington, Louisville, Cincinnati, St. Louis, Rochester, Nashville, Huntsville, Mobile, Milledgeville, and Natchez.

These same years also saw a rapid increase in the demand from Europe for American agricultural commodities, particularly cotton, grain, and meat products. The spread of the cotton culture throughout the old Southwest was immeasurably aided by the development of the cotton gin. At the same time, major changes in transportation occurred: the building of roads and canals and the widespread use of the steam boat, which enabled goods to be shipped to market more quickly and cheaply than ever before. This also led to a quickening of the transfer of information and communication between different parts of the country. During the early decades of the nineteenth century, a legal system emerged that encouraged and protected the country's economic development and transformation. Perhaps most important, the United States during these years underwent a major financial revolution based on the proliferation of banks, which made capital easily available, and an increase in the money supply, which replaced the older barter system that many small farmers had been using in economic transactions.

Taken together, these fundamental changes are referred to by a number of historians as "the market revolution," and it is clear that it had consequences that were good, bad, and controversial.[5] With it came the early development of a truly national economy, prosperity for many people, and an increase in people's standard of living. It also contributed in a major way to the urbanization of America and to the creation of a powerful and dynamic middle class, one that began to push for a broad variety of reforms which included attempts to bring under control the country's excessive consumption of alcohol; the establishment of a public educational system; improved sanitary conditions; better treatment for the insane, orphans, and criminals; and eventually the women's rights movement. On the other hand, the market revolution also contributed in a major way to the growth and expansion of slavery by turning cotton into the country's leading export commodity. It also created an inequality of wealth much greater than anything that had existed in the eighteenth century and brought widespread inflation, debt, and speculation. Moreover, as a consequence of the market revolution, the United States entered into the boom-bust cycle that would characterize the American economy throughout the nineteenth century and into the twentieth. It also tended to leave behind various workers, mechanics, small farmers, and farm laborers who did not have the business skills to achieve and maintain success, or who were simply unlucky.

Much of the country was divided over the significance of the market revolution. This division first became apparent in the struggle over the adoption of the U.S. Constitution in 1787–1788. The great majority of those who supported the adoption of the Constitution were found mainly in the country's commercial farming and urban areas, while those opposed were found mainly in backcountry areas, far from navigable waterways and thus lacking the cheap transportation necessary to participate in the market. This changed during the course of the market revolution. Many welcomed the economic growth it brought, but just as many were skeptical or hostile to it, while still others were unsure or ambivalent about its implications. A large number changed their positions as the country veered sharply between periods of prosperity and depression. These divisions continued well into the nineteenth century. One particularly astute historian has noted that the main division between the Jacksonians and their Whig opponents was that "the Whig party spoke to the explicit hopes of Americans, as Jacksonians addressed their diffuse fears and resentments."[6]

Many of the people hostile to the market revolution were not opposed to making money and getting ahead by means of hard work and frugality, but they were opposed to speculation, excessive debt, and the granting of special privileges through acts of incorporation. They were also critical of the market revolution because they found themselves increasingly subject to forces, both national and international, that they could neither understand nor control. Viewing the strong and active national government created by the U.S. Constitution as under the control of aggressive commercial interests, who not only had created the 2BUS but also favored a federal program of internal improvements, and perceiving the idea of privately controlled national corporations as dangerous, they rallied around the banner of states' rights. Indeed, the states were not so much attacking the 2BUS as they were defending themselves from it. This all came together with particular force in the reaction to the decision in *McCulloch v. Maryland* because it involved two national institutions, the 2BUS and the U.S.

Supreme Court, that were not amenable to popular control and that had become aggressive, intrusive, and coercive. These concerns also contributed in a major way to Andrew Jackson's election to the presidency in 1828. Moreover, Jackson's famous veto of the bill rechartering the 2BUS in 1832 was, on its most basic level, a response to John Marshall's decision in *McCulloch v. Maryland.*

Jackson's veto brought an end to the 2BUS; therefore, in a narrow sense, the Supreme Court's decision in *McCulloch v. Maryland* was short-lived in its impact. But on a more basic level, the significance of the decision has grown in the nearly two hundred years since it was handed down, so that it has become the foundational statement for a strong and active central government and the broadening of its powers. While the problem raised by federal-state relations remains a source of constant dispute, the context in which it has taken place has been altered in major ways by history, politics, and ideology. Further, changed social and economic circumstances have undercut the kind of loyalties that existed for most people in the early nineteenth century. This, of course, is a long and complicated story, one that does not lend itself to telling in a short space. Moreover, it is not the main purpose of this book, which is mainly to place the great case of *McCulloch v. Maryland* and the immediate reaction to it in their proper historical context. What all of this means, at least in historical terms, is that the original significance of an event and its results are often two different things.

ONE

THE U.S. SUPREME COURT
VERSUS THE STATES

The end of the War of 1812 was a major turning point in American history. The war itself had not gone very well. The country had been unprepared militarily, there were financial problems galore, there had been considerable opposition both from Federalists and from many Republicans, and President James Madison's administration had been so wracked by various personality and policy conflicts that the war effort was marked by chaos and inefficiency.[1] Yet despite all of this, the results of the war for Madison and the national republican wing of the Jeffersonian party were clear and glorious: a spirit of nationalism pervaded most parts of the United States (southern New England excepted), enhanced by Andrew Jackson's extraordinary, if belated, victory at the Battle of New Orleans. As Albert Gallatin observed in 1816:

> The war has been productive of evil and good, but I think the good preponderates. Independent of the loss of lives, and the losses in property by individuals, the war has laid the foundation of permanent taxes and military establishments, which the

Republicans had deemed unfavorable to the happiness and free institutions of the country. But under our former system we were becoming too selfish, too much attached exclusively to the acquisition of wealth, above all, too much confined in our political feelings to local and state objects. The war has renewed and reinstated the national feelings and character which the Revolution had given, and which were daily lessened. The people have now more general objects of attachment with which their pride and political opinions are connected. They are more American; they feel and act more as a nation; and I hope that the permanency of the Union is thereby better secured.[2]

On a more specific and political level, control of the federal government had fallen into the hands of a group of visionary and optimistic Jeffersonians who generally shared a common desire to encourage American economic development, a nationalist interpretation of the Constitution, and an elitist view of how the political process should operate. This group was mainly made up of a new and rising generation of Americans and was personified by Henry Clay, John C. Calhoun, John Quincy Adams, William Lowndes, Langdon Cheves, Samuel Smith, Nicholas Biddle, and Joseph Story. Their agenda included an expansion of national institutions that would have the power to override the activities of the state governments. Just how far some of these nationalists wanted to go in their antagonism toward local prerogatives is laid out in unusually frank terms by U.S. Supreme Court associate justice Joseph Story in a letter written in February 1815:

Never was there a more glorious opportunity for the Republican party to place themselves permanently in power. . . . Let us extend the national authority over the whole extent of power given by the Constitution. Let us have great military and naval schools; an adequate regular army; the broad foundation laid of a permanent navy; a National bank; a national system of bankruptcy; a great Navigation act, a general survey of our ports, an appointment of port wardens and pilots; Judicial Courts which shall embrace the whole Constitutional powers; national notaries; public and national justices of the peace, for the commercial and national concerns of the United States. By such enlarged and liberal institutions the Government of the United States will be endeared to the people, and the factions of the great states will be rendered harmless.[3]

I

The U.S. Supreme Court spearheaded the movement toward nationalism. Ever since its inception under the U.S. Constitution, adopted in 1788, it had been a source of political and ideological controversy. Unlike Articles I and II of the Constitution, which created the Congress and the office of the president and explicitly indicated how they were to be put into operation, Article III, which dealt with the federal courts, needed legislation to be put into operation. The Constitution mandated the creation of the Supreme Court, but did not give any indication as to its size or the qualifications of its members. The Constitution provided for federal judges to be appointed by the president with the approval of the U.S. Senate, but it was left up to Congress to decide whether or not some kind of lower federal court system was needed at all. It also indicated that the Supreme Court was to be mainly a court of appeals with original jurisdiction in only a few relatively minor matters, but did not delve into how appeals were to be made from the lower courts. As a result, the Judiciary Act of 1789 and the Process Acts that immediately followed it became one of the earliest and most significant pieces of legislation adopted by the First Congress. They provided that the Supreme Court should consist of a chief justice and five associate justices. Also, they organized an elaborate lower federal court system made up of district courts, which dealt mainly with admiralty questions, and circuit courts, which were courts of original jurisdiction in civil and criminal matters; both of these courts were to meet in different locales throughout the new nation. Although the Judiciary Act of 1789 was clearly a victory for the advocates of a strong and active national government, it was only a qualified victory: it did not give the federal courts exclusive jurisdiction on all matters dealing with federal law, since it also gave the state courts original and concurrent jurisdiction in many of those areas.[4]

The Judiciary Act of 1789 did explicitly deal with one question that had been the source of much debate since the Revolution and the creation of a central government under the Articles of Confederation: to what extent and in what manner could the federal government review and even reverse actions taken by the state governments that violated the powers and authority of the federal government? Under the Articles of Confederation written in 1777 and ratified in 1781, no provision was made to deal with this problem. It did not create a national judiciary, and while the Continental Congress under the Articles of Confederation had the power to create ad hoc courts to deal with disputes between different states, the decisions of the courts were nonenforceable. At the Philadelphia Convention which drafted the U.S. Constitution in the summer of 1787, the matter came up once again. The Virginia Plan, written by James Madison and presented by Edmund Randolph, which was the core document from which the Constitution eventually evolved, contained a provision granting to Congress the power "to negative all laws passed by the several states, contravening in the opinion of the National Legislature the articles of the Union," but it never made it to the final draft of the Constitution.[5] Instead, Article VI of the U.S. Constitution provided:

> This Constitution and the laws of the United States which shall be made in Pursuance thereof; and all Treaties made, or which shall be made, under the Authority of the United States, shall be the supreme law of the Land; and the Judges in every State shall be bound thereby, any thing in the Constitution or laws of any State to the contrary notwithstanding.

Often referred to as the supremacy clause of the U.S. Constitution, it would seem to have settled the matter, except that it did not indicate what judges or other bodies were to decide when a state law or judicial ruling was contrary to the Constitution, a federal law, or a treaty made by the national government. Congress explicitly dealt with this problem in section 25 of the Judiciary Act of 1789 by granting the U.S. Supreme Court the right to reverse state actions that involved the federal Constitution and the laws or treaties of the United States.[6] But this was not the same thing as having the power provided for in the Constitution itself. For if this power were contained in the Constitution itself, to elim-inate or alter it would necessitate an amendment to the Constitution, which requires a two-thirds vote of both houses of Congress and the approval of three-quarters of the states. These kinds of majorities are, of course, very difficult to obtain. On the other hand, the Judiciary Act of 1789 was legislative law that could be altered by a majority vote of both houses of Congress, or even challenged on the grounds that it was unconstitutional.

II

Federal-state relations were central to two key decisions handed down by the U.S. Supreme Court during the 1790s. According to the Constitution, federal courts had jurisdiction over "controversies between a state and citizens of another state." When a South Carolina creditor sued the state of Georgia, the state denied the Supreme Court's jurisdiction on the grounds that Georgia had sovereign immunity, and refused to appear. The Supreme Court decided in the South Carolina creditor's favor and handed down an ultranationalist opinion that denied Georgia's sovereignty.[7] The response came quickly, at least by eighteenth-century standards. The Eleventh Amendment to the Constitution was proposed and ratified in 1798, denying jurisdiction to federal courts in suits by citizens of another state or country "against one of the United States." In another decision, *Ware v. Hylton* (1796), the Supreme Court overturned state laws that impeded the recovery of debts owed by Americans to British creditors, since their collection had been guaranteed by the peace treaty with Great Britain (1783) that ended the Revolutionary War, on the grounds that it had supremacy over state laws.[8]

This spirit of nationalism was not unopposed. The United States in the late eighteenth and early nineteenth centuries also had a vigorous and persistent states' rights tradition. It had its origins in the different and unconnected ways that the various colonies had been settled and devel-oped. For many, the American Revolution bolstered this particularism because it had been fought against the only central government the Americans had ever known: Great Britain. Many others also associated localism with democracy and the protection of people's liberties. The most important manifestation of these views came with the adoption of the Articles of Confederation, which placed most power in the hands of the states. This concern was also at the heart of the opposition to the adoption of the U.S. Constitution in 1787–1788, because many feared the extent to which it undermined the authority of the states. These opponents, who have come to be known as Antifederalists, argued that giving the newly proposed central government the power of the purse (the ability to raise money through the levying of tariff duties and other taxes) and the power of the sword (the ability to enforce the central government's will through the federal judiciary and the military, if necessary) represented a dangerous concentration of authority.[9]

Nonetheless, after a sharp and at times bitter debate, all of the states eventually ratified the U.S. Constitution. Many of the Antifederalists who reluctantly voted for ratification were swayed by the consideration that, when they voted, the requisite nine states were already certain to approve the Constitution and implement the new government. This meant that the states where the Antifederalists had majorities (Virginia, New York, North Carolina, and Rhode Island) would not be able to go back to the way things were under the Articles of Confederation, but would be out of the union. The Antifederalists may have believed in states' rights and preferred the weak and nonthreatening central government established by the Articles of Confederation, but they did not believe in disunion or in becoming separate nations. After all, the official and often-forgotten title of the Articles of Confederation is "The Articles of Confederation and Perpetual Union," with the phrase "perpetual union" frequently reiterated throughout the document.[10]

The promise of amendments by the Federalists also convinced Antifederalists to go along with ratification. Along with unconditional ratification in many states (Massachusetts, Maryland, South Carolina, New Hampshire, Virginia, New York, North Carolina, and Rhode Island) came numerous proposals for amendments. These amendments fell into two categories. The first involved additions to the Constitution, which would restrict the federal government's authority over individuals in a number of important areas: freedom of religion;

freedom of the press; and the right to assemble, petition, and bear arms. There were also prohibitions against the quartering of troops and against unreasonable searches and seizures of evidence. Others guaranteed due process in criminal trials by requiring grand jury indictments, speedy public trials, the assistance of counsel, the right to a jury trial, and protection from excessive bails and fines and cruel and unusual punishments.[11]

The second group of amendments included substantive structural alterations to the Constitution. Their purpose was to check the centralizing tendencies in the new government and to make it more amenable to popular control. These amendments limited the federal government's power to levy taxes, defined and restricted the jurisdiction of the federal courts, shortened the term of office of U.S. senators, changed the way the president was elected, increased the ratio of representation in the House of Representatives, and stipulated that the militia remain under state control. Especially important was an amendment reserving to the states those powers not "expressly" granted to the federal government.[12]

This matter was immediately dealt with by the First Congress but, to the unhappiness of many Antifederalists, it was mainly the additions dealing with the rights of individuals that were adopted. Only what became the Tenth Amendment addressed the all-important problem of distributing power between the states and the federal government. But it was a watered-down version of what the Antifederalists wanted. It stipulated: "The powers not delegated to the United States by the Constitution nor prohibited by it to the States are reserved to the States respectively, or to the people." What the Antifederalists wanted was a restatement of the second Article of the Articles of Confederation, which designated that all powers not "expressly" granted to the federal government were retained by the states or the people, which would have sharply circumscribed any attempt to broaden, by construction, the many powers already explicitly granted to the federal government. Because of this, many Antifederalists opposed the Bill of Rights as finally proposed by Congress. One of them described these amendments as "mutilated and enfeebled," and another called it "good for nothing." As a result, the question of how power was to be distributed between the states and the federal government remained the central constitutional and political issue in American history until the Civil War.[13]

The Antifederalists were also particularly worried that many of the loose and open-ended phrases like the necessary and proper clause, the right to regulate interstate commerce, and the power to legislate for the general welfare would be used to dangerously increase the powers of the federal government. This manifested itself in the struggle over Alexander Hamilton's financial policies, which caused much unhappiness among states' rights proponents. At first, Jefferson and Madison opposed the secretary of the treasury's proposals to fund the national debt and to assume the debts of the states, but in the end they agreed to go along with them. On the other hand, in 1790 and 1791, the Virginia legislature, led by Patrick Henry, who had been a leading Antifederalist, adopted a resolution declaring the state to be

> the guardian of . . . the rights and interests of their constituents,
> as Sentinels placed by them over the ministers of the federal
> government, to shield it from their encroachments, or, at least
> to sound the alarm when it is threatened with invasion.

Arguing that the assumption of the states' debts was repugnant to the Constitution, the Virginia legislature requested that the law be repealed.[14]

Growing opposition to Federalist domestic and foreign policies led to a major constitutional crisis in 1798 during the administration of John Adams. Following the XYZ affair, Adams began building up the military and sought to suppress public criticism of his policies by signing the Alien and Sedition Acts into law. This development alarmed many Americans who feared the Federalists were determined to silence or even crush their domestic opposition. The question was how to effectively oppose these measures. Jefferson and Madison, seeking to express their disapproval through a proper and legally constituted forum, prepared two sets of resolutions to be introduced in the Kentucky and Virginia legislatures.[15]

These resolutions, adopted in the latter part of 1798, condemned the Alien and Sedition Acts as unconstitutional and put forth a theory of the origins and nature of the union very similar to the one endorsed in 1791 by the Antifederalist-controlled Virginia legislature, which had denounced Alexander Hamilton's plan to assume the debts of the states as unconstitutional. These resolutions argued that the federal government was one of limited and specifically delegated powers and was the result of a compact made between the states in 1787–1788. These resolutions also took specific issue with the Federalist claim that the U.S. Supreme Court was the exclusive and final arbiter of constitutional questions. The Kentucky Resolutions, drafted by Jefferson and the more directly and strongly worded of the two, asserted that, when the federal government exercised powers that had not been specifically assigned to it, a state "has an equal right to judge for itself . . . as of the mode and measure of redress." The Virginia Resolutions, written by Madison and more moderate in many ways, argued that in the matter of unconstitutional legislation the states "have the right and are in duty bound to interpose for arresting the progress of the evil." Moreover, the Kentucky Resolutions specifically argued that the Supreme Court was a creature of the Constitution, and to give it the power of judicial review was to make "its discretion and not the Constitution the measure of its powers."[16]

In actuality, the rhetoric of the Kentucky and Virginia Resolutions was a good deal more extreme than the resolutions' practical effect. They were not meant to be a prescription for action. Shortly after the adoption of the Virginia Resolutions, Governor James Monroe, who had opposed the adoption of the Constitution in 1788, indicated that no attempt would be made to prevent the enforcement of the Sedition Act in Virginia, and the trial of James T. Callender, a highly controversial journalist, took place without incident in Richmond before the federal circuit court. The Kentucky and Virginia Resolutions were issued not to foster disobedience to the law, but for political effect. Their purpose was to rally political opposition to Federalist policies, to reassert the link that existed in many people's minds between civil liberty and states' rights, and to offer an alternative theory about the origins and nature of the federal government. The theory challenged the constitutional basis for the Federalists' program of centralization and their claim that the Supreme Court was the final arbiter of federal-state relations. No other state at the time endorsed the Kentucky and Virginia Resolutions, but they were the rallying cry of the Republicans in the election of 1800, and in this way they were both important and successful. Throughout the remaining antebellum period, they were the essence of what became known as "the spirit of '98."[17]

III

Jefferson's great victory in the "civil revolution" of 1800 also gave his party control of both houses of Congress. For some, this was enough. But others, however, particularly those sympathetic to the old Antifederalist critique of the Constitution, who called themselves Old Republicans, wanted more. They wanted to make major alterations in the Constitution and reduce the jurisdiction of the federal courts so that the centralizing powers that had been unleashed by the achievement of 1787–1788 would never resurface. Jefferson actually had some sympathy for this point of view, while Madison did not. In the end, however, Jefferson opted not to go along with a direct assault on the Constitution; instead, he established the principle that when a new party came to power, it could change government policies and personnel, but not the government itself.[18]

As president, Jefferson did have a particularly difficult time with the national judiciary, which remained a Federalist stronghold whose members held their offices for life tenure during good behavior and therefore were not subject to popular control. The Federalist-dominated lame-duck Congress passed the Judiciary Act of 1801, which expanded both the size and powers of the national courts, but Jefferson responded by adopting a more moderate and measured course, bringing about a repeal of the Judiciary Act of 1801, while at the same time returning the national court system, with only minor modifications, to the way it had existed during the 1790s under the Judiciary Act of 1789, something the U.S. Supreme Court itself upheld in *Stuart v. Laird* (1803). Jefferson's response to the Supreme Court's decision in *Marbury v. Madison* (1803), which declared Section 13 of the Judiciary Act of 1789 unconstitutional, was also restrained. He did not like the long *obiter dicta* lecture it contained on why the commissions should have been delivered. Actually, in many ways, the decision was a victory for

Jefferson: it rejected Marbury's request for a writ of mandamus and did not order his administration to deliver the commissions. The decision also did not in any way try to reduce the powers of the president or Congress, but only rejected Congress's attempt to increase the powers of the Supreme Court by giving it original jurisdiction in cases involving writs of mandamus. Further, while the Supreme Court claimed the right to interpret the Constitution on matters before it, it did not claim its power to do so was either exclusive or final.[19] Jefferson did support impeachment proceedings against John Pickering, an insane and alcoholic district court judge, but only because he had no other way of removing him. He helped to initiate impeachment proceedings against Samuel Chase, an associate justice of the U.S. Supreme Court, but did not try to enforce party regularity, which contributed in a major way to Chase's acquittal. Annoyed by Chief Justice Marshall's subpoena to appear before the Supreme Court in Aaron Burr's treason trial and dismayed by some of his rulings, Jefferson sidestepped the former by sending over some documents and accepted the latter. To be sure, there were some tense moments, but in the end no fundamental changes in the U.S. Constitution occurred.[20]

Marshall also did his part during Jefferson's presidency to avoid a major confrontation with the Republicans, which he undoubtedly would have lost, by having the Supreme Court avoid making any politically explosive decisions. All of this changed in 1809, however, when Madison became president for, despite his states' rights rhetoric during the 1790s, he had never had much sympathy for the Old Republican wing of the party and its desire to make major alterations in the Constitution. The Old Republicans had also unsuccessfully tried to prevent his becoming Jefferson's successor in 1808.[21] No longer threatened by a hostile chief executive, the Supreme Court began to move more aggressively on the question of federal-state relations.

An important opportunity came in the case of *United States v. Peters* (1809), which originated in 1779 and involved a dispute among various Americans over the capture of a British supply vessel, the *Active*. A group of American sailors who had been impressed by the British into service, led by Gideon Olmstead, a Connecticut resident, managed to seize control of the *Active*, although they had not been able to entirely quell the resistance of the British crew. Nevertheless, Olmstead and his supporters were in the process of bringing the *Active* into an American port, where they expected to claim it as a prize, when it was overtaken and taken command of by the *Convention*, a privateer that had been fitted out by the state of Pennsylvania, and another privateer which also was in the vicinity. The captains of both of these ships claimed the *Active* as a prize, arguing that Olmstead had never really taken full control of the vessel. For his part, Olmstead disputed this, and the matter went before a Pennsylvania admiralty court, which by a jury decision divided the prize among Olmstead, the state of Pennsylvania, and the other two crews. Unhappy with the decision, Olmstead took the matter to the Continental Congress, since it had the power to create special tribunals to hear appeals from state admiralty courts. This tribunal proceeded to reverse the Pennsylvania admiralty court's decision and found for Olmstead. The Pennsylvania authorities, however, refused to accept the decision, arguing that the appeals tribunal did not have the power to review the facts and reverse a jury decision. The state legislature, however, acting on the side of caution, ordered that its share of the receipts from the sale of the *Active* be placed in the hands of the state treasurer, David Rittenhouse, who provided a bond for it.[22]

After the adoption of the Constitution, Olmstead took the matter into the newly formed federal courts, and in 1803 he got a district court to reverse the Pennsylvania ruling. The state, however, continued to refuse to hand the money over, Governor Thomas McKean arguing that the suit violated the Eleventh Amendment, since the state had been sued without its consent. His decision was strongly supported by the state legislature, which ordered him "to protect the just rights of the State from any process issued by a Federal Court." Meanwhile, the federal district court judge, Richard Peters, hoping to avoid a political confrontation at a time when Congress was engaged in the Pickering and Chase impeachments, decided not to try to enforce his ruling.[23]

Finally, in 1808, Olmstead took his case into the U.S. Supreme Court and requested that a writ of mandamus be issued against Judge Peters, requiring him to enforce his decree. In his decision, issuing the writ, Chief Justice Marshall made it clear that federal-state relations had become the central issue in the dispute and warned:

If the legislatures of the several states may, at will, annul the judgments of the Courts of the United States, and destroy the rights acquired under those judgments, the constitution itself becomes a solemn mockery, and the nation is deprived of the means of enforcing its laws by the instrumentality of its own tribunals. So fatal a result must be deprecated by all; and the people of Pennsylvania, not less than the citizens of every other State, must feel a deep interest in resisting principles so destructive of the Union and in averting consequences so fatal to themselves.[24]

The state of Pennsylvania, however, continued in its refusal to back down. When Judge Peters began process against Elizabeth Sargeant and Esther Waters, Rittenhouse's daughters and surviving heirs, who controlled the state's share of the funds from the sale of the *Active*, Governor Simon Snyder called out the state militia under the leadership of General Michael Bright, which surrounded the home where the daughters now lived and prevented the federal marshal from delivering the writ.

At the same time, Snyder wrote to President Madison, asking for his help in negotiating some kind of settlement. Making reference to Madison's role in drafting the Virginia Resolutions of 1798, he emphasized the need to "discriminate between opposition to the constitution and laws of the United States, and that of resisting the decree of a judge, founded . . . in a usurpation of power and jurisdiction not delegated to him by either." But Madison, in no uncertain terms, rejected the request. "The executive of the United States," he wrote, "is not only unauthorized to prevent the execution of a decree sanctioned by the Supreme Court of the United States, but is expressly enjoined, by statute, to carry into effect any such decree where opposition may be made to it."[25]

When federal troops were called out to enforce the process, Pennsylvania backed down. General Bright, who had carried out the governor's orders, was then arrested by federal marshals and was tried and convicted for his role in the confrontation, although President Madison quickly pardoned him for humanitarian reasons now that the authority of the federal government and the U.S. Supreme Court had been established.[26]

With a supportive chief executive behind it, the U.S. Supreme Court, under John Marshall's leadership, for the next fifteen years entered its most nationalist phase and began to make use of section 25 of the Judiciary Act of 1789 with increasing vigor. In 1810 in *Fletcher v. Peck*, the Court overturned a Georgia law and decision and also broadened the meaning of the contract clause of the Constitution to include public as well as private contracts. The problem at the heart of the case dated back to 1795, when a corrupt Georgia legislature had been bribed by land speculators to sell them, for a penny and a half an acre, over 35 million acres of Indian land in the Yazoo Territory, located in what is today Alabama and Mississippi. The following year, a reform legislature, elected by an irate citizenry, rescinded the act authorizing the sale. However, in the year following the original sale, much of the land had been sold to northern speculators, all of whom claimed they had no knowledge of the corruption involved, and many of whom had resold the land to parties even further removed from the original contract. In 1802, Georgia relinquished to the federal government its claims to the Yazoo Territory. The cession, however, provided that the national government assume the responsibility of satisfying the claims of the various second-, third-, and fourth-party purchasers of the Yazoo lands. A special high-level commission, consisting of his cabinet, was appointed by President Jefferson to investigate the matter. It recommended "a compromise on reasonable terms," whereby the federal government would set aside 5 million acres to satisfy the claimants and bring the matter to a successful conclusion. But the proposal was very controversial, with strong opposition coming from Old Republicans, who got Congress to reject it.[27]

The matter entered the federal court system in 1807 when a diversity-of-citizenship suit was deliberately created between Robert Fletcher of New Hampshire and John Peck of Massachusetts, from whom Fletcher had bought some of the Yazoo holdings, in order to bring a suit in a federal circuit court so as to get a ruling on the validity of the Georgia repeal law. When the law was declared unconstitutional, the decision was appealed to the U.S. Supreme Court, where

John Marshall, on behalf of a majority of the Court, upheld the circuit court's decision, indicating that a state legislature could not revoke a contract if it was a party, even if the contract were fraudulently obtained. Since it no longer controlled the lands involved in the decision, the state of Georgia did not take any formal position on the decision. Congress, however, once again moved to settle the matter and in 1814, when Old Republican influence was greatly diminished, appropriated $5 million to resolve the dispute.[28]

The U.S. Supreme Court handed down another section 25 decision in 1812 in the case of *New Jersey v. Wilson*. The case originated in a 1758 law by which the colony of New Jersey tried to clear the claims of the Delaware Indians to land within its boundaries. In return for abandoning their various claims, they were given a tract of land which would not be subject to state taxes. In the early nineteenth century, the Delaware Indians decided to move to New York to join other members of their tribe, and sold their land. The new owners claimed the tax immunity, and the state legislature responded by rescinding the 1758 grant and assessing a tax on the new proprietors. The legal dispute that followed was taken to the New Jersey Supreme Court, which upheld the legislature's action. The decision was appealed to the U.S. Supreme Court, which found the rescinding act to be in violation of the contract clause of the U.S. Constitution, and ruled that the tax immunity continued in effect. New Jersey made no formal response to the Court's decision. Instead, the state ignored it and continued to levy taxes on the land.[29]

IV

By far, the most significant section 25 decision handed down by the U.S. Supreme Court during this period came in the case of *Martin v. Hunter's Lessee* (1816). It was a landmark decision that established an important precedent and triggered a major controversy with the state of Virginia over the constitutionality of section 25 itself. Its origins can be traced back to the American Revolution, and involved the estate of Thomas, the sixth Lord Fairfax, who owned, as a consequence of a gift from King George II, over 5 million acres of land, a kind of proprietary colony in the Northern Neck of Virginia between the Potomac and

Rappahannock rivers that was considered extremely fertile and valuable. Fairfax, who returned to England at the time of the Revolution but who was considered a citizen of Virginia, died in 1781 and bequeathed his property to his nephew Denny Martin, a British subject who never took up residence in the Old Dominion. When this occurred, Virginia, under the leadership of Patrick Henry, denied the right of an alien to inherit property and passed a series of laws that sequestered the quit rents being paid by tenants and that removed various tax exemptions and other special privileges attached to the land. The state also assumed ownership of the waste or unappropriated lands of the estate, and had by 1786 begun to sell them.[30]

Martin challenged these developments in a number of different suits. His claim to the lands was further strengthened by the 1783 treaty of peace between the United States and Britain, which contained a clause prohibiting the confiscation of loyalist estates. For their part, most Virginians believed the treaty provision only affected laws adopted after 1783. They also questioned whether the treaty actually was in force, since the British had violated it by failing to withdraw their troops from certain forts that had been ceded to the United States. Moreover, the British had also failed to make compensation for slaves they had taken with them when they retreated at the end of the war, which had also been provided for in the treaty.

Virginia sold some of the lands it had confiscated from the Fairfax estate to David Hunter, a Winchester speculator, in 1789. Lord Fairfax's heirs refused to recognize Hunter's title to the land, and the latter sued to clear the title in the state district court at Winchester, which found for Martin. Hunter appealed the decision to the state's highest court, the Court of Appeals, in Richmond. Before a decision was handed down, Martin sold 160,000 acres of the claim to a syndicate of speculators that included John Marshall and his brother James. Then, in 1796, with Marshall's help, the state legislature offered a compromise. Martin and the syndicate would relinquish title to the undeveloped or waste lands in the Northern Neck in return for clear title to the manor lands which were the lands Lord Fairfax had developed for his own personal use. When both sides accepted the compromise it became law, which seemed to settle the matter.[31]

But the case was never dropped from the docket of the Virginia Court of Appeals, and it was revived, probably by Spencer Roane, a former opponent of the adoption of the U.S. Constitution and a son-in-law of Patrick Henry. Roane had become a prominent state politician in his own right and sat on the Court of Appeals. For him, the matter seems to have been a question of principle, and he wanted to see the fundamental constitutional and other legal issues raised by the case resolved in Virginia's favor. In *Hunter v. Fairfax's Devisee* (1809), the Virginia Court of Appeals reversed the lower court's decision and found for Hunter. The Martin-Marshall syndicate, which among other things wanted to collect quit rents on the land it owned, responded by appealing the decision to the U.S. Supreme Court on a writ of error under section 25 of the Judiciary Act of 1789.[32]

Because he owned some of the land involved, John Marshall recused himself from the case, although there is strong evidence to indicate he was active behind the scenes. The Supreme Court's decision in *Fairfax Devisee v. Hunter* (1813) was handed down by Joseph Story, an ultranationalist who was very learned in the law and who had been appointed to the High Court in 1811 by President Madison over Thomas Jefferson's strong objections. Speaking for a three-member majority with only one justice dissenting, Story reversed the decision of the Virginia Court of Appeals. He denied the legitimacy of the various statutes under which Virginia had taken custody of the Fairfax lands and argued that Martin's inheritance was protected not only by the common law of descent, but by the anticonfiscation clause of the 1783 peace treaty, which had been reiterated in the Jay treaty of 1794. He made no mention of the legislative Act of Compromise of 1796. Story aggressively concluded his opinion by addressing the Virginia Court of Appeals in the following manner: "You therefore are hereby commanded that such proceeding be had in said cause, as according to right and justice, and the laws of the United States, and agreeable to said judgment and instruction of said Supreme Court."[33]

Story's opinion brought a strong reaction from Roane and the Virginia Court of Appeals. They fully understood that the case involved more than the reversal of their court's opinion or even a "command" and "instruction" from the U.S. Supreme Court, as controversial as these were. For many members of Virginia's revolutionary generation, a host of additional issues were involved: loyalism, the right of the state to control its own destiny and purge itself of the vestiges of feudalism, the hated Jay treaty which they viewed as a formal recognition of British ability to control the high seas, and the great fear of consolidation. The Virginia Court of Appeals convened in 1814 to confront what it called the "mandate" handed down by the U.S. Supreme Court. To help consider the matter, the Virginia court "invited the members of the bar to investigate it," and it was discussed "in a full and able manner." Following this, "it received the long and deliberate consideration of the Court" itself. Although the court's opinion was ready a short time later, its publication was delayed. The War of 1812, then in its third year, had aroused bitter opposition in New England, where rumors of secession were rife. Although many Virginians advocated states' rights, they had no intention of aiding those who were actually hindering the war effort.[34]

Following the end of the war, the Virginia Court of Appeals published its unanimous decision in *Hunter v. Martin, Devisees of Fairfax* (1815). In it, the court argued that section 25 of the Judiciary Act of 1789, which allowed appeals from state courts to the U.S. Supreme Court in matters dealing with the Constitution, federal laws, or treaties, was unconstitutional. The four judges delivered their opinions *seriatim*, but Roane's was the most substantial. He reiterated the position that the Old Dominion had taken on the origins and nature of the union during the great crisis of 1798–1799: the union was a compact of the states, a view that had been validated by the election of 1800, "producing a new era in the American Republic." Sovereignty, Roane argued, was divided between the states and the national government, and the latter only had limited and specifically delegated powers. Since the U.S. Constitution had provided no final umpire on constitutional questions, nor specifically granted Congress the power to bestow such a role on the Supreme Court, the federal and state courts each had the right to rule on such questions, and neither could bind the other on matters before it. This latter point was crucial. In no other way could the states be protected from encroachments by the central government. "No calamity," he argued, "would be more to be deplored by the American people than a vortex in the general government, which would ingulf [*sic*] and sweep away, every vestige of the state constitutions."[35]

The U.S. Supreme Court's response came the next year in *Martin v. Hunter's Lessee* (1816). Once again Marshall did not sit, although Story, who wrote the majority opinion, later indicated that the chief justice had "concurred in every word."[36] In his decision, Story strenuously defended the constitutionality of section 25 of the Judiciary Act of 1789 and the right of the U.S. Supreme Court to review the final judgments of state courts which impacted on the powers of the federal government. In opposition to the compact theory, Story argued that the U.S. Constitution was created not by the states but by the people, the ultimate source of political and constitutional authority. He cited the supremacy clause and argued that "the Constitution has presumed . . . that state jealousies and state interests, might sometimes obstruct, or control . . . the regular administration of justice." Since state prejudices had undermined the central government under the Articles of Confederation, state courts could not be allowed to be the final interpreters of the Constitution, for different judgments would be given in different states, and "these jarring and discordant judgments" would inevitably undermine the federal government and the union. Uniformity, Story believed, was absolutely essential for the future well-being of the nation, and this could only be assured through federal judicial review of state actions.[37]

The use of section 25 by the U.S. Supreme Court to overturn state court decisions and to enforce its will on the states established important legal precedents and was controversial mainly in narrow legal circles, but it did not have a broad impact and only touched on real interests in at best a limited way. Indeed, the actual outcomes had already been settled even before they were heard in the cases involving the Fairfax lands in Virginia where, as far as we can tell, the legislative compromise, which by then had been in effect for twenty years, remained operative, and the Supreme Court's decision was disregarded, as in *New Jersey v. Wilson*. Or settled by some other means, as in *Fletcher v. Peck*. What little controversy the outcomes engendered was pushed aside by the preoccupation with the events that led to the War of 1812, by the difficulties in fighting that war, and for political reasons.

The war itself, to be sure, strengthened the cause of nationalism, but it was not until after its end that this nationalism found its most concrete and specific manifestations. And of these, by far the most important, far-reaching, and controversial issue for the next two decades was the creation of what has come to be known as the Second Bank of the United States (2BUS).

TWO

THE SECOND BANK OF
THE UNITED STATES

The creation of the Second Bank of the United States (2BUS) in 1816 was the most important and specific manifestation of the nationalist thrust that followed the end of the War of 1812. It raised fundamental constitutional issues and had a major impact on the economic and political development of the country. The debate unleashed by its creation and the implementation of its policies in one form or another involved all of the constituent elements of the national government—the powers of the executive, the Congress, and the federal judiciary, as well as the role of the states in a federal system—and would take almost twenty years to fully resolve.

I

The creation of a national bank has a long and complicated history dating back to the adoption of the U.S. Constitution which, in Article I, section 10, had prohibited the states from using anything but gold and silver for money. The First Bank of the United States (1BUS) had been created in 1791 under Alexander Hamilton's leadership. Using the Bank of England as a model, the purpose of the 1BUS was to provide a national circulating medium, to make loans to the federal government to cover deficits, to be a source of credit for businesspeople, and to be a profitable business opportunity which would obtain the loyalty of many of the country's wealthiest citizens to the newly established national government. It was chartered for twenty years and capitalized (the amount invested in the bank by its stockholders) at $10 million with 80 percent of its stock purchased by private investors and the remainder by the U.S. government. It was to serve as the federal government's fiscal agent (the place where the public's money would be deposited and from which it would be disbursed) and to issue a currency redeemable in specie (gold and silver) that could be used to pay taxes, tariff duties, and fees due to the federal government and to purchase federal lands. Moreover, allowing investors to pay for three-fourths of their stock purchases in the 1BUS with public securities made the bonds recently issued by the new federal government to redeem the national debt even more attractive. Headquartered in Philadelphia, it had the power to create branches in the major commercial centers of the country.[1]

From the moment Hamilton introduced the measure, it was controversial. In Congress, Madison led the opposition, arguing that the creation of a national bank was unconstitutional and illegitimate because there was no provision for it in the Constitution and that the Constitutional Convention that had created the Constitution in the summer of 1787 had actually rejected a proposal to give the federal government the power to create such a corporation. Opponents of the measure also warned that it would concentrate too much power in the hands of the federal government. But Congress, on Hamilton's urging, adopted the measure anyway.[2]

President George Washington was unsure how to proceed, and before he decided what to do with the bill he asked the members of his cabinet to prepare written opinions on the constitutionality of incorporating a national bank. This led to one of the great exchanges in American constitutional history. Thomas Jefferson, who was secretary of state, delivered his opinion on February 15, 1791. He argued that the bill was unconstitutional, advancing what has become known as a narrow, or "strict constructionist," view of the powers of Congress. Jefferson maintained that the power to incorporate a bank was not a power expressly granted to Congress. The bank would be a monopoly, and in its operation would violate in various ways the rights of the states which were protected by the Tenth Amendment, which provided that "*all powers not delegated to the United States nor prohibited by it to the states, are reserved to the states, or to the people.* To take a single step beyond the boundaries thus specially drawn around the powers of Congress is to take possession of a boundless field of power, no longer susceptible of any definition." He warned that if the president signed the bill into law, it would indicate that Congress had "a power to make laws, paramount to the laws of the states; for so they must be construed to protect the institution from the control of the state legislatures; and so probably they will be construed."[3]

Jefferson rejected the argument that the 1BUS could be considered constitutional because in Article I, section 8, the Constitution had granted Congress the power "to make all laws which shall be necessary and proper for carrying into execution" its delegated powers. The bank, he asserted, was not "necessary" but "convenient," and he warned that given Congress's long list of delegated powers ("to lay taxes," "to borrow money," "to regulate commerce," "to provide for the general welfare"), there is "no one which ingenuity may not torture into a convenience in some way or other, to some one." The Constitution, Jefferson argued, "restrained them [members of Congress] to the necessary means; that is to say, to those means without which the grant of the powers would be nugatory."[4]

Hamilton's answer came on February 23, 1791. He called Jefferson's objections "ill-founded." As a substitute, he developed what has become known as the doctrine of "implied powers," or a "broad construction," of the Constitution. As a sovereign power, the United States had the implied right to create corporations. Hamilton took specific issue with Jefferson's definition of the word "necessary," arguing that it meant "*needful, requisite, incidental, useful or conducive to*," and that this was the true meaning "to be understood as used in the Constitution. The whole turn of the clause containing it indicates, that it was the intent of the Convention, by that clause to give a liberal latitude to the exercise of specified powers." The bank, Hamilton argued, was related to Congress's power to levy taxes and regulate trade, for it facilitated that power's implementation. He declared, in phrases that were to be appropriated and made even more eloquent by Chief Justice John Marshall in *McCulloch v. Maryland* (1819): "If the *end* be clearly comprehended within any of the specified powers, and if the measure have an obvious relation to that *end*, and is not forbidden by any particular provision of the Constitution, it may safely be deemed to come within the compass of the national authority." Finally, toward the end of his opinion, Hamilton observed that "as the bill under consideration contemplates the government in the light of a joint proprietor of the stock of the bank, it brings the case within the provision of the clause of the Constitution which immediately respects the property of the United States."[5]

Although he remained uncertain as to how to proceed, Washington, in the end, supported Hamilton's view of the constitutionality of the 1BUS, mainly on the grounds that his support should go to the cabinet officer whose department was most directly involved in the outcome of the decision. In the decade that followed, the 1BUS generally acted in a partisan fashion, siding with Hamilton and his supporters by lending them money and servicing their financial needs, while refusing to do business with his enemies. But after Thomas Jefferson became president in 1801, fearful of political repercussions, it stopped acting in a partisan fashion. At the same time, as an economic institution, the 1BUS was very successful: it performed its functions without any problems and paid high dividends, while the value of its stock increased rapidly. It also became a highly respected financial institution, not only in the United States but also on the international scene, especially in London and Amsterdam, which were the most important banking centers in Europe. Further, it was a safe and efficient depository of government funds, transferring them around the country as needed, and it regularly made short-term loans to the federal government, especially during Hamilton's tenure as secretary of the treasury. The 1BUS was also a very conservatively run institution, even by late eighteenth-century standards. It lent money mainly to successful, well-known, and highly respected individuals, and then only for very short terms, thirty or sixty days, renewable depending on economic circumstances and forecasts. This allowed the 1BUS to maintain high specie reserves. As a consequence, it almost exclusively serviced the leading members of the mercantile and financial communities in the country's urban areas. The problem with this was that it was no help to the overwhelming majority of Americans, who lived in rural areas and engaged in agricultural pursuits. These people needed longer-term loans to purchase land and slaves and to plant crops and raise livestock, loans that would take at least a year, and usually longer, to pay off.[6]

Under the leadership of the Jeffersonians, mainly during the first decade and a half of the nineteenth century, in many rural areas smaller banks were created that were willing to make longer-term loans. These also were privately controlled banks, usually referred to as state or local banks because of the manner in which they were chartered. Many were capably run institutions that successfully serviced specific local areas, but there were many that were not very sound. Like the national bank, they issued bank notes or money when they made loans and often did so without adequate amounts of specie to back up their notes. The 1BUS helped to keep the more disreputable banks in check by refusing to accept their notes or by sharply discounting their value. This, of course, created widespread resentment toward the 1BUS by many local banks, which wanted to expand their operations but did not have adequate capital to do so.[7]

When the charter of the 1BUS came up for renewal in 1811, President Madison and Secretary of the Treasury Albert Gallatin quietly made it known that they favored renewal. But they ran into a strong alliance of states' rights and local banking interests, which killed the measure. Shortly thereafter, the War of 1812 began, and the federal government quickly found itself facing enormous difficulties as it tried to finance the struggle. The federal government's major source of income was tariff duties, but these quickly dried up when the British navy blockaded the coast. This, combined with the fact that government bonds could only be sold at heavy discounts, seriously hindered the war effort. Following the demise of the 1BUS, the number of local banks rapidly increased, and with it came monetary instability since there was no central agency to monitor their activities. In addition, the lack of a national bank led to fiscal chaos during the War of 1812, as many of the soundest local banks were in New England (where antiwar feeling was strongest), and they refused to lend money to the federal government, while local banks in other parts of the country ended up suspending specie payments when Washington, D.C., was burned in August 1814 because they had issued more bank notes than they could redeem. However, the support of two wealthy financiers, Stephen Girard of Philadelphia and John Jacob Astor of New York, who bought substantial amounts of bonds and treasury notes issued directly by the federal government, kept the war effort alive.[8]

At the same time, Girard and Astor, as well as other wealthy merchants and financiers who supported the war effort, began a movement to encourage the establishment of a new national bank. Their main contact with the Madison administration was Alexander J. Dallas, a Pennsylvania lawyer who had extensive commercial ties with mercantile interests throughout the country, who was about to become Madison's secretary of the treasury, and who was known to sympathize with their point of view. In his first report to Congress on October 17, 1814, Dallas indicated that the country's finances had reached a crisis point. He pointed in particular to "the inadequacy of our system of taxation to form a foundation for public credit; and the absence even from that system of the means which are best adapted to anticipate, collect, and distribute the public revenue." The government, he argued, lacked adequate funds to effectively prosecute the war, and the lack of a national circulating medium was a "copious source of mischief and embarrassment." As a solution, Dallas proposed the incorporation of a new national bank, similar in many ways to the 1BUS, only larger, that would be required to loan the federal government money if it needed it.[9]

In concluding his report, Dallas turned his attention to the constitutional issues involved in creating a new national bank. He had earlier privately indicated his belief that the events of the post-1811 period had proven the necessity of a national bank and that the opposition to it on constitutional grounds was now discredited and maintained only "by a few raving Printers and rival Banks. It may have been doubtful in 1792 [1791], but it is certain in 1814 that a national bank is essential to the fiscal operations and credit of the Government."[10] He treated the subject more tactfully in his report to Congress by arguing that "precedent" and necessity had established the constitutionality of a national bank. As Dallas put it: "In the administration of human affairs, there must be a period when discussion shall cease and decision shall become absolute." Opponents of a national bank, Dallas argued, could have obtained an amendment to the Constitution prohibiting its creation, but they had not. As a consequence:

> [W]hen, therefore we have marked the existence of a national bank for a period of twenty years, with all the sanctions of the legislative, executive, and judicial authorities; when we have seen the dissolution of one institution, and heard a loud and continued call for the establishment of another; when, under the circumstances, neither Congress nor the several states have resorted to the power of amendment; can it be deemed a violation of the right of private opinion, to consider the constitutionality of a national bank as a question forever settled and at rest?[11]

Although there was by now considerable support for the creation of a national bank, some sharp differences quickly emerged over important details. What the Madison administration, led by Dallas, wanted was a bank capitalized at $50 million which would be required to lend the federal government up to $30 million. There were to be fifteen directors of which five, including the bank's president, were to be appointed by the president of the United States. The federal government was to subscribe $20 million payable in special 6 percent bonds issued to finance the war. Private subscriptions were to be paid over three months, one-fifth in specie and the balance in war debt bonds and recently issued treasury notes that the government had issued to pay its creditors. Under this arrangement, the bank would clearly be under the control of the federal government and would be required to provide the money and credit necessary for the Madison administration to sustain the war effort.[12]

Substantial opposition to Dallas's proposal quickly emerged. Many Federalists, led by Daniel Webster, Rufus King, Joseph Hopkinson, and

William Gaston, feared that the proposed bank would be too much under the control of a Jeffersonian-dominated federal government and that it would be used for partisan purposes. Others, including these same Federalists plus a number of Republicans led by John C. Calhoun, William Lowndes, and Langdon Cheves, questioned whether such an institution, whose stock would be purchased mainly with rapidly depreciating government bonds and treasury notes, would be financially sound. Taken together, these two groups formed a majority in Congress, at least temporarily. Stressing that the interests of the federal government and the proposed bank would not always be the same, they altered Dallas's proposal for a national bank in a number of significant ways. In particular, they eliminated the provisions that allowed the federal government to appoint directors and to order it to suspend specie payments, and that required it to make loans to the federal government. In other words, they reduced the federal government's power over the bank in order to make sure it remained under private control.[13]

Dallas was distraught and angry when he saw the bill adopted by Congress. He wrote to a friend, "I asked for a Bank to serve the Government during the war; and they gave me a commercial bank to go into operation after the war."[14] He promptly advised Madison to veto the measure, which the president proceeded to do. In his veto message, Madison indicated that he rejected the bill because the bank created by it would not help revive the public credit nor help the federal government meet its financial obligations by facilitating the raising of revenue and making loans to do it. At the same time, Madison went out of his way to disassociate himself from those who opposed the bank on constitutional grounds since this was now "precluded in my judgment by repeated recognitions under varied circumstances of the validity of such an institution in acts of the legislative, executive, and judicial branches of the Government, accompanied by indications in different modes, of a concurrence of the general will of the nation."[15] To be sure, there still remained a small and shrinking group of Old Republican purists who believed a national bank was unconstitutional, but they were generally ignored in the events that led up to the creation of the 2BUS. Instead, the early debate on the creation of a new national bank is revealing because it indicates that the major issue was whether the bank was to be under the control of the federal government or whether it was to be an independent and essentially private operation.

Less than two weeks after Madison's veto, news arrived that a peace treaty had been signed with Great Britain, ending the War of 1812. This, combined with the news of Andrew Jackson's great victory at New Orleans (which took place after the war was officially ended), enormously improved the country's economic climate and brought about a revival of public credit, a boost in the income from tax duties, and the beginnings of an increase in the value of government bonds. This sharply reduced the tensions that existed between the president and Congress over the kind of national bank to be created, since the federal government no longer needed bank loans to pay its bills.

Both sides agreed, however, that problems remained and that the creation of some kind of national bank was necessary. The state banks refused to resume specie payments, and the lack of some kind of national circulating medium created all kinds of difficulties and unnecessary expenses. In 1815, Gallatin complained that the value of the various local currencies fluctuated every fifty miles, and he later observed that, at that time, "the currency of the United States, or, to speak more correctly, of the several states [local banks] varied, during the suspension of specie payments, not only from time to time, but at the same time from state to state, and in the same state from place to place."[16]

In his annual message to Congress on December 5, 1815, Madison stressed the need for a uniform national currency and suggested that "the probable operation of a national bank will merit consideration." Since the federal government was rapidly becoming solvent and no longer needed to create the bank in order to finance its operations, its desire to control the financial policies of the bank was no longer a central concern. The bill creating the 2BUS passed in the House 80–71 and in the Senate 22–12, the opposition coming mainly from Federalists and from Republicans representing state banking interests fearful of the new institution's mammoth economic power and concerned over who would control it. Madison signed it into law on April 10, 1816. As finally created, the new bank was clearly, if not entirely, a victory for those people who wanted it to be much more a private rather than a public enterprise.[17]

II

The 2BUS is usually described as being similar to the 1BUS, only larger. There is some truth to this. It was capitalized at $35 million. Its charter was for twenty years, and 80 percent of its capital stock was to be held by private interests, while the federal government was to subscribe the remaining 20 percent. The charter of the 2BUS authorized it to be the federal government's fiscal agent and to act as a depository for government funds without having to pay interest for their use. Its charter provided that the central office of the 2BUS would be located in Philadelphia and that it would have the power to establish branches wherever it chose in the United States.[18]

But there are also important differences between the 2BUS and the 1BUS that are usually not stressed. In return for its charter, the 2BUS was to pay the federal government $1.5 million in three equal yearly installments, and the question of what to do with this money soon became an important political and constitutional issue in itself. Further, the president of the United States was now given the power, with the consent of Congress, to name five of the twenty-five directors instead of their all being elected by the stockholders, as was the case with the 1BUS. The biggest difference, however, was the contexts that existed at the times the two different banks were created. In 1791, only 3 state or local banks existed, and in the beginning almost no tension developed between them and the 1BUS. In 1816, there were around 246 local and state banks, most of which had suspended paying specie as a consequence of the economic difficulties that flowed from the War of 1812, and it is clear that one of the main purposes for creating the 2BUS was to force these banks to resume specie payments.[19]

Local banking interests were at best wary and, in many cases, even hostile to the creation of such an overwhelmingly formidable economic institution as the 2BUS. The great fear was that it would impose its will on them by obtaining large amounts of their bank notes, which the 2BUS could accumulate as a federal government depository, and then present them to the issuing banks and demand specie. While this may have helped to control inflation and produce a more stable currency, it would sharply cut into the earning capacity of local banks since it was through the circulation of their notes, issued by means of loans, that these institutions made their profits. This concern was especially widespread in the South and West, and even in South Carolina, whose most important leaders on the national level had supported the creation of the 2BUS.[20]

Another concern was that the 2BUS, through its branches, would also compete with the local banks for business. Louis McLane, president of the Wilmington branch of the Farmers Bank in Delaware, who was later to become Andrew Jackson's secretary of the treasury during the early phase of his war against the 2BUS, opposed its creation in 1816 because he believed "there is not business for it, unless by the prostration of some other institution, and here will be our chief danger."[21]

The creation of the 2BUS, with the power to create branches wherever it pleased, would also pose a major fiscal threat to many state governments. Following the end of the War of 1812, most states had moved to bring the chaotic financial situation that had come about as a consequence of the demise of the 1BUS and the proliferation of local banks under some kind of control. Unincorporated banks were prohibited or forced to incorporate. This process allowed the states to reap substantial financial rewards. Banks were required to pay bonuses for their charters, agreed to provide funds for educational and internal improvement projects, and allowed state governments to acquire ownership of portions of their stock, which usually sharply increased in value and paid high dividends. Branches of the 2BUS, which would not be subject to state regulation, clearly posed a threat to this important source of income, which for many states amounted to about 20 percent of their revenue stream.[22] Michael Lieb, an important Pennsylvania politician, expressed these concerns with great clarity when he tried unsuccessfully to get his state to levy a tax on the 2BUS and its Pittsburgh branch because they adversely affected the income from the other banks chartered by the state of Pennsylvania and therefore the income of the state itself:

> The State has imposed a tax on its own institutions, and it is incumbent upon the State to protect its own offspring. The principle of equality requires that the Bank of the U.S. should participate in the tax, otherwise advantages would be extended to it, not enjoyed by the State Banks. The establishment of the

U.S. Bank must operate to the injury of our State institutions, and diminish the profits of the State arising out of them. The increase of banking capital has diminished the value of the stock which the State holds in its own institutions, and the revenue arising from it must experience a proportional diminution; to supply the loss, then, the U.S. bank ought to indemnify the State by a contribution equal to that exacted from the State banks.[23]

The creation of branches of the 2BUS also threatened the power of various local elites. Since there were no general incorporation laws at the beginning of the nineteenth century, the incorporation of a bank required a special act of the legislature. This, of course, made the incorporation of a bank a political act, and the successful requests for bank charters invariably went to wealthy and well-connected members of the ruling group, while those out of power would often favor the establishment of a branch of the 2BUS as a way to pursue their own interests. This is precisely what happened in Tennessee, where a group of out-of-power politicians petitioned for the creation of a branch of the 2BUS to be located in Nashville, only to be thwarted when the state adopted a law imposing a high tax of $50,000 on all banks not chartered by the state. This prevented the establishment of a branch of the 2BUS in Tennessee until 1827, when the law was finally repealed.[24]

Considerable concern also existed over the fact that the branches of the 2BUS would be beyond the control of the local communities and the states in which they operated. The charter for the 2BUS required it to establish a branch in the District of Columbia and "wheresoever they shall think fit," although it had the option of using state banks as repositories for federal funds if approved by the secretary of the treasury. Total control of branches was located in the parent bank in Philadelphia. It appointed and removed all of the directors of the branch offices, and while each branch's board of directors had the right to select its own president, in practice this was done in Philadelphia by means of instruction. The main office also set policy for the branches and made all of the rules and regulations under which the branches would operate. Most important of all, the cashier, who was the main operating officer of the branch, was also selected by the main office.[25]

Clashes with the local banks began almost immediately when the 2BUS went into operation in 1817 and pressed the local banks to resume specie payments. Dallas wanted this to occur by February 20, 1817, and a joint resolution by Congress declared that all payments to the federal government after this date would have to be made either in specie, in treasury notes, in notes of the 2BUS, or in the notes of local banks that would pay specie on demand.[26] The local banks, fearing that this would ruin them, refused to accept this date. In doing this, they ended up having considerable support from William H. Crawford, who had succeeded Dallas as secretary of the treasury and who at that time was considered the heir apparent to incoming President James Monroe. He therefore was particularly sensitive to the political complications that would follow any attempt to implement such a policy. In the end, an arrangement was brokered with many of the most important commercial banks in New York City, Philadelphia, Baltimore, and Richmond, which nominally kept the February date, but which in actuality required the 2BUS to pay out specie for its own notes until July 1. This arrangement, however, did not include the many banks in the South and West. It also sharply slowed down the accumulation by the 2BUS of specie, which was needed to underwrite its own operations and to make payments on the international scene.[27]

Another source of conflict emerged when the 2BUS tried to pressure the local banks to transfer to it the deposits of funds made by the federal government before it went into operation, and which the local banks had used as a basis for issuing their own loans and notes. In addition, the 2BUS wanted to discriminate against the notes of local banks that could not be redeemed in specie by sharply discounting them. These policies were also vigorously opposed by the local banks. They argued that it could ruin them since they lacked adequate specie reserves, or would at least force them to contract their loans, thereby creating economic havoc in the various communities they served. A group of bankers representing various local banks in western Pennsylvania, western Virginia, and eastern Ohio warned in particular of the problems that would ensue from placing them "in the power of an institution the Directors of which are not at all identified in the feeling or interest with the western banks or country."[28] A Boston banker similarly observed:

> [T]he call for money has been so great in this place since the peace that we have been induced, and in a manner obliged, to discount [make loans] freely to the mercantile interest, to manufacturers and other businesses, to enable them to support the extreme pressure which they are under, and it will be extremely injurious to be obliged to call suddenly on those persons.[29]

Once again, the pleas of local banks found a sympathetic ear in Crawford. He was motivated by economic considerations as well as political ones. Requiring local banks to pay out their limited specie reserves would force them to contract their loans, slowing down or even ending the boom times that characterized most of 1816, 1817, and the first half of 1818, and would make it difficult, if not impossible, for many people, especially in the South and West, to pay for the lands they had purchased on credit from the federal government and to pay their taxes. Crawford recognized that the growing tensions between the 2BUS and the local banks had become difficult and explosive. In no uncertain terms, he warned William Jones, the president of the 2BUS, and a number of its directors to move cautiously:

> In whatever point of view I have been able to consider the subject it appears fraught with mischief to the community, calculated to draw upon the bank [the 2BUS] the public indignation and effect its extinction at the end of [its] charter. It places the bank and community in a state of open hostility, continually exciting to acts of mutual aggression upon the rights and interests of each other. In such a contest the Government will have no alternative. It cannot hesitate upon the course which public duty requires it to take. Its weight and influence must be exerted to save the community.[30]

Crawford's position was based on his recognition of an important political reality: in 1817, the local banks were very popular and had strong political support. These included numerous debtors, who benefited from the inflation these banks had helped to create, and stockholders, including numerous members of state legislatures, who had prospered from rising stock prices and the dividends paid by these banks. In addition, these banks contributed in a major way to the agricultural prosperity the country enjoyed following the end of the War of 1812, as their easy loan policies allowed numerous people to purchase land, plant crops, and purchase slaves. The capital these local banks provided also helped to underwrite the development and expansion of various boom towns and commercial centers throughout the country. These included Pittsburgh, Lexington, Louisville, Cincinnati, St. Louis, Rochester, Nashville, Huntsville, and Milledgeville.

Although people recognized that many of the local banks lacked adequate capital and specie reserves to back up the loans they made and the currency they issued, and that their policies were a major source of inflation, very few were inclined to make an issue of it, while those who did were ignored or worse. Condy Raguet, a state senator from Pennsylvania who had a good understanding of how banks operated, explained the situation in these terms to the British political economist David Ricardo:

> The whole of our population are either stockholders of [local] banks or in debt to them. It is not the *interest* of the first to press the banks and the rest are *afraid*. This is the whole secret. An independent man, who was neither a stockholder or debtor, who would have ventured the banks to do justice, would have been persecuted as an enemy of society.[31]

In a special report to the House of Representatives on banking, Secretary of the Treasury Crawford described the situation in similar terms:

> On the part of the [local] banks, mutual weakness had produced mutual forebearance [*sic*]. The extensive diffusion of bank stock among the great body of citizens, in most of the states, had produced the same forebearance among individuals. To demand specie of the banks, when it was known they were unable to pay, was to destroy their own interests, by destroying

the credit of the banks in which the productive portion of their own property was invested. In favor of forebearance was also added the influence of the great mass of debtors. To this portion of the community all other evils were light when compared with the imperious demands of the banks.[32]

III

Given their popularity, political connections, and economic power, the local banks were a formidable force in immediate post–War of 1812 America. They presented intractable political and economic obstacles to the implementation of the policies the supporters of the 2BUS favored. But in addition to this, the 2BUS had other problems that were related to its organization and actual operation in its early years, and they were mainly self-made.

To start, the 2BUS failed to obtain an adequate amount of specie for the purchase of its stock. According to its charter, one-fifth of the stock ($7 million) was to be paid for in gold and silver, and the balance ($28 million) in government securities, in three installments six months apart. This would have been difficult and expensive since both specie (always scarce in the United States) and the securities of the federal government were selling at a premium. In order to accommodate a number of its stockholders, the 2BUS instead accepted various promissory notes, in many cases secured by stock held in the 2BUS. This was a clear violation of its charter. It also meant that the 2BUS started business low in specie and in a financially vulnerable position. According to one estimate, it had only $2 million in specie, $14 million in government securities, and $12 million in IOUs. To compensate for this, the 2BUS had to purchase specie abroad, starting in the summer of 1817 and throughout 1818, paying a premium since Central and Eastern Europe, especially Austria and Russia, were preparing to go on the gold standard and were competing for specie.[33]

Another problem was the election of William Jones as the first president of the 2BUS. He was essentially a political appointee, having served without any distinction as both secretary of the navy and acting secretary of the treasury under President Madison, who strongly supported his quest for the post. He was also controversial. Stephen Girard, in particular, opposed Jones on the grounds that he was not a "man of solid means," for he had gone through bankruptcy only two years earlier.[34] Although it is not clear that Jones was corrupt, he proved to be an ineffective administrator who could easily be manipulated and who made a number of significant financial mistakes. He also was preoccupied with seeing the 2BUS quickly become profitable, which would raise the value of the stock he owned in it, thus alleviating his personal financial difficulties.[35]

In addition to the problems that were to flow from Jones's mismanagement, the board of directors of the 2BUS fell under the control of people, a number of whom were unscrupulous and dishonest, who were more interested in making a profit than they were in controlling inflation, reforming the currency, or establishing financial stability. The charter of the 2BUS specifically limited private stockholders, no matter how large their holdings, to a maximum of thirty votes, which included both Girard and Astor, who had substantial holdings of stock in the 2BUS. While both men expected to make a profit from the venture, they were also committed to the creation of a sound monetary system. Yet despite their business skills, they found themselves quickly isolated by a group of speculators and devious business types, mainly centered in Baltimore, who underwrote the purchase of stock in the 2BUS by a large number of individuals who then gave them their proxies, which allowed them to gain control of the board of directors.[36] As a consequence, Girard severed his ties with the 2BUS and, along with Astor, became a formidable opponent of it and engaged in various machinations to discredit it.[37]

These speculators were after quick profits. As a consequence, key officers of the 2BUS immediately indicated that they had no intention of emulating the sound and cautious policies that had made the 1BUS such a financially responsible institution. James McCulloch, the cashier at the Baltimore office, observed in March 1817 that the lending policies of the 1BUS had been mistaken for "instead of expanding its views as the country and its trade grew, it pursued a timid and faltering course, and invited by its measures, the erection of rival institutions [the local banks] to share its business, and contaminate the character of the country's medium."[38] Jones was in complete agreement. He indicated in July 1817, "I am not at all disposed to take the late Bank of the United States as an exemplar in practice because I think its operations were circumscribed by a policy less enlarged, liberal and useful than its powers and resources would have justified."[39] What this meant, in effect, was that the 2BUS was going to compete with, not restrain, local banks by providing easy credit to further fuel the prosperity that had developed following the end of the War of 1812. It also meant that the 2BUS would make long-term loans.

An immediate manifestation of this policy occurred when the 2BUS opened nineteen branch offices in fourteen states in 1817. They were located in the following cities:

Portsmouth, N.H.	Savannah, Ga.
Boston, Mass.	New Orleans, La.
Providence, R.I.	Cincinnati, Ohio
Middleton, Conn.	Chillicothe, Ohio
New York, N.Y.	Lexington, Ky.
Baltimore, Md.	Louisville, Ky.
Washington, D.C.	Pittsburgh, Pa.
Richmond, Va.	Fayetteville, N.C.
Norfolk, Va.	Augusta, Ga. (never
Charleston, S.C.	established)

As a result of the establishment of these branches, which the two succeeding presidents of the 2BUS, Langdon Cheves and Nicholas Biddle, found to be excessive, the tensions between the 2BUS and the local banks and their communities were further exacerbated.[40]

Jones also mismanaged the relationship between the branches and the home office in Philadelphia, for he viewed the branches simply as an extension of the 2BUS in Philadelphia. He therefore allowed the individual branches to have unlimited power to make loans and issue notes which could be redeemed for specie at any office of the 2BUS. As a result, the capital of the 2BUS was steadily transferred to the South and West throughout 1817 and 1818, for that is where the demand for credit was greatest. Moreover, many of the loans made at the time were for long-term ventures that were secured by personal notes and real estate holdings: town lots, buildings, farm land, and the value of future commodity sales, which could not easily be liquefied in times of financial crisis. This was to cause major problems since specie was really needed by the 2BUS in Philadelphia to make payments to England on the Louisiana debt and for the large importation of manufactured goods that had taken place following the end of the War of 1812, specie which the 2BUS now did not have.[41]

IV

The debate that emerged among politicians, various members of the business community, and even the general public over the creation and the early policies of the 2BUS was driven mainly by economic considerations. Constitutional questions were either held in abeyance or ignored, and if they were raised at all it was by a minority of Old Republicans, who were marginalized and politically weak. However, the creation of the 2BUS did indirectly lead to a major constitutional discussion of another issue. It emerged from the question of how to spend the bonus money the 2BUS was required to pay the federal government in return for its charter, and it involved the legitimacy of a federal program of internal improvements. In addition to being important in themselves, the constitutional issues raised by a federal program of internal improvements foreshadowed in a number of important ways the constitutional issues that were eventually to emerge in connection with the 2BUS.

The internal improvements issue can be traced back to the Jeffersonian ascendancy that followed the election of 1800. In his second inaugural address, in March 1805, Jefferson urged the creation "in time of peace" of a nationally financed system involving "rivers, canals, roads, arts, manufactures, education, and other great objects within each State." The following year, in his sixth annual message, he again urged the adoption of such a program for "by these operations new channels of communication will be opened between the States: the lines of separation will disappear, their interests will be identified, and their union cemented by new and indissoluble ties." It revealed, among other things, Jefferson's concern after the Louisiana Purchase of integrating the West into the union.[42]

This program clearly had strong nationalist implications. Some precedents for it existed. The Ohio Enabling Act of 1802, under which that state entered the union in 1803, provided that 5 percent of the proceeds from the sale of its public lands be used to build roads to connect it with the East. A national road was also begun whose route stretched from Cumberland, Maryland, into Pennsylvania and through western Virginia into the Old Northwest. But neither was on such a scale or as elaborate as what was now being proposed. To this end, Jefferson instructed his secretary of the treasury, Albert Gallatin, to prepare a report about the building of a national system of roads and canals.[43]

At the same time, while Jefferson strongly favored a federal system of internal improvements on policy grounds, he recognized that it involved numerous complicated problems that had not previously been carefully thought through. Who was to choose the various sites and routes that were involved: the states or the federal government? Who would control or maintain the roads and canals: the states or the federal government? Should the states have a veto power over the decisions of the federal government that affected their lands and citizens? Jefferson had major doubts that the federal government had the authority to act without consulting the states on these issues. He therefore wanted some kind of amendment to the Constitution granting the federal government the power to act in these areas.[44]

As it turned out, difficulties in foreign affairs and the economic hard times that dominated the end of Jefferson's second administration forced the issue to be postponed. It was taken up again by President Madison in his annual message in December 1815. The War of 1812 had fully exposed the inadequacies of the country's transportation system, and he recommended that a system of roads and canals throughout the country be established and that this "can be executed under the national authority," because it would require "a national jurisdiction and national means." He also observed "that any defect of constitutional authority which may be encountered can be supplied in a mode which the Constitution itself has providently pointed out," meaning the adoption of an amendment. In the same message, he also urged the creation of a "national seminary of learning" within the District of

Columbia, which, among other things, would serve "as a model instructive in the formation of other seminaries."[45]

Congress responded favorably when, under the leadership of Calhoun, a measure was introduced that became known as the Bonus Bill. It provided that the dividends that the federal government received for its stock in the 2BUS, as well as the $1.5 million bonus for its charter, be set aside to create a permanent fund for building roads and canals. Earlier, Calhoun had made it clear that he favored a program of extensive government spending. In arguing for maintaining the high level of taxation established during the War of 1812, he asserted "it was preposterous to say, that we should not lay taxes on the people. . . . gentlemen ought not to give into the contracted idea, that taxes were so much money taken from the people: properly applied, the money proceeding from taxes, was money put out to the best possible interest for the people."[46]

When the Bonus Bill came up for a vote in Congress, Calhoun was dismissive of the constitutional objections that were raised against a federal program of internal improvements. In a statement he undoubtedly would come to regret when he became the leading advocate of the doctrine of nullification, he observed that he "was no advocate for refined arguments on the Constitution. The instrument was not intended as a thesis for the logician to exercise his ingenuity on. It ought to be construed with plain, good sense; and what can be more express than the Constitution on this very point?"[47]

Strong support for the Bonus Bill also came from the powerful Speaker of the House, Henry Clay. More of a political animal, Clay was less dismissive of the constitutional objections to the bill than was Calhoun. Unlike Calhoun, who directly confronted the constitutional issues, Clay tried to finesse them. He stressed instead "the importance and utility of internal improvements" and argued that all that was required at this time was to create a fund for them without making actual appropriations about which constitutional questions might emerge. In other words, "Congress could at some future day examine into the constitutionality of the question, and if it has the power it would exercise it; if it has not, the Constitution, there could be very little doubt, would be so amended as to confer it." By so neutralizing the constitutional questions swirling around the implementation of a federal program of internal improvements, Clay was able to bring about the passage of the Bonus Bill. Nonetheless, the vote was extremely close, 86–84 in the House and 20–15 in the Senate.[48]

On March 3, 1817, in his last act as president, Madison vetoed the Bonus Bill. In a very short message, he made it clear that his objections were exclusively based on constitutional considerations and not policy ones. He denied that a national system of internal improvements could be justified by the necessary and proper clause or by the federal government's power to regulate commerce. Nor could it be legitimized by Congress's right "to provide for the common defense and general welfare." For to do so "would have the effect of giving to Congress a general power of legislation instead of the defined and limited one hitherto understood to belong to them." Moreover, it would also subject the states to the total control of Congress since, according to the supremacy clause of the Constitution, its acts were the supreme law of the land, whereas Madison believed that the power of determining the boundary between the states and the national government belonged to the judiciary and not to Congress. He concluded his brief message by indicating his belief that the power to create a federal system of internal improvement "can not be deduced from any part of it [the Constitution] without an inadmissible latitude of construction and a reliance on insufficient precedents." He also asserted his belief "that the permanent success of the Constitution depends on a definite partition of powers between the General and the State Governments, and that no adequate landmarks would be left by the constructive extension of the powers of Congress as proposed in the bill."[49]

What motivated Madison to take this position? How could he reconcile the creation of the 2BUS, which he strongly advocated and of which he approved, with the interpretation of the Constitution he had just asserted in vetoing the Bonus Bill? Was Madison, now that he was permanently leaving public office, simply reverting to the states' rights position he had adopted in the 1790s? Or did fundamental differences exist between the law that created the 2BUS and the Bonus Bill as well as the purposes and the circumstances which had brought them about? It is the latter that definitely seems much closer to the truth.

Although based on a loose interpretation of the Constitution, the law that provided for the 2BUS created a definite and discrete institution; in other words, you knew what you were getting when you created the 2BUS, or at least thought you did. The federal system of internal improvements as defined and defended in the Bonus Bill, on the other hand, was open-ended and lacking in details as to how extensive it might be. Although the debate on the Bonus Bill focused on roads and canals, could it be extended by construction or precedent to also include a national educational system and federally funded literary and scientific societies scattered throughout the country, which is the way Jefferson had earlier described a federal system of internal improvements? In fact, this broad definition of a federal system of internal improvements may have been part of the reason Jefferson and Madison wanted an amendment to the Constitution in order to legitimize the granting of such broad powers to the federal government. President John Quincy Adams (1825–1829) was later to define a federal program of internal improvements in similarly broad terms, although he believed that Congress did have the power under the Constitution to create such a program and that an amendment was not needed.[50]

Another difference between the creation of the 2BUS and the Bonus Bill was that Madison viewed the former as a necessity while the latter was merely a matter of good policy and desirable. The financial difficulties that faced the federal government after the failure to recharter the 1BUS forced many people, even those who had constitutional reservations, to view the creation of the 2BUS as indispensable to the well-being of the country. The same could not be said for the building of a system of roads and canals, no matter how useful they might prove to be.

Beyond this, the political circumstances in April 1816, when the 2BUS was chartered, and those that existed almost a year later when Madison vetoed the Bonus Bill, were distinctly different. In early 1816, the Fourteenth Congress voted to increase the salaries of its members, something the overwhelming majority felt was overdue since they were still receiving payment at the same rate ($6 per diem and a travel allowance) that had been established back in 1789, which had by then been substantially eroded by inflation. What they were totally unprepared for was the intense and widespread reaction of their constituents, which manifested itself in the fall 1816 congressional elections. Incumbents ran into so much hostility in their home districts that a large number decided not to run for reelection; a substantial number who did run for reelection was defeated; and many of those few who succeeded in being reelected had to promise to work for a repeal of the "salary grab act," as it came to be known. The result was that two-thirds of the House of Representatives was replaced in what was the largest single turnover in Congress up to that time.[51]

Congressional salaries were the central issue in the election of 1816, but it is clear that it also brought a halt to the enactment of any further nationalist legislation. In his seventh annual address, Madison had recommended the creation of a national university in Washington, D.C., but the congressional committee that considered the matter reported in March 1817 that it be indefinitely postponed and that they be discharged because "all further consideration had become useless. . . . The measure, if indeed it were a good one, had fallen upon evil times and into inauspicious hands."[52] There had also been some hope for a major increase and restructuring of the federal judiciary that would create a separate system of circuit courts which as Thomas Todd, an associate justice of the U.S. Supreme Court, observed, would "relieve us from the arduous duty of attending the Circuit Courts, but that unfortunate measure the Compensation bill has almost blasted every hope."[53] William G. Blount, a member of the House of Representatives from the Knoxville district in Tennessee, who voted against the chartering of the 2BUS, was the only member of the state congressional delegation returned in the ensuing election. He blamed his colleagues' defeat to a considerable extent on their votes for the bank. The man he told this to, Jonathan Roberts of Pennsylvania, observed: "The temper of the times require[s] prudence."[54] Madison undoubtedly was aware of all of these developments, and they may well have contributed to his decision to veto the Bonus Bill.

Madison's decision to veto the Bonus Bill probably also had a personal dimension to it, although here the evidence is circumstantial; and while it was not the main cause of his opposition, it did tend to intensify it. Calhoun, as one of the leading members of the War Hawks, had been very critical of Madison's handling of the events leading up to the War of 1812, especially his unwillingness to engage in military preparations and his not going to war earlier. Calhoun believed the events leading up to the War of 1812 represented "the commence[ment] of a new era in our politicks," as a new generation, more aggressive and self-assured, was taking over the leadership of the country.[55] Nor was Madison very happy, as his veto message indicated, with Calhoun's glib dismissal of the constitutional problems involved in a federal program of internal improvements. Madison also undoubtedly did not approve of Calhoun's arrogance when, following the congressional elections of 1816, Calhoun unsuccessfully opposed the repeal of the Compensation Act, arguing in Federalist-like fashion that Congress did not necessarily have to obey the expressed will of its constituents.[56] The day before Madison sent to Congress his veto message on the Bonus Bill, he called Calhoun in to personally inform him about his decision. By vetoing the Bonus Bill, Madison was demonstrating that the older generation of the founders still had to be reckoned with, that constitutional considerations still mattered, and that the will of the people, the very essence of republican government, still had to be taken into account. Madison clearly had strong feelings on the issue, for he ignored a request from Henry Clay to neither veto nor sign the Bonus Bill, and leave the decision up to his successor.[57] It is clear that Madison wanted his opinion to be known in what was to be his last official pronouncement on a constitutional issue.

Strong support for Madison's position on internal improvements came from his successor, James Monroe. In his inaugural address, delivered on March 4, 1817, only a day after Madison's veto message, the new president went out of his way to indicate that, while a federal program of roads and canals was necessary, it would require a "constitutional sanction." He reiterated his position in his annual message to Congress on December 2, recommending "the adoption of an amendment to the Constitution, which will give to Congress the right in question." He also urged that the amendment should also grant to Congress a right to "institute like-wise seminaries of learning."[58]

Henry Clay quickly responded, making it clear that on this issue there would be no compromise. He completely rejected the idea of an amendment to the Constitution because of the likelihood it would be defeated, not because a federal program of internal improvements was unpopular, but because it would probably lead to an unnatural alliance between those opposed to the program and those who believed Congress already had the authority to implement it. The failure to get an amendment, of course, would make it impossible to simply legislate such a program in the future. He also reiterated his belief in the need for Congress to have what he called "constructive powers" under the Constitution for "we cannot forsee [sic] and provide specifically for all contingencies. Man and his language are both imperfect." After stressing the great value of a federal program of internal improvements, Clay denounced the particularistic prejudices of the states' rights opponents of the program and criticized Madison for ignoring established precedents, such as the building of the national road and the lessons of the recent war on the country's need for an internal system of roads and canals, and for unexpectedly reversing (in Clay's view) his position on internal improvements after he had urged Congress to take up the matter. He also criticized incoming President James Monroe, who endorsed Madison's position, for precipitously dealing with the issue in his annual address when there was no actual measure before him.[59]

Meanwhile, in the fall of 1817, the House of Representatives had appointed a special committee chaired by Henry St. George Tucker to also consider the question of a federal program of internal improvements. It reported a short time later, calling it "a great Constitutional question" and denied "that the expressions in the Message of the President [Monroe] of an opinion unfavourable to the Constitutional powers of the General Government should be permitted to have any influence on the disposition of Congress to legislate on this interesting subject." The report endorsed the creation of a national program of roads and canals "with the consent of the states." Eschewing "what is called a liberal construction of the Constitution," it justified such a program in terms of precedent and military necessity. The report concluded by recommending a reenactment of the Bonus Bill which had been vetoed by Madison and which Monroe had indicated would be unacceptable. After a long and desultory debate, Congress adopted a resolution asserting that Congress had the power "to appropriate money for the construction of post roads, military *and other* roads, and of canals, and for the improvement of water courses." By close votes, however, the House rejected three other resolutions asserting the authority of Congress "to construct" post and military roads, canals for commerce between the states, and canals for military purposes, so long as compensation be provided for any private property confiscated. What all of this meant was that, despite the extensive debate over the constitutionality of a federal program of internal improvements, no action had been taken, especially since President Monroe remained adamant in his opposition to such a program without a constitutional amendment.[60]

Although the struggle over a federal program of internal improvements ended in 1818 with an unproductive standoff between Congress and the executive, it still was significant. It raised once again many of the great constitutional questions that had been at the center of the debate over the creation of the 1BUS in 1791 and its rechartering in 1811, but that had been pushed aside by the economic urgency that surrounded the creation of the 2BUS in 1816. These included strict versus broad interpretations of the Constitution where the powers of Congress were concerned. It also involved the issue of states' rights and the related question of the right of the federal government to create institutions that would operate within state boundaries and the jurisdictional problems that would flow from this. This had been an unimportant issue where the 1BUS was concerned, but it certainly was very relevant to the operation of the 2BUS, which had been given the right to create branches wherever it pleased. Finally, the debate over a federal program of internal improvements also raised the question of the role of precedent in deciding constitutional disputes.

THREE

THE STATES VERSUS
THE SECOND BANK OF THE
UNITED STATES

The crisis for the 2BUS finally began in the summer of 1818. This was the beginning of the Panic of 1819 and the depression that dominated the early 1820s. The causes of these economic difficulties had their origins in developments on the international scene. For by 1818, Europe had begun to recover from the economic disruptions caused by the wars of the French Revolution as well as by a run of bad weather, and now was capable of feeding itself. This led to a sharp decline in its demand for American food products. In addition, English manufacturers, discontented over rapidly rising cotton prices in the United States, began to look to India as an alternative source of supply. In the long run, Indian cotton did not prove to be a viable alternative to the tougher fiber grown in the United States, but in the short run it did lead to the collapse of the American cotton market. Moreover, Eastern Europe's continued demand for gold and silver helped to raise the price of specie and placed a strain on reserves throughout the world.[1]

I

Within the United States, the impact of the Panic of 1819 was intensified by the easy credit that had been extended by both the local banks and the 2BUS, which now had to call in their loans and demanded payment in specie in order to meet their own obligations. As commodity prices fell, businesses failed, unemployment rose, creditors moved against debtors, and there was widespread foreclosure on lands and farms that had been bought with loans that could no longer be paid. The Panic of 1819 and the depression that followed was national in scope, but it had its hardest impact in those areas of the country that had undergone the greatest economic expansion in the 1815–1818 period: western Pennsylvania, western Virginia, Ohio, Kentucky, Tennessee, Alabama, Mississippi, Louisiana, Georgia, and South Carolina. Finally, in late 1818, the 2BUS, as the fiscal agent for the federal government, also had to make a major payment, much of it in specie, on the bonds issued to pay for the Louisiana Purchase.[2]

The 2BUS responded to these developments in a number of different ways. To stop the drain of specie from its eastern branches, it required that the notes issued by its branches could only be redeemed at the branch that issued them. Salutary in many ways, the policy undercut the claim that the 2BUS provided a truly national currency. Moreover, in addition to curtailing its loans, the 2BUS demanded payment in specie for the balances due to it from local banks in order to meet its obligations on the international scene. For example, it required that the local banks in Cincinnati, where the sale of public lands had been particularly feverish after the War of 1812, pay off what they owed in specie at the rate of 20 percent per month. In Georgia, a local banker, responding to similar pressure, described the demand as "unprecedented." These developments forced those local banks that wanted to survive to, in turn, contract their loans and press their debtors for payment in specie. A substantial number of local banks defaulted and were forced out of business as a consequence of the broader results of the Panic of 1819: economic stagnation, deflation, unemployment, ruin, and widespread distress and misery. During this time, the 2BUS became widely unpopular and was generally viewed as the cause of the country's economic difficulties, when in fact its new policies mainly reflected and aggravated more fundamental economic pressures.[3]

Congress responded on November 18, 1818, by appointing a special committee to investigate the operations of the 2BUS. The ensuing report was unfavorable to the bank and further hurt its reputation. The committee found that the 2BUS had violated its charter by failing to require the payment of specie for its stock, by paying dividends to stockholders who had not completed the purchase of their stock, by allowing numerous irregularities to take place during the election of its board of directors, by making questionable loans, by generally being poorly managed, and by not paying sufficient attention to its public responsibilities. The committee did not make any specific recommendations on how to proceed, but left the matter up to Congress.[4]

Although many people in Congress, including the chair of the investigating committee, John C. Spencer of New York, wanted to move directly against the 2BUS and revoke its charter or enter legal proceedings against it, they could not muster a majority. Instead, supporters for the continuation of the 2BUS effectively argued that such an institution was a necessity in order to prevent a return to the situation that had existed during the War of 1812, when the government was financially dependent on local banks for loans and other services, inflation was rampant, and nothing resembling a national currency existed. What was needed, the advocates of a national bank argued, was new leadership and a reform of the 2BUS's policies. In Congress, this point of view was effectively espoused by William Lowndes of South Carolina, Louis McLane of Delaware, and Thomas Sergeant of Pennsylvania, and it was privately supported by Clay, Crawford, and President Monroe.[5] A short time later, Secretary of State John Quincy Adams recorded a conversation with Monroe where the president indicated:

> With respect to the bank, he said no man had a more convincing experience of its absolute necessity than he had during the late war, when [as secretary of war and as secretary of state] he had been obliged to borrow money on his own responsibility whenever he could obtain it, and which at one place was at one stage of depreciation, and another at another.

As to the constitutional objections to incorporating a national bank, Monroe pointed out, "Mr. Madison and Mr. Jefferson himself had considered them as settled by twenty years of practice and acquiescence under the first bank."[6]

In other words, there was strong support among the Washington establishment for a continuation of the 2BUS. An additional explanation for this may be that the bank had been an important source of loans for many people who had gotten into economic difficulties. As one member of the board of directors advised: "it is all important to accommodate the Members of Congress."[7] Among the people who asked the 2BUS for help at various times were Senators Thomas Worthington of Ohio and Wilson Cary Nicholas of Virginia; Daniel D. Tompkins, vice president of the United States; and former president James Madison.[8]

On January 21, 1819, despite the fact that the board of directors had just reelected him president of the 2BUS, Jones resigned. He was temporarily replaced by James C. Fisher of Philadelphia, who became acting president and who a short time later wrote to a knowledgeable critic of the 2BUS's activities under Jones's leadership that he was

> perfectly in accord in sentiment with you, that unless the Speculative Directors resign or are put out of the Bank, it will injure the National Credit. I am happy to say that the last election for Directors has been so managed as to leave out all the speculators except two or three, and they have lost all their influence, so that if the Bank can now be placed on safe ground it may yet prove of immense benefit to the Country.

He also gave assurances that "measures are now abt. to be adopted by the present Board . . . to try to do what is right and honorable."[9] The board started by electing Langdon Cheves of South Carolina, who had joined the board of directors of the 2BUS in January and who had the backing of the Monroe administration, as president on March 6, 1819, and he immediately launched a searching investigation into all of the bank's activities.[10]

Congress's decision not to revoke its charter had saved the 2BUS, but it did nothing to alleviate its unpopularity at the local level, where the most direct assaults on the 2BUS originated and where a number of fundamental constitutional questions were raised. Indiana in 1816 and Illinois in 1818 had included provisions in their constitutions prohibiting the establishment of any banks not chartered by the state. Maryland in February 1817 levied a tax of $15,000 per year on the branch of the 2BUS in Baltimore. Georgia in December 1817 levied a tax of 331/4 cents on every $100 of bank stock of out-of-state banks, which it made clear in a separate resolution was meant to apply to branches of the 2BUS. That same month, Tennessee adopted a tax of $50,000 on any bank not having a state charter. North Carolina in December 1818 levied an annual tax of $5,000 upon the Fayetteville branch of the 2BUS. In January 1819, Kentucky adopted a yearly tax of $60,000 each on the Lexington and Louisville branches of the 2BUS, and Ohio levied an annual tax of $50,000 on the 2BUS branches in its state. And the legislature of Pennsylvania in early 1820 proposed an amendment to the U.S. Constitution that would limit the 2BUS and its branches to the District of Columbia, a proposal that was supported by Tennessee, Ohio, Indiana, and Illinois.[11]

In treating these developments, scholars have viewed them as part of a common movement fueled by "hatred and enmity" toward the 2BUS and as "practically annihilatory" in their effect.[12] This is an oversimplification at best, for these measures were very much a mixed bag in terms of their timing, purpose, and effect. The measures adopted were not part of a concerted movement against the 2BUS. They were disconnected as most movements involving states' rights by their very nature tended to be. The purpose of the measures in Indiana, Illinois, and Tennessee was to prevent the establishment of branches of the 2BUS in these states and had nothing to do with the hard times created by the Panic of 1819; it is doubtful that there was much popular support for or against them. The purpose of the Kentucky and Ohio taxes was to drive the existing branches out of their states, and they had considerable popular support and represented a real threat to the operation of the 2BUS. On the other hand, the purpose of the relatively low taxes levied by Maryland, North Carolina, and Georgia was to raise revenue, not to destroy the activities of the branches of the 2BUS in their states, and they also did not attract much public attention. As such, they were significantly different from what was going on in Kentucky and Ohio and raised very different constitutional issues. Henry Clay agreed. A strong supporter of the 2BUS, he also was its lead attorney in Kentucky and Ohio, and he wrote:

> It follows, of course, that the General Government had the right to charter the Bank (of which alone it is the judge) [and] the States cannot have a right to destroy the efficacy of the charter[.] —It may be another question (on which I do not now offer any opinion) how far they have the power to lay a tax bona fide for the purpose of revenue and which shall be only equal to the tax imposed on similar monied institutions within their jurisdictions respectively.[13]

A similarly ambivalent position was taken by the New York legislature in 1823. It rejected Pennsylvania's proposal for a constitutional amendment to restrict the activities of a national bank to the District of Columbia on the grounds that "the extreme embarrassment" suffered by the federal government during the War of 1812 had made its creation, along with branches in the different states, a necessity. Nonetheless, the writers of the report also recognized that the 2BUS was "a powerful monied institution extending over the widespread union above the power and in no manner subject to the direction of the state governments." Moreover, while it did not explicitly endorse the legitimacy of state taxation of the various branches of the 2BUS, it did sympathize with the view "that wished that the power now exercised by Congress in establishing a national bank, with the branches in the several states, had been used with some limitation, subjecting them to such taxation in the respective States as the local banks were or might be subjected to."[14]

Sectional considerations also played a role in explaining the reaction to the 2BUS. This is because the 2BUS played a different role in different parts of the country. In New England and in the mid-Atlantic states of New York, eastern Pennsylvania, New Jersey, Delaware, and Maryland, where many sound local banks existed by the end of the second decade of the nineteenth century, the 2BUS did not have much "regulating" to do and for the most part played only a relatively minor role in the economies of these areas. Therefore, there did not exist much hostility or even concern about its existence or operations. If anything, the branches of the 2BUS established in these states were considered a welcome addition because they helped to facilitate economic transactions with the federal government. Not surprisingly, therefore, when Pennsylvania proposed its amendment to the U.S. Constitution to limit the national bank's activities to the District of Columbia, the proposed amendment was explicitly rejected by the legislatures of New Hampshire, Vermont, Massachusetts, Connecticut, New York, New Jersey, South Carolina, and Georgia. On the other hand, in the West, in western Pennsylvania, Ohio, and Kentucky, where many unsound banks existed, many of which failed or went out of business in the aftermath of the Panic of 1819, the branches of the 2BUS played a much more dominant and controversial role, and because of this engendered a more intense and extreme opposition. The situation in 1819 in the states of North and South Carolina and Georgia was more complicated, for there existed in these states a small number of generally sound, well-run, and highly capitalized banks with branch systems of their own. However, because their business involved a greater percentage of high-risk, long-term loans where land was put up for security, repayment was seasonal in nature, and the course of exchange was mainly to the Northeast, they were at greater risk when hard times came. Many people in these states at first welcomed the establishment of a branch of the 2BUS because it would be a source of additional capital during boom times and would be especially useful in the making of interregional payments, but they quickly became disillusioned when it began to press the state banks for specie to the point where it threatened to ruin them and adversely affected the local economies.

II

The Maryland tax is particularly significant since it is the origin of the great Supreme Court case of *McCulloch v. Maryland*. This alone should have made scholars particularly curious about it, but this has not been the case. Moreover, the closer one looks at the Maryland origins of the case, the "curiouser and curiouser" it becomes.

A close examination of the Maryland law, particularly in regard to its timing, its provisions, and its purpose, reveals that its objectives were different from those of the laws passed by Ohio, Kentucky, and Tennessee, which were meant to force the withdrawal of the branches of the 2BUS or to prevent their establishment within their boundaries. To begin with, the Maryland law was introduced in late 1817 and adopted in February 1818, a half year before popular opinion had turned against the 2BUS in opposition to its policy of contracting loans and demanding specie from local banks. Also, the tax levied by the Maryland law only amounted to $15,000, which was substantially less than the amounts levied by Ohio, Kentucky, and Tennessee.[15] Moreover, as Hezekiah Niles pointed out, "all the banks in the city are in like manner taxed."[16] Given that the volume of business of the Baltimore branch was so much larger than that of the western branches, it is clear that the tax did not threaten the viability of the Baltimore branch of the 2BUS as a profit-making institution in Maryland. The following table indicates the amounts of the loans made by the most active branches of the 2BUS in June 1818:[17]

Philadelphia	$10,832,000
Baltimore	9,289,000
Richmond	3,041,000
Charleston	2,786,000
New York	2,016,000
Cincinnati	1,825,000
Lexington	1,620,000
New Orleans	1,441,000
Norfolk	1,403,000
Washington, D.C.	1,392,000

When some of the officers of the 2BUS expressed dismay at the levying of the Maryland tax, both William Crawford and George Williams, a director of the Baltimore branch, believed that the best course for the 2BUS to follow was simply to pay the tax rather than to try and fight it and get involved in a morass of political and constitutional problems.[18]

The purpose of the Maryland tax was not to destroy or even attack the Baltimore branch of the 2BUS, but to raise revenue. The state had been unusually hard hit by the War of 1812. The unsuccessful defense of Washington, D.C., had fallen mainly on the Maryland militia, and it proved expensive, the cost being estimated at nearly a half million dollars. Although the federal government was expected to eventually pay for most of this, it was going to be a slow and difficult process to accumulate the necessary documentation. In addition, the federal government had its own financial problems during the years 1815–1817 and was in no hurry to deal with Maryland's claims. This left Maryland in dire financial straits. To meet its various financial obligations, the state levied a series of taxes on auction houses, state banking institutions, and other private corporations in order to raise money. This was the driving force behind Maryland's levying a $15,000 per annum tax on the Baltimore branch of the 2BUS. What the state wanted, according to Joseph Hopkinson, who was one of the attorneys for Maryland in *McCulloch v. Maryland*, was for the 2BUS to submit "to the jurisdiction of the laws of the State, in the same manner with other corporations and other property; and all this might be done without ruining the institution, or destroying its national uses."[19]

The Maryland law did not attract much public attention when it came up in the legislature. The measure passed the House of Delegates by a vote of 36–17 and the Senate by a much closer margin of 5–4, where the opposition was mainly from Federalists led by Virgil Maxcy and Roger Brooke Taney.[20] At no point did the law's supporters decry the constitutionality of the 2BUS, or even deny it had the right to create branches on the local level. The only constitutional issues raised came from the opposition and were not directed at the 2BUS but at the proposed tax. As one observer put it: "some members considered it impolitic, and some impolitic and unconstitutional."[21]

There is other evidence to indicate that Maryland did not desire to drive the Baltimore branch of the 2BUS out of the state nor to threaten in any other way the existence of the 2BUS. When Congress investigated the activities of the 2BUS and then debated whether to revoke or begin legal proceedings to take away its charter, not a single member of the Maryland congressional delegation supported these measures; instead, they favored the more conservative and less threatening approach of reforming the 2BUS from within.[22] Also, when the legislature of

Pennsylvania in March 1819 introduced a resolution calling for an amendment to the U.S. Constitution that would limit Congress's ability to incorporate banks and other moneyed corporations to the District of Columbia, the Maryland legislature did not endorse it.[23] In short, opposition to the 2BUS in Maryland in 1818, 1819, and beyond did not go very deep. In fact, the only effect of the Maryland tax on the Baltimore branch of the 2BUS, as Hopkinson was later to argue, was "its profits will be diminished by contributing to the revenue of the state; and this is the whole effect that ought, in a fair and liberal spirit of reasoning, to be anticipated."[24]

In large part, the accepting attitude of Maryland toward the 2BUS is to be explained by the nature of the state's politics. In 1818, the state was roughly evenly divided between the Republican and Federalist parties. This was a major anomaly because by this time, in most other states, especially in the southern, western, and mid-Atlantic regions, the Federalist party had been disgraced and was in rapid decline as a consequence of its obstructionist activities during the War of 1812 and support for the Hartford Convention. In Maryland, however, after the War of 1812, the Federalists were able to maintain their control of the Eastern Shore, Annapolis, and the state's rural southern and western counties; indeed, Federalists had even captured control of the governorship and the legislature for a short while after the end of the War of 1812. This was because the Federalist party in Maryland differed from its New England counterparts in that, while it was critical of the Madison administration's handling of the war effort, it did not engage in obstructionist tactics, nor did it espouse the rhetoric of states' rights and secession. The Republican party in Maryland, on the other hand, was centered in Baltimore and the surrounding counties. Its members belonged to the commercial and national wing of the party, and they were among the leading advocates of the creation of the 2BUS, whose branch in Baltimore they controlled and ran for their own interests.[25]

What is completely lacking in Maryland in 1817 and 1818 are any spokesmen for the more agrarian and Old Republican wing of the Jeffersonian party. Led by people like Nathaniel Macon, John Randolph, and John Taylor on the national level, the Old Republicans urged a return to the true principles of the "revolution of 1800," which had been articulated in the Kentucky and Virginia Resolutions of

1798–1799. These Republicans were critical of the nationalist leanings of the Jefferson and Madison administrations, and they were among the few who had opposed, on constitutional grounds, the chartering of the 2BUS and, of course, a federal program of internal improvements. It was their point of view that offered the theoretical underpinnings—the doctrine of states' rights and the compact theory of the union—that were the basis of the attack on the 2BUS in Kentucky, Ohio, Tennessee, Pennsylvania, and, later, Virginia.

III

None of this means that the 2BUS and its Baltimore branch were happy or even accepting of the Maryland tax. The alternatives available to them were limited, however. George Williams, a director on the boards of both the 2BUS in Philadelphia and the Baltimore branch, in a letter to William Jones recounted a recent conversation he had with Secretary of the Treasury William Crawford on the matter of the tax.

> [Crawford] had no doubt but the Bank was subject to the payment of this tax as well as all other burthens which the Govt. [of Maryland] might deem necessary to impose upon other Banking institutions and that he feels confident if an attempt had been made in Congress to have exempted this institution from the tax it would have defeated the bill.

Williams then added, "sound policy would dictate yielding this point."[26]

As it turned out, the officials of the 2BUS decided not to pay the Maryland tax, or any of the other taxes levied by the state for that matter, but to literally make a federal case out of it and take the matter up to the U.S. Supreme Court. How this came about was explained by the governor of the state of Maryland, Charles Ridgely, in his annual address to the legislature in December 1818. It is definitely worth quoting in its entirety because it is not only the official account of what occurred, but also the only account. After noting that the tax applied to all banks not chartered by the state, he continued:

> The penalties of the law applying equally to the branch of the bank of the United States, established in Baltimore, a demand

was early made on that bank. It was found, however, that considerable difficulty would be experienced in proving the particular offences, so as to recover the penalty attached; especially as from the nature of that institution the notes of a branch in any other state, could be and were issued in payment. The bank, however, having early determined to start a suit, negotiations were entered into, as it professed a sincere desire to bring the question of Constitutional right before the legal tribunals of the country (for which their right to resort was unquestionable), and to wave at once all legal delays and carry it to the highest appellate jurisdiction, the Supreme Court of the United States, an amicable arrangement was entered into.

A suit being brought into the Baltimore County Court, judgment was entered for the state; and an appeal taken to the court of appeals for the western shore which met in June last, upon a case stated, so as to rest the question upon the constitutionality of the act. A decision in favour of the state was there had by consent, and the appeal carried up to the Supreme Court of the United States. In the meantime the president of the bank had lodged in the council chambers a memorandum by which, in the event of the suit being determined in favour of the state, the penalty is not to be extracted, but the bank is bound to paying into the state treasury the sum of fifteen thousand dollars specified in the act, for the year commencing on the first day of May last, the day on which the act went into operation; and the same sum annually, as long as the act continues. . . . In the event of the suit's being determined against the state, no costs are to be exacted, and no further steps taken, under the said act against the bank.[27]

The central issue in the dispute between Maryland and the 2BUS was not the constitutionality of the bank but the constitutionality of the state's tax on the bank. It is also clear that, at least in its origins, *McCulloch v. Maryland* did not involve the fierce controversy between the forces of nationalism and the forces of states' rights that was going on in a number of other states that levied taxes against the 2BUS. Indeed, what was involved here was a very "amicable controversy."[28]

To what extent was the Supreme Court itself involved in the collusion that culminated in the hearing of *McCulloch v. Maryland*? Here, the evidence is circumstantial and far from conclusive. What we know for sure is that on the first Monday of August 1818, Chief Justice Marshall witnessed the decision to hear the case on appeal, and the appeal was signed on August 28, 1818, by E. B. Caldwell, clerk of the U.S. Supreme Court and Gabriel Duvall of Maryland, an associate justice of the Supreme Court and presiding judge of the Fourth Judicial Circuit.[29]

This is the only direct evidence of any contact with the case by members of the U.S. Supreme Court before it was officially heard in late February 1819. But this should not rule out the possibility that some kind of indirect contact may have taken place between certain members of the High Court and representatives of the 2BUS and/or the state of Maryland. Nathaniel Williams, an attorney for the bank in Maryland, may have played a key role here. He was a close friend and confidant of Associate Justice Joseph Story. Story was a particularly energetic and aggressive nationalist who frequently worked behind the scenes to make things happen.[30] Another contact may have been E. W. duVal, a nephew of Gabriel Duvall, another member of the High Court who was from Maryland. Gabriel Duvall is, perhaps, the least heralded justice ever to sit on the U.S. Supreme Court. This dubious honor is probably well earned, since he served for nearly twenty-five years without writing a major opinion. Still, he should not be discounted, since he was a consistent supporter of the nationalist decisions handed down by Marshall and Story. For his part, E. W. duVal was in constant contact with William Jones, the president of the 2BUS in Philadelphia, and during the actual trial of *McCulloch v. Maryland* he provided Jones with a steady account of the proceedings. Among other things, he hoped to be appointed as cashier of the St. Louis branch when it opened.[31] A third possibility is William Pinkney, considered by many at the time to be the country's leading practitioner before the Supreme Court. He knew its members well. He also was a leading member of the Maryland bar, an experienced diplomat, and an important politician soon to be elected as U.S. senator from Maryland. He became the lead attorney for the 2BUS in *McCulloch v. Maryland*.[32]

There are probably several reasons that the 2BUS pushed the Maryland case as opposed to that from some other state where the bank had been taxed. To begin with, Maryland was one of the earliest states to tax the bank, and this, combined with the state's willingness to cooperate in getting the matter before the Supreme Court as soon as possible, would allow the Court to hand down a quick decision, which could serve as an important precedent for local and federal courts in other states. There is evidence that this is what a number of the 2BUS's supporters hoped would happen, and indeed this is what did happen.[33]

Another reason the 2BUS may have had for initiating the case in Maryland is that it is obvious from Governor Ridgely's account to the legislature of the agreement between the state and the bank that, unlike the other states that had taxed the 2BUS's branches, Maryland was willing to recognize the Supreme Court's jurisdiction in the case and accept it as the final arbiter in federal-state disputes. This was made explicit when, following the Supreme Court's decision in *McCulloch v. Maryland*, the new governor of the state, Charles Goldsborough, a Federalist, reported the results of the case to the legislature in the following manner: "although the case has been decided against the state, we have the satisfaction of being assured that her claim was ably supported, and that nothing was wanted in zeal and talents of the counsel, to have procured a different determination of the Court."[34] From this point on, as far as Maryland was concerned, the matter was now settled. The Supreme Court's decision was accepted as final by Maryland, and the state completely withdrew from the controversy that continued to swirl about the 2BUS in other parts of the country. It is also worth noting that, by early 1819, the federal government had begun to reimburse Maryland for many of the expenses it had incurred during the War of 1812, and this went a long way toward relieving the financial pressure that had caused the state to tax the Baltimore branch of the 2BUS in the first place.[35]

To represent the state in *McCulloch v. Maryland*, Maryland selected three very capable and experienced lawyers: Joseph Hopkinson of Pennsylvania, Walter Jones of Washington, D.C., and its own attorney general, Luther Martin. They were all Federalists and nationalists and therefore not disposed to attack the authority of the U.S. Supreme

Court to hear the case nor the Supreme Court's claim that it was the final arbiter in federal-state constitutional disputes. From this, it is only logical to assume that the case would involve a full hearing of the numerous complicated issues that were raised by the controversy over the 2BUS. At the top of the list would be the question of to what extent the 2BUS was an agency of the federal government. This was relevant because 80 percent of its stock was held by private interests, and they selected 80 percent of its board of directors. The bank also was a profit-making institution that paid dividends to its shareholders, and the value of its stock fluctuated in value according to the demands of the market. Nor were any of its directors, even those appointed by the federal government, or its president considered to be federal office holders. Another significant issue was the question of whether a distinction could be made between a tax levied against a branch for the purpose of raising revenue and one whose purpose was to make the operation of the branch so unprofitable as to drive it from the state. Also immediately relevant was the problem of "foreign corporations" in a federal system of government. *Foreign corporation* was the term used to describe a private corporation chartered outside the state. The ability of the 2BUS to establish its branches wherever it pleased raised this issue, which was of great importance to many of the opponents of the 2BUS. It also involved more than simply branches of a federally chartered national bank, but also lotteries, insurance companies, and other private corporations that might be chartered on the national level, and the issue would be raised directly a short time later in the case of *Cohens v. Virginia* (1821).

Yet, a full discussion of the issues did not take place. This is because even before the case was heard by the U.S. Supreme Court, a successful effort was made to sharply limit and skew the discussion of the constitutional issues that had been raised by the attempt of Maryland to tax the Baltimore branch of the 2BUS. Thus, upon learning that Daniel Webster was to be his co-counsel in *McCulloch v. Maryland*, Pinkney wrote to him about what he referred to as the case involving "the affair of the Bank of the United States (relative to the power of Maryland to tax it)" and indicated that it had been his "intention to have asked from you an Interchange of Ideas in that Cause." But then he significantly added, "I now suppose it will not be necessary, since it is said that little else than the thread bare topics connected with the constitutionality of the Bank will be introduced into the argument, which is expected to take place early in the next term of the Supreme Court."[36] What Pinkney does not indicate is who "said" this and how it was relayed to him. Was it a member of the Supreme Court itself? Was it part of the instructions he received from the bank? Or was the source someone else? And why did it carry so much weight with Pinkney? It is doubtful that anyone else but Chief Justice John Marshall had the stature, the influence, or the power to operate behind the scenes to channel a case as important as this one in a particular direction.

FOUR

MCCULLOCH V. MARYLAND

In December 1818, Associate Justice Joseph Story indicated that the upcoming "term of the United States Supreme Court will probably be the most interesting ever known," since it would deal with "several great constitutional questions."[1] These included the constitutionality of a New York insolvency law in *Sturges v. Crowninshield* and *Dartmouth College v. Woodward*, a very important contract clause case. And, of course, the right to tax the Bank of the United States. The significance of *McCulloch v. Maryland* was widely understood at the time, and the small room in the basement of the Capitol Building where the High Court began hearing the case on February 22, 1819, "was full almost to the point of suffocation, and many went away for lack of room."[2] In recognition of the importance of the issues to be decided, the Supreme Court waived its standing order that limited each party in a case to two lawyers and increased the number to three on each side. What followed was an unusually perceptive and searching exploration of the issues, both broadly and narrowly defined, raised by the case.

The Supreme Court consisted of seven justices at this time. Chief Justice John Marshall and Joseph Story, both outspoken nationalists, dominated its proceedings. Bushrod Washington, Brockholst Livingston, Gabriel Duvall, and Thomas Todd were more passive and invariably went along with their decisions. The seventh justice, William Johnson, was much more independent. But while he had important differences with Marshall and Story, they were not over such questions as the need for a strong and active central government, the need for an independent judiciary, or the sanctity of contracts. Rather, they were on the less important issues of the role of *seriatim* opinions, the relative powers of Congress and the federal judiciary, and the extent of the jurisdiction of the federal courts. Whatever Johnson was, he was not an advocate of states' rights.[3]

In addition to Webster and Pinkney, the 2BUS had also secured the services of William Wirt, who at the time was not only a practicing attorney, but also attorney general of the United States. Webster was only just emerging as a major force in early American constitutional law, but Pinkney and Wirt were the leading figures practicing law before the U.S. Supreme Court. As one congressman observed in a different context, only several weeks before the beginning of *McCulloch v. Maryland*, "The inquiry will be by the people, not the merits of the cause pending in court, but what attorneys are employed? Have Mr. Wirt and Mr. Pinkney been secured? If they have, the result cannot be doubted."[4]

I

Daniel Webster, on behalf of the 2BUS, made the first presentation. His argument is particularly important because Chief Justice Marshall in his opinion borrowed a number of the more memorable phrases from it and, even more important, accepted Webster's formulation of the central constitutional issues that had to be resolved by the U.S. Supreme Court.

Webster began by asserting that there were two key issues central to the case. The first was whether the 2BUS was constitutional or not. To this, Webster answered with a resounding yes. In making his argument, he cited and endorsed Alexander Hamilton's discussion of the issue in 1791. He also argued for the role of precedent. The national legislature had affirmed the creation of national banks in both 1791 and 1816. Moreover,

> the executive government has acted upon it; and the courts of law have acted upon it. Many of those who doubted or denied the existence of the power, when first attempted to be exercised, have yielded to the first decision, and acquiesced in it, as a settled question. When all branches of the government have thus been acting on the existence of this power nearly thirty years, it would seem almost too late to call it in question.[5]

Following Hamilton's reasoning, Webster also justified the constitutionality of the 2BUS by using the necessary and proper clause. Like Hamilton, he defined "necessary" broadly, to mean what was "*Best* and *most useful* to the end proposed" and rejected the claim that it meant "*absolutely* indispensable." The 2BUS, it was clear, was a "suitable instrument" to aid in the operation of the federal government: it collected and distributed the federal revenue and helped to regulate the currency of the country. It was not up to the Court to decide if it were the best possible means to accomplish these purposes. This decision was "within the discretion of Congress."[6]

Webster also defended Congress's right to create a corporation: "Corporations are but means. They are not ends and objects of government. No governments exist for the purpose of creating corporations as one of the ends of its being. They are institutions established to effect certain beneficial purposes; and, as means, take their character generally from their end and object." From this, it flowed naturally that since "Congress has duties to perform and powers to execute," it also has the right to choose

> the means by which these duties can be properly and most usefully performed, and those powers executed. Among other means, it has established a bank; and before the act establishing it can be pronounced unconstitutional and void, it must be shown, that a bank has no fair connection with the execution of any power or duty of the national government, and that its creation is consequently a manifest usurpation.[7]

The second major question in *McCulloch v. Maryland*, according to Webster, was the right of the state governments to tax the 2BUS. He pointed out that the Constitution was *"the supreme law of the land"* and therefore could control "all State legislation and State Constitutions" and that the Supreme Court had "the ultimate power of deciding all questions arising under the constitution and laws of the United States." Webster argued that the "only inquiry, therefore, in this case is, whether the law of the state of Maryland imposing the tax be consistent with the free operation of the law establishing the bank and the full enjoyment of the privileges conferred by it?"[8]

To this question, Webster responded with a clear no, for "if the states may tax this bank, to what extent shall they tax it, and where shall they stop? An unlimited power to tax involves, necessarily, a power to destroy; because there is a limit beyond which no institution and no property can bear taxation." He warned that if the states shall have the right to tax the 2BUS, the "consequence is inevitable. The object in laying this tax, may have been *revenue* to the State. In the next case, the object may be to *expel the bank from the state.*"[9]

The implications of giving the state the power to tax the 2BUS, Webster asserted, therefore were far reaching. If they could do this, then the states could move against other federal institutions operating within their boundaries.

> Can they tax proceedings in the Federal Courts? If so, they can expel those judicatures from the states. As Maryland has undertaken to impose a stamp tax on the notes of the bank, what hinders her from imposing a stamp tax also on permits, clearances, registers, and all other documents connected with imposts and navigation? If by one she can suspend the operations of the bank, by the other she can equally shut up the custom house.[10]

The Maryland law, Webster asserted, had to be overturned for it was a direct assault on the authority of the federal government. Webster concluded:

> Nothing can be plainer than that, if the law of Congress establishing the bank be a constitutional act, it must have its full and

complete effects. Its operation cannot be either defeated or impeded by acts of state legislation. To hold otherwise, would be to declare, that the Congress can only exercise its constitutional powers subject to the controlling discretion, and under the sufferance, of the state governments.[11]

Not only had Webster followed Pinkney's instructions, but he was confident that his argument would have the desired results. Writing shortly after he had made his presentation, Webster in a letter to a close friend indicated "of the decision I have no doubt."[12]

Hopkinson followed Webster on behalf of Maryland. In a tightly constructed and carefully crafted argument, he presented the fullest and in many ways the most subtle description of the issues that had been raised by *McCulloch v. Maryland*, as well as a powerful case for the right of a state to tax the branches of the 2BUS. Responding to Webster's claim that the 2BUS was constitutional, he denied its constitutionality. In doing this, he did not merely restate the position that Madison and Jefferson had taken in 1790–1791. Instead, he offered an original and very different argument based on historical context and circumstances. The creation of the 1BUS in 1791 had been constitutional, because it had been necessary at the time. But then, he added, "a power, growing out of a necessity which may not be permanent, may also not be permanent. It has relation to circumstances which change in a state of things which may exist at one period and not at another."[13] A national bank was necessary in 1791 because there were no alternatives. Its purposes at the time, following Hamilton's argument, were to augment the active and productive capital of the country, to make gold and silver the basis of a paper circulation, to provide loans to the federal government, to generally facilitate the payment of taxes and transmit funds for the federal government, and to aid in commercial transactions. Hopkinson argued that these needs legitimized the creation of a national bank in 1791 because there only existed three banks, with limited capital, at the time, and they could not have provided the services required by the government. But circumstances had changed, and by 1816 there was a substantial amount of banking capital "vested in banks of good credit, and so spread over the country, as to be convenient and competent for all the purposes enumerated in the argument." The five years following the expiration of the 1BUS's charter had demonstrated that there were now enough state-chartered banks "of a sound and unquestioned credit and permanency to meet the financial needs of both the government and the commercial needs of the country." This, Hopkinson asserted, vitiated the necessity of another national bank and strongly implied that the federal government and other supporters of the creation of the 2BUS had greatly exaggerated the monetary and banking crisis of 1815–1816.[14]

Hopkinson next raised another central issue in the debate over the constitutionality of the 2BUS, one that had been totally avoided by Webster: whether the bank had the authority to "establish its branches in the several states, without the direction of Congress, or the assent of the States." To be sure, this power had been granted to the 2BUS when it was chartered in 1816. But was it constitutional? Two key issues, Hopkinson argued, were involved here. First, were the branches necessary, and second, who was to be the judge of this necessity?

Hopkinson argued that branches were not necessary for the bank to perform its services for the federal government. These services as well as the creation of a national circulating medium "can as well be done, and, in fact, [are] done, by the state banks."[15] Hopkinson believed that the branches of the 2BUS were "established with a single view to trading, and the profit of the stockholders, and not for the convenience or use of the federal government; and, therefore, they are located at the will of the directors, who represent and regard the interests of the stockholders, and are such themselves." Was it right therefore that "the State rights of territory and taxation are to yield for the gains of a money-trading corporation; to be prostrated at the will of a set of men who have no concern, and no duty, but to increase their profits?"[16] This, Hopkinson continued, was an enormous, unjust, and arbitrary power to have granted to the directors of the 2BUS, who hold it "without any control from the government of the United States; and, as is now contended, without any control of the State governments." It was indeed "a most extravagant power to be vested in a body of men, chosen annually by a very small portion of our citizens, for the purpose of loaning and trading with their money to the best advantage."[17]

Simply put, even if branches were necessary, Hopkinson argued, the power to decide where and when they were to be created did not belong in the hands of a small group of people motivated by self-interest and who were not responsible to anyone for their actions. What was the remedy? It was better that the 2BUS be limited to the District of Columbia, where the authority of the federal government was absolutely clear, and if branches had to be created, then the consent of Congress should be required since that body at least was responsible to the will of the people. Most important of all, the rights of the states had to be protected from the activities of a private corporation with unlimited powers. Hopkinson concluded this portion of his presentation by asking:

> [W]ill it be tolerated, that twenty directors of a trading corporation, having no object but profit, shall, in the pursuit of it, tread upon the sovereignty of the State; enter it without condescending to ask its leave; disregard, perhaps, the whole system of its policy; overthrow its institutions, and sacrifice its interests?[18]

Hopkinson next turned his attention to the claim that the branches of the 2BUS had a right to be tax exempt. Or, as Hopkinson put it, could a private "trading association with independent powers and immunities" come to a state "with rights of sovereignty paramount to the sovereignty of the State, and privileges possessed by no other *persons, corporations* or *property* in the State?"[19] He pointed out that the right of a state to raise revenue was the "highest attribute of sovereignty." He also noted here that the Maryland tax was not an attempt to destroy the bank nor even to deny the government the use of its services. Instead, the purpose of the tax was to raise revenue from the bank's profits.[20]

Hopkinson further argued that banking activities had generally been considered a legitimate object of taxation throughout the United States. And again he reiterated the argument that in no sense was the 2BUS an agency of the federal government. The United States was only a stockholder and did not have control of the bank's "direction and management." It was a Bank of the United States in name only: "strip it of its name, and we find it to be a mere association of individuals, putting their money into a common stock, to be loaned for profit, and to divide the gains." The government's involvement was "for gain also," since it could make use of the bank's services "without owning a dollar in it. It is not, then, a Bank of the United States, if by that we mean an institution, belonging to the government, directed by it, or in which it has a permanent indissoluble interest." As for the federal government's connection with the Bank of the United States, it was only a stockholder, and this stock could be sold at any time. "How, then," Hopkinson asked, "can such an institution claim the immunities of sovereignty . . . ?"[21]

Continuing, Hopkinson noted that the only explicit limitation on the power of state taxation was in Article I, section 10, of the U.S. Constitution, which declared that "no state shall, without the consent of Congress, lay any imposts or duties, on imports or exports, except what may be absolutely necessary for executing its inspection laws." In fact, the issue of state taxation had been raised during the ratification debate in 1787–1788, and assurances had been given, in the *Federalist* papers, that a state's power of taxation, except in the area of import and export duties, was "sacred and inviolable." Now, a state's power to tax a branch of the 2BUS was being denied as a consequence of "implications and obscure constructions of indefinite clauses in the constitution."[22]

Hopkinson next proceeded to argue that the power of "construction" of the U.S. Constitution was at the heart of the debate over the 2BUS. The bank itself, after all, had been created as a consequence of a broad construction of the Constitution. Now, building upon this, and also by construction, it was being contended that the bank, through its branches, had the right

> to enter a territory of a state without its assent; to carry on its business when it pleases and where it pleases, against the will and perhaps in contravention of the policy, of the sovereign owner of the soil. Having such great success in the acquirement of implied rights, the experiment is now pushed further; and not contented with having obtained two rights in this extraordinary way, the fortunate adventurer assails the sovereignty of the State, and would strip from it its most vital and essential power.[23]

Hopkinson also argued that the power to tax banks was a concurrent power shared by the states and the federal government. Other areas where the federal and state governments had concurrent powers to levy taxes, he observed, were licenses to sell alcohol, land taxes, poll taxes, and the entire range of internal duties. By levying a tax on the branch of the 2BUS at Baltimore, Maryland was only exercising a constitutional right. In making this argument, Hopkinson took specific issue with Webster's claim that "a right to tax is a right to destroy," which had been offered as a reason to reject the right of a state to tax branches within its boundaries. The proponents of the bank have warned, Hopkinson observed, of "distressing inconveniences ingeniously contrived; supposed dangers; fearful distrusts; anticipated violence and injustice from the States and consequent ruin to the bank."[24] Hopkinson denied the appropriateness of this argument for the Maryland tax, which was the specific issue before the Supreme Court. For in Maryland, he pointed out, "we only require that the bank shall not violate State rights, in establishing itself, or its branches; that it shall be submitted to the jurisdiction and laws of the State, in the same manner with other corporations and other property, and all this may be done, without ruining the institution; or destroying its national uses."[25]

Finally, Hopkinson warned against the hostile and aggressive posture and confrontational manner that the proponents of the 2BUS and their nationalist allies had taken against the rights of the states. Under a federal system of government, he pleaded, "mutual forbearance and discretion in the use of power" were essential in revenue matters. He then added:

> [A]ll our relations in society, depend upon a reasonable confidence in each other. It is peculiarly the basis of our confederation, which lives not a moment after we shall cease to trust each other. If the two governments are to regard each other as enemies, seeking opportunities of injury and distress, they will not long continue friends.[26]

Hopkinson was followed by William Wirt, who spoke on behalf of the 2BUS. He did not add anything new to the issues as they had been laid out by Webster, but he did strengthen the arguments. He began by focusing on the issue of the bank's constitutionality, which he argued "ought not now to be questioned." The matter had been settled by the creation of the 1BUS in 1791. Not only had that bank been created by Congress, but it had been signed into law by the president, and its existence had been recognized by the federal judiciary, which had enforced various laws on its behalf. The creation of a national bank, he argued, "must be considered as ratified by the people, and sanctioned by precedent."[27]

Wirt also defended the use of the necessary and proper clause to create the 2BUS. The fiscal chaos of 1811–1816 had made clear both the utility and necessity of a national bank. In making this argument, Wirt totally rejected the "strict and literal" interpretation of the Constitution that had been espoused by the bank's opponents. The federal government was sovereign and with sovereignty came the right to create corporations. To require the federal government to only exercise those powers expressly provided in the U.S. Constitution would be a mistake. To do so would, Wirt asserted, in a phrase that was to resonate strongly in Chief Justice Marshall's final decision, destroy the Constitution's "simplicity and load it with all the complex details of a code of private jurisprudence."[28]

Having made the case for the constitutionality of the 2BUS, Wirt proceeded to defend the necessity of its being granted the power to establish branches throughout the country. Otherwise, it could not effectively carry out the duties assigned to it. He then went on to declare the Maryland tax on the Baltimore branch to be unconstitutional, not because federal law was supreme, but because if the states were allowed to tax federal institutions, they would have the ability to undermine the operations of the entire federal government. Wirt asserted: "If they may tax an institution of finance they may tax the proceedings of the Courts of the United States. If they may tax to one degree, they may tax to any degree; and nothing but their own discretion can impose a limit upon this exercise of their authority."[29]

Jones, on behalf of Maryland, spoke next. He questioned the constitutionality of the 2BUS. He only made passing reference to the compact theory on the origins and nature of the union, the Tenth Amendment, and the idea that the federal government had only been granted limited and delegated powers. His emphasis was on the dangers inherent in allowing Congress to increase its powers by implication. Describing the 2BUS as essentially "a commercial institution, a partnership incorporated for the purpose of carrying on the trade of banking," he warned that its establishment set a precedent for a variety of "vexatious monopolies."[30] The U.S. Constitution had not granted the federal government "unlimited discretion" to create private corporations. The Constitution of the United States

> [did] not imply the power of establishing a great banking corporation, branching out into every district of the country, and inundating it with a flood of paper money. To derive such tremendous authority from implication, would be to change the subordinate into fundamental powers; to make the implied powers greater than those which are expressly granted; and to change the whole scheme and theory of government.[31]

He then linked the legitimacy of the 2BUS to the even broader constitutional issues raised by a federal program of internal improvements. He warned that if the federal government could create the 2BUS under a broad interpretation of the necessary and proper clause, this power could also "be exercised to create corporations for the purpose of constructing roads and canals; a power to construct which has been also lately discovered among other secrets of the constitution, developed by this dangerous doctrine of implied powers."[32]

Following this, Jones turned his attention to the constitutionality of Maryland's tax. He argued that the power to tax was the essence of sovereignty, and the only limit on the power of the states in this area contained in the Constitution was the prohibition against import and export duties, and he denied that others could "be added by implication." Both the states and the federal government had the right to levy taxes on the same object, especially on a corporation primarily engaged in "the trade of banking." In such a case, "mutual confidence, discretion, and forbearance, can alone qualify the exercise of the conflicting powers, and prevent the destruction of either." Admitting that this could create difficult and antagonistic situations and might be "an imperfection in our system of government," he pointed out that the federal "system was established by reciprocal concessions and compromises between the State and Federal government[s]. Its harmony can only be maintained in the same spirit." He concluded by pointing out that while the 2BUS acted as an agent of the federal government in performing services for it, it was essentially a private corporation of a "mercantile character . . . and their property thus employed became subject to local taxation, like other capital employed in trade."[33]

Martin presented the closing arguments for Maryland. He was currently the state's attorney general and at the end of a long and distinguished career. He had been a member of the Constitutional Convention of 1787 that had written the U.S. Constitution, but he refused to endorse it and opposed its adoption. He switched to the Federalist party during the 1790s and played a key role in defending Associate Justice Samuel Chase in the latter's impeachment trial in 1805. He had a reputation for being an extremely effective trial lawyer. He had not aged well, however, since he was a chronic alcoholic, and he had a reputation for being difficult and unpleasant. Still, he brought a strong historical perspective to the issues involved in *McCulloch v. Maryland*, and his focus on the dangers to the liberties of the people from the attempt by some to increase the powers of the federal government through construction and implication resonated well with the critics of the 2BUS.[34]

Martin began by noting that the opponents of the adoption of the Constitution had expressed these fears in 1787–1788. The danger had been denied at the time by the advocates of ratification, and "this apprehension was treated as a dream of distempered jealousy." Nonetheless, the Tenth Amendment was adopted, though it was only declaratory of the sense of the people as to the extent of the federal government's powers. He then observed: "We are now called upon to apply that theory of interpretation which was then rejected by the friends of the new constitution, and we are asked to engraft upon it powers of vast extent, which were disclaimed by them, and which, if they had been fairly avowed at the time, would have prevented its adoption." Martin then added, "[T]he power of establishing corporations is not delegated to the United States."[35]

Martin also defended Maryland's right to tax the property of private corporations operating within its territory. The state had not taxed the U.S. government, but had levied a "stamp tax upon the notes issued by a banking house within the State of Maryland."

Because the United States happens to be partially interested, either as dormant or active partners, in that house, is no reason why the State should refrain from laying a tax which they have, otherwise a constitutional right to impose, any more than if they were to become interested in any other house of trade, which should issue its notes, or bills of exchange liable to a stamp duty by a law of the States.[36]

Martin also took issue with the argument "that a right to *tax*, in this case, implies a right to *destroy*." He pointed out that "the whole subject of taxation is full of difficulties, which the [Philadelphia] Convention found it impossible to solve in a manner entirely satisfactory." The members of the convention had found it "impracticable, or inconvenient," to simply divide different forms of taxation between the states and the federal government. In the end, they only denied the states the power to levy taxes on imports and exports. Congress was given the power to tax all other subjects, but at the same time the states had

a concurrent right to tax the same subjects to an unlimited extent. This was one of the anomalies of the government, the evils of which must be endured, or mitigated by discretion and mutual forbearance. The debates in the State conventions show that the power of State taxation was understood to be absolutely unlimited, except to imposts and tonnage duties. The states would not have adopted the Constitution upon any other understanding.[37]

Martin concluded by denying the analogy that if the state of Maryland could tax the notes of the Baltimore branch of the 2BUS it could also tax the "judicial proceeding, and the custom house papers of the United States." The latter, he pointed out, "are not [private] property, by their very nature; they are not the subjects of taxation; they are the proper instruments of national sovereignty, essential to the exercise of its powers, and in legal contemplation altogether extra-territorial as to State authority."[38]

William Pinkney, arguing on behalf of McCulloch and the 2BUS, made the final presentation to the U.S. Supreme Court. He had relatively little formal education but an enthusiasm for learning, and during his long stays in England as a diplomat he spent considerable time educating himself to read Greek and Latin, listening to speeches by cultured and well-educated individuals in Parliament and the courts, and carefully studying the English language. As a result, he became an unusually effective public speaker; indeed, he often mesmerized and overwhelmed juries and others who listened to him, and his presentations in court usually attracted considerable public attention. His oratorical abilities caused John Marshall to call him "the greatest man I ever saw in a Court of Justice." His fellow Marylander Chief Justice Roger Brooke Taney recalled many years after Pinkney died, "I have heard almost all the great advocates of the United States, both of the past and present generation, but I have seen none equal to Pinkney."[39]

Pinkney's speech on behalf of the 2BUS is generally considered to be a tour de force. It drew extraordinary praise from Justice Joseph Story, a flinty New Englander, not inclined to enthusiasms. "I never in my whole life heard a greater speech," he wrote. "[I]t was worth a trip from Salem to hear it. . . . his eloquence was overwhelming."[40] Unfortunately, all we know of it is from the sharply abbreviated version contained in the *Supreme Court Reports*, and while impressive that version does not do justice to it, given the praise it received.[41] The reason for this is that Pinkney never wrote out his speech, which required the court reporter, Henry Wheaton, "to abstract it as well as I could" from his notes. Wheaton considered this to be particularly unfortunate since people would fail to get "some notion of the peculiar diction and manner of Pinkney."[42]

Pinkney began by immediately confronting the question of "whether the act of Congress establishing the bank was consistent with the Constitution." He argued in the affirmative by asserting a nationalist interpretation of the origins of the union, by underscoring the role of the people in its creation, and by denying that the states were in any way a source of the federal government's authority. "The Constitution," he claimed, "acts directly *from* the people. No state, in its corporate capacity, ratified it; but it was proposed for adoption to popular conventions. It springs from the people. . . . The state sovereignties are not the authors of the Constitution of the United States." The Constitution of the United States represents the supreme will of the people and is the supreme law of the land. The significance of this argument was clear: the federal government, on behalf of the people, had the right to create the 2BUS, and the states could not object.[43]

Pinkney also justified the creation of the 2BUS in 1816 by using the precedent argument. A national bank had been created in 1791 and had been buttressed by various additional laws adopted by Congress. Political expediency and other considerations had prevented its rechartering in 1811 and had led to the veto of an attempt to re-create it in 1815. But in 1816, the federal government had given its assent to the establishment of a new national bank, and the judiciary had recognized its existence by enforcing various federal criminal laws that had been adopted to protect its operations.[44]

Did Congress have a right to create a corporation? Here, Pinkney followed the argument Hamilton used in 1791 when he justified the creation of a national bank because it helped the federal government to carry out its fiscal responsibilities. Although the Constitution did not explicitly grant the federal government the right to create corporations, it had not prohibited it either. The attempt to limit the federal government's implied powers by adding the word "expressly" to the Tenth Amendment had been rejected because the members of the First Congress recognized:

> [I]t was impossible for the framers of the Constitution to specify prospectively all these means, both because it would have involved an immense variety of details, and because it would have been impossible for them to foresee the infinite variety of circumstances in such an unexampled state of political society as ours, forever changing and forever improving.[45]

Pinkney also briefly confronted the charge that the 2BUS was not a government agency but a privately controlled money-making corporation. This had come about merely as a consequence of necessity, he argued, for the bank "could not be rendered effectual . . . but by mixing the property of individuals with that of the public. The bank could not otherwise acquire credit for its notes. Universal experience shows, that, if altogether a government bank, it could not acquire, or would soon lose, the confidence of the community."[46] Pinkney also very briefly defended the bank's right to create branches without acquiring the permission of the states in which they were to be located: "The branches . . . are identical with the parent bank. The power to establish them is that species of subordinate power, wrapped up in principal power, which Congress may place at its discretion."[47] What Pinkney did was to quickly pass over the two most controversial aspects of the 2BUS without examining at all how it had actually operated in 1816, 1817, and 1818.

Pinkney next turned his attention to what he called "the last and greatest, and only difficult question in the cause . . . that which respects the assumed right of the State to tax the bank, and its branches, thus established by Congress." Pinkney's response was direct and simple: Congress's power to create a bank was supreme, and the states did not have a right to undo it. He argued that there existed

> a manifest repugnancy between the power of Maryland to tax and the power of Congress to preserve, this institution. . . . This law of Maryland acts directly on the operations of the bank and may destroy it. There is no limit or check in this respect, but in the discretion of the State legislature. That discretion cannot be controlled by the national councils. Whenever the local councils of Maryland will it, the bank *must* be expelled from the state. A right to tax without limit or control, is essentially a power to destroy. If one national institution may be destroyed in this manner, all may be destroyed in the same manner.[48]

Pinkney took issue with the claim that the purpose of the Maryland tax on the 2BUS branch in Baltimore was merely an attempt to raise revenue, and therefore was not a threat to its existence. He argued that it was not possible to make this distinction. In particular, he denied it was possible to find "any intelligible, fixed, defined boundary" for the power of a state to tax the bank's operations. Instead, he asserted that if a comparison were made between "this act of Maryland with that of Kentucky which is yet to come before the Court . . . the absolute necessity of repressing such attempts in their infancy, will be evident. Admit the constitutionality of the Maryland tax, and that of Kentucky follows inevitably."[49]

Pinkney concluded by revealing the underlying assumption behind the opposition to recognizing the right of the states to levy any kind of tax on the branches of the 2BUS: "the local interests of the States are in perpetual conflict with the interests of the Union; which shows the danger of adding power to the partial views and local prejudices of the states." The taxes on the 2BUS could not be allowed to stand for they were "as much a direct interference with the legislative faculty of Congress, as would be a tax on patents, or copy rights, or custom house papers, or judicial proceedings." If this were allowed to happen:

> [T]he whole machine of the national government might be arrested in its motions, by the exertion, in other cases, of the same power, which is here attempted to be exerted upon the bank: no other alternative remains, but for this Court to interpose its authority, and save the nation from the consequences of this dangerous attempt.[50]

II

Marshall, on behalf of a unanimous court, delivered his decision on March 6, 1819, only three days after the completion of the various oral arguments. The speed with which it came down is certainly remarkable, but it does not in itself justify the claim made by some that Marshall's eloquent and carefully reasoned ruling had been prepared beforehand. First of all, there is no positive evidence to support what is in effect a very serious charge. But also Marshall's decision in structure, focus, and wording owed too much to the arguments made by Webster, Wirt, and Pinkney on behalf of the 2BUS to lend credence to the view that he had written it before he actually heard the case.

Marshall began his opinion by emphasizing the significance of the case. "The constitution of our country," he noted, "in its most interesting and vital parts, is to be considered; the conflicting powers of the government of the Union and of its members, as marked in that constitution, are to be discussed; and an opinion given, which may essentially influence the great operation of the government." The Supreme Court, Marshall indicated, was approaching the issues that had been raised in the case with "a deep sense of its importance, and of the awful responsibility involved in its decision." It was, however, imperative that the issues raised "be decided peacefully, or remain a source of hostile legislation, perhaps of hostility of a still more serious nature." It was up to the Supreme Court to settle the matter for "on the Supreme Court of the United States has the Constitution of our country devolved this important duty."[51]

Turning his attention to the question of whether Congress had the power to create a national bank, Marshall immediately made it clear that the matter was settled. "It has been truly said," he noted:

> that this can scarcely be considered as an open question, entirely unprejudiced by the former proceeding of the nation respecting it. The principle now contested was introduced at a very early period of our history, has been recognized by many successive legislatures, and has been acted upon by the judicial department, in cases of peculiar delicacy, as a law of undoubted obligation.

He then observed that in cases of "daring usurpation" of the Constitution, precedent ought not to be binding, but in other areas where

> the great principles of liberty are not concerned . . . the practice of government ought to receive a considerable impression from that of practice. An exposition of the constitution, deliberately established by legislative acts, on the faith of which an immense property has been advanced ought not to be lightly disregarded.[52]

In rendering his decision, Marshall first considered the question "has Congress the power to incorporate a bank?" To answer it, Marshall followed the argument made by Webster and Pinkney and proceeded to examine the origins and nature of the federal union created in 1787–1788. He pointed out that the Constitution had been submitted to and approved by the people through specially elected state ratifying conventions. As a consequence, "[f]rom these conventions the constitution derives its whole authority: the government proceeds directly from the people; is 'ordained and established' in the name of the people."[53] By asserting this, Marshall was advocating a nationalist theory of the origins and nature of the union and rejecting the claim made in the Kentucky and Virginia Resolutions of 1798–1799 that the federal government was a product of a compact between the states and had only specifically granted and limited powers. Marshall argued that the compact theory of the union made sense for understanding the Articles of Confederation, which was a "league" or "alliance" of sovereign states. But this government had proved to be inadequate, and "to form a more perfect union" and to create "an effective government, possessing great and sovereign powers," the Constitution had been adopted. "The government of the Union," Marshall intoned in clear and strong terms, ". . . is emphatically, and truly, a government of the people. In form and in substance it emanates from them. Its powers are granted by them, and are to be exercised directly on them, and for their benefit."[54]

As Hamilton had done in 1791 in making the case for the constitutionality of the 1BUS, Marshall resorted to a broad interpretation of the Constitution to justify Congress's authority to incorporate the 2BUS. He began this part of his argument by forcefully asserting the supremacy of the federal government over the states. He admitted that the federal government was one of enumerated powers and could only exercise those powers granted to it. But, he added, there could be no doubt "that the government of the Union, though limited in powers, is supreme within its sphere of action."[55] The Constitution, Marshall observed, was the supreme law of the land:

> This would seem to result necessarily from its nature. It is the government of all; its powers are delegated by all; it represents all, and acts for all. Though any one state may be willing to control its operations, no state is willing to allow others to control them. The nation, on those subjects on which it can act, must necessarily bind its component parts. But this question is not left to mere reason; the people have, in express terms, decided it by saying this constitution, and the laws of the United States, which shall be made in pursuance thereof, "shall be the supreme law of the land," and by requiring that the members of the state legislatures, and the officers of the executive and judicial departments of the state shall take the oath of fidelity to it.[56]

Marshall recognized that the power to charter a corporation had not been specifically enumerated in the Constitution, but he also noted that there was nothing in the Constitution to exclude it. This included the Tenth Amendment, which unlike a predecessor provision in the Articles of Confederation did not include the word "expressly," and therefore allowed "incidental or implied powers." The inclusion of the word "expressly" in the Articles of Confederation had caused all kinds of "embarrassments," and it was to avoid these problems that the Constitution had taken the form it did. He then forcefully argued the case for a broad interpretation of the Constitution:

> A constitution to contain an accurate detail of all the subdivisions of which its great powers will admit, and of all the means by which they may be carried into execution, would partake of a legal code, and could scarcely be embraced by the human mind. It would probably never be understood by the public. Its nature, therefore, requires, that only its great outlines should be marked, its important objects designated, and the minor ingredients which compose those objects be deduced from the nature of the objects themselves. That this idea was entertained by the framers of the American constitution, is not only to be inferred from the nature of the instrument, but from the language. Why else were some of the limitations, found in the ninth section of the 1st article introduced? It is also, in some degree, warranted by their having omitted to use any restrictive term which might prevent its receiving a fair and just interpretation. In considering this question, then, we must never forget that it is a constitution we are expounding.[57]

Marshall totally rejected the idea of a strict interpretation of the Constitution as espoused by states' rights advocates. Such a reading of the Constitution, he argued, would make it unworkable. Marshall argued that the necessary and proper clause had been included among the powers of Congress, and not in the section dealing with its limitations, and was meant to enlarge, not reduce, the ability of Congress to execute its enumerated powers. He explained his position in the following manner:

The subject is the execution of the great powers on which the welfare of a nation essentially depends. It must have been the intention of those who gave these powers, to insure, as far as human prudence could insure, their beneficial execution. This could not be done by confiding the choice of means to such narrow limits as not to leave it in the power of Congress to adopt any which might be appropriate, and which were conducive to the end. This provision is made in a constitution intended to endure for ages to come, and, consequently, to be adapted to the various crises of human affairs. To have prescribed the means by which government should in all future time, execute its powers, would have been to change, entirely, the character of the instrument, and give it the properties of a legal code. It would have been an unwise attempt to provide, by immutable rules, for exigencies which, if foreseen at all, must have been seen dimly, and which can be best provided for as they occur. To have declared that the best means shall not be used, but those alone without which the power given would be nugatory, would have been to deprive the legislature of the capacity to avail itself of experience, to exercise its reason, and to accommodate its legislation to circumstances.[58]

From the premises Marshall developed about the origins and nature of the Constitution, he proceeded to justify the creation of the 2BUS. The Constitution had delegated certain specified powers to the federal government: to lay and collect taxes, to borrow money, to regulate commerce, to declare and conduct war, and to raise and support armies and navies. Marshall believed that it was in the best interests of the country that Congress should have the means to exercise these delegated powers. In particular, the bank was a convenient, useful, and essential instrument in the implementation of the nation's fiscal policies. In promulgating this argument, Marshall made clear that he envisaged the United States to be a dynamic, powerful, and ever-growing nation:

The sword and the purse, all the external relations, and no inconsiderable portion of the industry of the nation, are entrusted to its government. It can never be pretended that their vast powers draw after them others of inferior importance, merely because they are inferior. Such an idea can never be advanced. But it may with great reason be contended, that a government entrusted with such ample powers, on the due execution of which the happiness and prosperity of the nation so vitally depends, must also be entrusted with ample means for their execution. The power being given, it is the interest of the nation to facilitate its execution. It can never be their interest, and cannot be presumed to have been their intention to clog and embarrass its execution by withholding the most appropriate means. Throughout this vast republic, from the St. Croix to the Gulf of Mexico, from the Atlantic to the Pacific, revenue is to be collected and expended, armies are to be marched and supported. The exigencies of the nation may require that the treasure raised in the north should be transported to the south, that raised in the east conveyed to the west, or that this order should be reversed. Is that construction of the constitution to be preferred which would render these operations difficult, hazardous and expensive?[59]

In making the case for a broad and expansive interpretation of the powers of the federal government, Marshall expressed his belief that the necessary and proper clause had been included in the U.S. Constitution "to remove all doubts respecting the right [of Congress] to legislate on that vast mass of incidental powers which must be involved in the constitution, if that instrument be not a splendid bauble."[60] Having made this point, Marshall concluded this section of his argument with a magnificent peroration:

> We think the sound construction of the constitution must allow to the national legislature what discretion, with respect to the means by which the powers it confers are to be carried into execution, which will enable that body to perform the high duties assigned to it, in the manner most beneficial to the people. Let the end be legitimate, let it be within the scope of the constitution, and all means which are appropriate, which are plainly

adapted to that end, which are not prohibited, but consist with the letter and spirit of the constitution, are constitutional.[61]

Having developed at length, and with great force, the view that the Constitution had created a strong and active federal government and had given Congress great discretion to implement its enumerated powers, Marshall upheld the constitutionality of the 2BUS. On the other hand, like Pinkney had in his oral presentation, Marshall quickly and superficially passed over the complicated constitutional questions raised by the dispute over whether the 2BUS had the right to create branches within the states without their permission. All he did was argue that the branches were "conducive to the great accomplishment of the object" for which the 2BUS had been created. "The great duties of the bank are prescribed; those duties require branches; and the bank itself may we think, be safely trusted with the selection of places where those branches shall be fixed."[62]

In the second part of his opinion, Marshall turned to the question of "whether the state of Maryland may without violating the constitution tax" a branch of the Bank of the United States. He started by noting that the Constitution, through the supremacy clause contained in Article VI, clearly established that federal law took precedence over state law. This basic principle, according to Marshall, "so entirely pervades the constitution, is so intermixed with the materials which compose it, so interwoven with its web, so blended with its texture, as to be incapable of being separated from it without rendering it into shreds."[63] Marshall then proceeded to elaborate on this crucial point still further:

> This great principle is, that the constitution and the laws made in pursuance thereof are supreme; that they control the constitution and laws of the respective states, and cannot be controlled by them. From this, which may be almost termed an axiom, other propositions are deduced as corollaries, on the truth or error of which, and on their application to this case the cause has been supposed to depend. These are 1st. that a power to create implies a power to preserve. 2d. that a power to destroy, if wielded by a different hand, is hostile to, and incompatible with these powers to create and preserve. 3d. That where

the repugnancy exists, that authority which is supreme must control, not yield to that over which it is supreme.[64]

Marshall then rejected the right of Maryland to tax the notes of the 2BUS. He recognized that the power of the states to tax was a vital part of their sovereignty. But they were nonetheless subordinate to the U.S. Constitution, and their power to tax did not extend to federal agencies. Using Webster's language, he asserted that "the power to tax involves the power to destroy." If the states were allowed this power, it would transform the nature of the federal government by making them "capable of arresting all the measures of the [national] government, and of prostrating it at the foot of the states." Viewing the 2BUS as an extension of the federal government, Marshall asserted:

> If the states may tax one instrument, employed by the government in the execution of its powers, they may tax any and every other instrument. They may tax the mail; they may tax the mint; they may tax patent-rights; they may tax the papers of the custom house; they may tax judicial process; they may tax all the means employed by the government, to an excess which would defeat all the ends of government. This was not intended by the American people.[65]

At the end of his opinion, Marshall entered the judgment of the Supreme Court. He declared "the act of the legislature of Maryland is contrary to the constitution of the United States and void." He also "reversed and annulled" the judgments of both the Maryland Court of Appeals and the Baltimore County Court. He did not, on the other hand, mention the constitutionality of the 2BUS, the origins of the union, nor the meaning of the necessary and proper clause, because they had not been the issues on which the Maryland courts had delivered their rulings.[66]

III

There is no question that Marshall's decision in *McCulloch v. Maryland* was a major effort, and that taken on its own terms it was important, forceful, far reaching in its implications, and truly eloquent at many points. Yet it was also in many ways contrived, inadequate, and misleading in its treatment of many of the key issues involved in the case and, despite occasional assertions to the contrary, almost totally dismissive of the rights of the states. Marshall's focus on such questions as the origins and nature of the union, the meaning of the necessary and proper clause, and the constitutionality of the 2BUS, fully two-thirds of the decision, was essentially *obiter dicta*. The real issue of the case was the legitimacy of Maryland's levying a tax on the Baltimore branch, and in the course of which Maryland had not challenged its constitutionality, asserted a strict interpretation of the Constitution, nor espoused the compact theory of the origins and nature of the union. Why then did Marshall make them so central to his decision? No hard evidence exists to explain this. But they clearly were issues to which he had given considerable thought and about which he had strong feelings, but he had never had the opportunity to rule on them before *McCulloch v. Maryland*. Probably also he wanted to make clear the Supreme Court's position on these issues so that it might have an impact on other constitutional questions beginning to emerge at this time, most notably the debate on the question of a federal program of internal improvements.

Intense reaction to Marshall's expansive view of the powers of Congress under the Constitution was, of course, to be expected from advocates of states' rights and from opponents of the 2BUS. At the same time, even those sympathetic to the outcome of the case appear to have been uneasy with the extreme nature of the decision. Only the New England papers, still under the control of former Federalists, fully endorsed it. The moderate and nationalist wings of the Republican party were much more cautious. For example, the *National Intelligencer*, the semi-official organ of the Monroe administration (and before that of the presidencies of Jefferson and Madison) and an open supporter of the 2BUS, described the decision, which it published, as "important," "interesting and elaborate," but did not actually endorse it, a procedure that was followed by most pro-2BUS newspapers in the mid-Atlantic, western, and southern states.[67]

Basically, the Monroe administration was willing to accept the High Court's ruling in *McCulloch v. Maryland* but was unwilling to support it. Its perspective was privately expressed by Secretary of the Treasury Crawford when he indicated his hope that "the opinion of the Supreme

Court . . . will I trust lead to" a reducing of tensions "upon the delicate subject." He also indicated his belief that the states did have a right to tax the branches, "but that under the right to tax, they could not be permitted to obstruct the exercise of the chartered powers." Even though the Supreme Court was unwilling to make a distinction between the right to tax and the right to destroy, he would still "have no difficulty in acceding to the conclusion of the court, . . . and in this decision I am entirely disposed to acquiescence."[68]

A sharper criticism of the opinion came from James Madison several months after Marshall delivered it. As we have seen, Madison was a strong nationalist and had been very supportive of the U.S. Supreme Court during his presidency. Indeed, it is not too much to say that Madison's becoming president in 1809 created the safe political environment, which had not existed during Jefferson's presidency, that allowed the Supreme Court to begin to issue its most important nationalist rulings during the second decade of the nineteenth century. Yet Madison was critical of the decision handed down in *McCulloch v. Maryland*. He believed "the occasion did not call for the general and abstract doctrine interwoven with the decision of the particular case." The real danger of Marshall's decision, Madison believed, was

> the high sanction given to a latitude in expounding the Constitution which seems to break down the landmarks intended by a specification of the power of Congress, and to substitute for a definite connection between means and ends, a legislative discretion as to the former to which no practical limit can be assigned.[69]

Among other things, the decision seemed to sanction a federal program of internal improvements. Jefferson, Madison, and Monroe supported such a program on policy grounds but, because it was broadly conceived and open-ended, they believed the jurisdictional problems raised by it were so complex and controversial that they could only be clarified through an amendment to the Constitution. Basically, what *McCulloch v. Maryland* did was to align the Supreme Court of the United States with those aggressive younger nationalists, like Clay, Calhoun, and John Quincy Adams, who were arguing that a constitutional amendment was not necessary to pave the way for a federal program of internal improvements since Congress already had the power to enact such a program. Madison feared that if Marshall's argument in *McCulloch v. Maryland* were followed, it would give unlimited authority to Congress in most economic matters. As he put it:

> In the great system of Political Economy having for its general object the national welfare, everything is related immediately or remotely to every other thing; and consequently a Power over any one thing, if not limited by some obvious and precise affinity, may amount to a power over every other. Ends and means may shift their character at the will & according to the ingenuity of the Legislative Body. What is an end in one case may be a means in another; nay in the same case, may be either an end or means at the Legislative option.[70]

The link between Marshall's decision in *McCulloch v. Maryland* and the federal program of internal improvements became clear in 1822 when President Monroe vetoed a bill authorizing the federal government to repair turnpikes and collect tolls on the Cumberland or National Road. To support his veto message, Monroe prepared a substantial treatise entitled "Views of the President of the United States on the Subject of Internal Improvements," in which he reiterated his belief that a constitutional amendment was required for Congress to extend its power over turnpikes that already existed within the states. He circulated this pamphlet among a number of government officials, including members of the Supreme Court. Marshall sent a polite and ambiguous response, indicating "this is a question which very much divides the opinion of intelligent men." After praising the president's effort, he noted "a general power over internal improvements if to be exercised by the union would certainly be cumbersome to the government, & of no utility to the people. But to the extent you recommend, it would be productive of no mischief, and of great good."[71] Joseph Story's reply was more circumspect, for he indicated: "Upon the constitutional question, I do not feel at liberty to express my opinion as it may hereafter perhaps come for discussion before the Supreme Court."[72]

Justice William Johnson, however, was much more forthcoming. In an undated letter, he indicated that he had discussed the matter with his "brother judges and is instructed to make the following report":

> The judges are deeply sensible to the mark of confidence bestowed on them in this instance and should be unworthy of that confidence did they attempt to conceal their real opinion. Indeed to conceal or disavow it would now be impossible as they are all of opinion that the decision on the bank question completely commits them on the subject of internal improvements as applied to post-roads and military roads. On the other points it is impossible to resist the lucid and conclusive reasoning contained in the argument.
>
> The principle assumed in the case of the Bank is that the grant of the principal power carries with it the grant of all adequate and appropriate means of executing it. That the selection of these means must rest with the general government and as to that power and those means the Constitution make[s] the government of the U.S. supreme.

Johnson concluded his report by "suggesting to the President that it would not be unproductive of good, if the Sec'y of State were to have the opinion of this Court on the bank question printed and dispersed through the Union."[73]

A short time after he delivered the decision in *McCulloch v. Maryland*, it became clear to Marshall that it was going to receive little public support. He was particularly concerned about an assault upon the decision being planned in his home state of Virginia. To Joseph Story, he fretted, "It would I understand be attacked in the papers with some asperity; and as those who favor it never write for the publick it will remain undefended & of course be considered as *damnably heretical*."[74] A few days later, with considerable bitterness, he complained to Justice Bushrod Washington on the silence of the Monroe administration, which clearly was pro-2BUS, on the decision:

> They have no objection to a decision in favor of the bank, since the good patriots who administer the government, wished it,

& would probably have been seriously offended with us had we dared to have decided otherwise, but they required an obsequious silent opinion without reasons. That would have been satisfactory, but our heretical reasoning is pronounced most damnable. We shall be denounced bitterly in the papers & as not a word will be said on the other side we shall undoubtedly be condemned as a pack of consolidating aristocrats. The legislature and executive who have enacted the law but who have the power & places to bestow will escape with impunity, while the poor court who have nothing to give & of whom nobody is afraid, bears all the obloquy of the measure.[75]

Actually, the general uneasiness on the part of people who agreed with the outcome in *McCulloch v. Maryland* but who were unwilling to defend its view of the origins and nature of the Constitution, as well as its expansionist definition of the implied powers of Congress under the necessary and proper clause, had considerable justification in fact, for it was, in the context of its time, an extremely nationalist interpretation of the Constitution. The baseline for Marshall's constitutional thought was the great struggle that had taken place over the ratification of the Constitution in 1787–1788, and despite an occasional empty reassurance that the rights of the states needed to be recognized and respected, he viewed the advocates of states' rights as essentially opponents of the national government created by the Constitution, who wanted to undo the victory of 1787–1788. From Marshall's perspective, the proponents of states' rights were essentially Antifederalists and supporters of the Articles of Confederation, and he believed that the 1780s had been mainly a period of state obstructionism, economic chaos, and anarchy which was leading to disunion and a collapse of America's republican experiment in liberty.[76]

In 1805, in *United States v. Fisher*, Marshall had dismissed the argument for a narrow definition of the necessary and proper clause as essentially "an objection to the Constitution itself."[77] Moreover, a few months after he handed down the *McCulloch* decision, he privately warned that if the principles of the opponents of the decision "were to prevail, the Constitution would be converted into the old confederation."[78] Indeed, at this extremely nationalist point in Marshall's judicial career, he had a strong bias against the view that the U.S. Constitution had created a truly federal system in which the states played an integral and coordinate part. This probably more than anything else explains why Marshall in his *McCulloch* decision so totally passed over the complicated and controversial issue of whether the 2BUS should have the power to create branches wherever and whenever it wanted, and whether the branches were to be totally immune from any kind of state regulation.

Marshall's decision also failed to deal adequately with the various issues that arose from the private nature of the 2BUS and that it was mainly a profit-making institution. To be sure, in Marshall's rather superficial attempt to deal with the issue, he made a valid point: the 2BUS never would have been able to go into operation in 1816 without substantial input of capital from the private sector because the federal government was essentially broke. But he totally ignored what had occurred between the creation of the 2BUS in 1816 and the summer of 1818 when the bank was under the complete control of a president and board of directors whose main interest was in making profits, increasing the value of its stock, paying high dividends, and making unsecured loans to themselves and their friends. Moreover, when hard times began in the summer of 1818, the 2BUS's exclusive concern was with its own survival, which it accomplished by severely contracting its credit, which in turn intensified the impact of the Panic of 1819 and created further distress and misery.

The 2BUS's policies in the years that immediately followed its inception more than justified the view, especially on the local level where its branches operated, that it was not only a formidable competitor but also an alien institution beyond any control, one that was capable of being intrusive and coercive and that was more interested in pursuing and protecting its own interests than it was in helping the government or serving the interests of the people. This was a given fact since, from its beginning, it was clear that the private investors who controlled the 2BUS expected a good return on the investments they had made to get the bank started. This was clearly understood by Secretary of the Treasury Crawford, for he wrote to Langdon Cheves, who succeeded Jones to the presidency of the 2BUS and opted to continue the policy of contraction: "The first duty of the Board [of Directors] is to the stockholders, the second is to the nation."[79] The tension between these two considerations became particularly obvious during the economic difficulties that flowed from the hard times of late 1818 and 1819, when the policies adopted by the 2BUS had a severe impact on the local economies of the West and South, prompting banking historian William Gouge to write several years later with considerable accuracy that, during this time, "the Bank was saved and the people were ruined."[80] Yet, despite all of this, Marshall in *McCulloch v. Maryland* depicted the 2BUS as first and foremost a government institution.

Meanwhile, in sharp contrast to the relative silence from those who favored the 2BUS but not the decision, there was a barrage of criticism from those who opposed the outcome of the case. The initial attack came from Hezekiah Niles, editor of *Niles' Weekly Register*, the first national news magazine, which had a broad circulation among educated readers throughout the country. He warned against the decision as an attempt to consolidate power on the national level and viewed it as an assault on the rights of the American people because "the sovereignty of the states is indispensable to the preservation of liberty." Moreover, as a consequence of the *McCulloch* decision, Niles believed, "a deadly blow has been struck at the *sovereignty of the states*, and from a quarter so far removed from the people as to be hardly accessible to public opinion."[81]

Especially dangerous, according to Niles, were the two main principles established by the decision. The first was that "Congress has an unlimited right to grant acts of incorporation." The second was that "a company incorporated by Congress is exempted from the common operation of the laws of the state in which it may be located." He warned that, as a result of the decision, more national corporations with exclusive privileges were sure to follow, and he urged people to be "truly alarmed at a *judicial* decision which threatens to annihilate the sovereignties of the states; which will sanction any species of *monopoly*, and make the productive many subservient to the unproductive few."[82]

A short time later, the *Argus of Western America*, published in Frankfort, Kentucky, and edited by Amos Kendall, ran a series of essays, all critical of the Supreme Court's *McCulloch* decision. Although less visible than *Niles' Weekly Register*, it was an important western paper, and its editor was a rising political star who would eventually emerge as one of Andrew Jackson's leading political advisors and arguably his most important speech writer. Kendall took sharp issue with Marshall's failure to recognize that the states had played a central role in the creation and functioning of the federal government. He denounced the Court's expansive definition of the necessary and proper clause, warning:

> if they be correct if Congress may exercise all powers which in their wisdom, their whim or caprice, they may aver to be necessary and proper to promote the general welfare, then is the Constitution, not indeed a "splendid bauble" but *a splendid imposition* palmed by the Chief Justice and his associates upon an unsuspecting community?[83]

Kendall viewed Marshall's decision as so wide ranging in its implications as to be dangerous. He believed the decision was the culmination of Marshall's desire, ever since the Constitution's adoption in 1788, to expand the powers of the federal government. He decried the decision because "it appears to lay the foundation for the exercise of a mass of implied powers by the Congress of the United States which the utmost stretch of the human mind can neither grasp nor define," and he urged that it be resisted. The decision, Kendall argued, was an "attempt to remove the restrictions which the people have imposed on the powers of Congress and the means of carrying them into execution."[84]

Turning his attention from the Court's decision and the dangers it posed to states' rights and a strict interpretation of the Constitution, Kendall next focused on the profit-making nature of the 2BUS, which he described as mainly "a business carried on by individuals for individual gain."[85] The immense powers of the 2BUS, transcending even the powers of Congress, went way beyond what was necessary for it to perform the services it rendered to the federal government. Moreover, as a private corporation, the decision meant that it could no longer be popularly controlled. What Congress had created, in fact, was "a corporation of prodigious wealth and extensive power, pervading every section of the Union and exempt from state taxation, whether employed as an agent of the government or not." The end result was a corporation "dangerous to the authority of the states and destructive of the liberties of the people."[86]

Niles and Kendall highlighted the main concerns of those hostile to the opinion handed down in *McCulloch v. Maryland*. But there were also other concerns about the case that could be raised. Why had the case come before the Supreme Court so quickly when it usually took much longer to get a hearing on important constitutional questions? Was it appropriate to use the Maryland situation to rule against the very real threat to the branches that existed in Kentucky and Ohio? It is therefore necessary to examine more fully the developments in Virginia and Ohio, where in different ways the sharpest, most sustained, and most searching opposition to the opinion developed.

FIVE

VIRGINIA'S RESPONSE TO MCCULLOCH V. MARYLAND

An interesting and far-ranging, if anomalous, discussion of the U.S. Supreme Court's decision in *McCulloch v. Maryland* occurred in the state of Virginia. The political leadership of the Old Dominion approached constitutional issues with an unusual seriousness of purpose, especially where the issue of states' rights was concerned. Indeed, building upon a strong Antifederalist heritage, the Virginia Resolutions of 1798 and 1799, and the opposition to *Martin v. Hunter's Lessee*, many believed that the state had a special mission to scrutinize the activities of the national government, and especially the U.S. Supreme Court, to expose all attempts to consolidate power on the national level, and to correctly define the exact nature of American federalism.

The debate that followed was both unusual and significant. It was unusual because, despite reservations about the constitutionality of the 2BUS, the Old Dominion's leadership had taken a pragmatic approach to its creation and accepted it. In fact, even with the coming of hard times in 1818–1819, the state never taxed its branches. Instead, the debate focused on the powers of the Supreme Court and the broader and long-range significance of the decision handed down in *McCulloch v. Maryland*. It was in many ways a continuation of the debate that had taken place in the Old Dominion in 1788 over the ratification of the Constitution. The debate was also particularly significant because the main defense and explication of the decision came in a series of essays anonymously penned by John Marshall himself.

I

The group that dominated Virginia politics during the second decade of the nineteenth century has come to be known as the Richmond Junto. It was essentially an informal and loose association of about twenty members brought together by personal friendships, family ties, business connections, and a common desire to control the dispensation of patronage under the oligarchic government structure of the Old Dominion. All of its members came from the Tidewater and Piedmont areas of the state, and while they owned plantations they were also judges, lawyers, bankers, and editors, who mainly operated out of Richmond.[1]

The principal members of the group included Spencer Roane, who was the dominant figure on the Virginia Court of Appeals. He had been a strong and important supporter of James Madison's presidential ambitions, and he had a special interest in constitutional questions. In particular, he was an implacable foe of John Marshall and the U.S. Supreme Court's determination to review the decisions of state courts involving federal questions and its attempt to broaden the powers of the federal government.[2] Thomas Ritchie, who had studied law under Roane and was also his cousin, became editor of the *Richmond Enquirer*, a newspaper that thrived economically as a consequence of being the main recipient of the state's printing contracts. Compared to many other newspapers of the time, it was unusually high-toned and knowledgeable about state and national politics; it dominated the Virginia market and had considerable visibility outside the state as many of its editorials and other pieces were reprinted in newspapers throughout the country.[3] Wilson Cary Nicholas, an effective behind-the-scenes political operative, served both in the U.S. Senate and the House of Representatives, where he was a strong political ally of Jefferson and

Madison. An inveterate and unsuccessful land speculator, he was in constant need of money and resigned his seat in Congress to become the collector of customs at Norfolk. He also eventually became governor of Virginia and the president of the branch of the 2BUS in Norfolk.[4]

Other significant figures in the Richmond Junto included Dr. John Brockenbrough, president of the Bank of Virginia; his brother William Brockenbrough, a judge of the General Court of Virginia; Phillip Norbonne Nicholas, brother of Wilson Cary Nicholas and president of the Farmers' Bank of Virginia; John Hay, James Monroe's son-in-law; Peter V. Daniel, a member of the Council of State and a future associate justice of the U.S. Supreme Court; James Barbour, a U.S. senator, former governor of the Old Dominion, and future member of President John Quincy Adams's cabinet; P. P. Barbour, his brother, a member of the House of Representatives, who also would serve on the U.S. Supreme Court; Dr. William Foushee, postmaster of Richmond; Andrew Stevenson, a former Speaker of the Virginia House of Delegates and a member of the U.S. House of Representatives, of which he eventually became Speaker; and a number of other successful lawyers and wealthy planters.[5]

Not all members of the Richmond Junto shared the same political principles. James Barbour, for example, became an outright nationalist following the end of the War of 1812, while most members, and especially Roane, tended to be moderate states' rights men. P. P. Barbour, on the other hand, believed the act creating the 2BUS to be unconstitutional. Despite their political differences on specific issues, they tended to remain friends and to look out for each other's interests.[6] Nor were they ideologues, constitutional purists, or extremists like John Taylor or John Randolph. And they were not antibusiness, narrow agrarians, or archconservatives; in fact, on almost all issues, they were cautious, pragmatic, and middle-of-the-road. They supported the strict separation of church and state, a state-funded public education system, and an internal improvements program so long as it was responsibly financed. They also believed in some reforms in the state's constitution and in concessions to the western counties, which were inadequately represented in the legislature. And while they viewed the proponents of abolition as essentially troublemakers, they did not defend slavery as a positive good and recognized that it was incompatible with the principles of the American Revolution.

Their moderate and pragmatic approach to issues is clearly revealed in their attitude toward state banking and the 2BUS. Most of them viewed banks as a necessary evil. They saw them as a powerful and dangerous force that could lead to the creation of a moneyed aristocracy capable of accumulating an extraordinary amount of power that would undermine the republic and destroy the people's liberties. But most members of the Richmond Junto also believed that it was not possible to do without banks since the result would be economic stagnation.[7] Their solution to the problem was to create a branch banking system that would lend itself to a form of centralized control. Under this system, banking in Virginia turned out to be a carefully regulated and financially responsible operation. State laws and banking policies limited the number of shares an individual could own. Also carefully controlled and monitored were the amount of notes issued and the specie reserves needed to back them up. Loans from the banks were not easily obtained, invariably were for short terms, and had strictly enforced due dates that were difficult to extend.[8]

The Bank of Virginia, chartered in 1804, was headquartered in Richmond with branches at Norfolk, Fredericksburg, and Petersburg. The end of the embargo in 1809, when some semblance of prosperity returned, combined with the failure of the 1BUS to be rechartered, created a demand on the state level for an increase in banking services. Virginia responded in 1812 with the creation of the Farmers' Bank of Virginia. Headquartered in Richmond, it had branches in Norfolk, Lynchburg, Winchester, Petersburg, and Fredericksburg. Both of these banks were required to lend money to the state so that it could purchase stock in them, and the dividends received from this as well as various taxes levied on the capital of the banks and other fees were used to create special educational and internal improvement funds.[9]

Virginia's conservatively run banks served the state well during the War of 1812. In the end, however, they were forced to suspend specie payments, for while they had adequate amounts of specie to back up their notes, the suspension of specie payments by local banks in other states required them to do so in order to prevent the draining away of their specie reserves.[10] William Gouge, whose important and influential treatise entitled *A Short History of Paper Money and Banking in the United States . . . with Consideration of the Effects on Morals and Happiness* (1833) critically surveyed state banking activities during the first third of the nineteenth century, denigrated developments in most of the mid-Atlantic, southern, and western states, but praised Virginia for "being the first state that took effectual measures towards reforming the currency," and predicted that it "will probably be one of the first to establish a perfectly sound system of credit and currency."[11]

On the other hand, the Virginia banking system did not adapt particularly well to the business expansion that occurred throughout most of the country from 1815 to mid-1818. Neither the Bank of Virginia nor the Farmers' Bank had any branches in the counties west of the Blue Ridge Mountains. As a consequence, a number of private banking operations emerged that provided a circulating medium and other financial services for the rapidly increasing number of people in that area who were being swept into the market economy. However, these independent and unchartered local banks were illegal, and the state quickly moved to tighten its laws in order to force them out of business or to formally apply for charters. In the legislative session of 1816–1817, there were twenty-two applications for charters, of which a special committee recommended fifteen for incorporation. The opponents of this development, who came mainly from the eastern part of the state, however, only would agree to the creation of two new mother banks with branches: the Northwestern Bank of Virginia in Wheeling and the Valley of Virginia Bank in Winchester. This measure was adopted by the very close vote of 80–78, which indicated that the state continued to be determined to limit and control banking operations within its borders.[12]

At the same time, while the Old Dominion's leadership had been at the forefront of the opposition to the rechartering of the 1BUS in 1811, mainly on constitutional grounds, by 1816, with the exception of a few purists, many acquiesced in the chartering of the 2BUS. This included Spencer Roane who, while he remained skeptical about whether the members of Congress "have the power to do it," also recognized that with the proliferation of local banks "a national bank . . . or a national currency must be resorted to, or the consequences cannot be foreseen or estimated."[13] Roane's support for a national bank continued even after its mismanagement during William Jones's presidency was revealed and Congress was considering taking away its charter. Writing less than a month before the Supreme Court handed down its decision in *McCulloch v. Maryland*, Roane agreed with "the necessity of supporting the bank" for he feared "a great and general distress would pervade all classes . . . from winding it up too hastily."[14]

In many ways, the creation of the 2BUS in 1816 was not an unwelcome development in Virginia, for with it came a number of economic benefits. Shortly after its incorporation, the 2BUS created branches in Richmond and Norfolk, which proved to be among the busiest offices in the country. This infusion of capital into the state relieved the pressure to create even more local banks or to have the existing ones expand their loans and issue more currency. This in turn allowed the state to continue to pursue its conservative banking policies and maintain control over the operations of its own banks. As a consequence, unlike many other states, there was, before 1819, no significant interest in Virginia to levy a tax on the 2BUS nor to drive it from the state. Moreover, even among those most sharply opposed to the 2BUS on constitutional grounds, there was no movement to tax it out of existence, at least in the beginning.[15]

II

Despite Virginia's generally accepting attitude toward the 2BUS before 1819, it immediately became clear that Marshall's opinion in *McCulloch v. Maryland* was going to receive a hostile reception in the Old Dominion. A clear indication of the nature of the opposition came in the *Richmond Enquirer* on March 23, 1819, when it published the decision, for Ritchie indicated that, while the decision was impressive, it was also unacceptable. Referring to the Virginia Resolutions of 1798 and 1799, which opposed the Alien and Sedition Acts, he asserted: "This opinion must be controverted and exposed. Virginia has proved itself the uniform friend of state rights—again she is called to come forth." A week later, on March 30, the first of two essays signed "Amphictyon" appeared, with Ritchie's strong endorsement, while the second one came out on April 2.[16]

These essays, written by Judge William Brockenbrough, took direct issue with the two main points of Marshall's opinion, which he claimed was an assault upon the entire concept of states' rights by denying the compact theory of the origins and nature of the union and by espousing an expansive view of the powers of Congress under the necessary and proper clause of the U.S. Constitution. In the first essay, Amphictyon pointed out that, for the U.S. Supreme Court to make its decision, it had not been necessary to have offered its opinion on these points, and therefore what was asserted was "merely *obiter*, extrajudicial, and not more binding or obligatory than the opinion of any other six intelligent members of the community."[17] Amphictyon then proceeded to reassert the compact theory of the union and pointed to the Tenth Amendment as proof that the federal government was limited to the powers actually enumerated in the Constitution. The states, Amphictyon argued, had to play the role of "sentinels of the public liberty" for "every government which has ever yet been established feels a disposition to increase its own powers," and unless restrained "by an enlightened public opinion . . . will inevitably conduct the freest government to the exercise of tyrannic power." In the course of arguing this, he rejected the claim that the power to restrain the federal government lay in the hands of the federal judiciary: "The supreme court may be a perfectly impartial tribunal to decide between two states, but cannot be considered in that point of view when the contest lies between the United States, and one of its members." Since the states had been the parties that had created the federal government, it was up to them to determine whether the compact had been dangerously violated.[18]

In his second essay, Amphictyon disputed Marshall's argument that "necessary and proper . . . ought to be construed in a liberal, rather than a restricted sense."[19] Approaching the issue in historical terms, he pointed out that "the danger arising from the implied powers has always been seen and felt by the people of the states." It was precisely this fear that had been at the heart of the Antifederalists' opposition to the adoption of the U.S. Constitution because they believed

that the powers of the federal government would be enlarged so much by the force of implication as to sweep away every vestige of power from the state governments. The progress of the government from the commencement of it to this day, proves that the fears are not without foundation. To counteract that irresistible tendency in the federal government to enlarge their own dominion, the vigilance of the people and state governments should constantly be exerted.[20]

Arguing for a narrow definition of the necessary and proper clause, Amphictyon claimed that a broad definition of Congress's powers would create "a government of almost unlimited powers." Marshall's decision, he asserted, was a direct assault on the rights and powers of the states. It undercut what he claimed was the original purpose of creating the Constitution:

to protect us from foreign nations and from internal dissentions. For this purpose it may lay taxes, borrow money, raise armies, govern the militia, build ships, and exercise every power which it is necessary should be exercised to attain those great and desirable objects. The purse and the sword are placed in its hands. The state governments have all residuary power; everything necessary for the protection of the lives, liberty and property of individuals is left subject to their control; the contracts of every class of society, agricultural, mercantile, or mechanical, are regulated by their laws, except in those cases the states fully surrendered the power. This residuary power was left in the hands of the states for wise purposes. It is necessary that the laws which regulate the daily transactions of men should have a regard to their interests, their feelings, even their prejudices. This can better be done when the territory is of moderate dimensions, than when it is immense; it is more peculiarly too in the situation of our society, where we have been always accustomed to our laws, and our own legislatures, and where the laws of one state will not suit the people of another. It is still more important that this division of legislative power into external and internal should be rigidly adhered to, and its proper distribution religiously observed, when we reflect that the accumulation of these powers into the hands of one government would render it too strong for the liberty of the people, and would inevitably erect a throne upon the ruins of the people.[21]

What Amphictyon called an "enlarged construction" of the Constitution needed to be opposed, he argued, because it would soon spill over into a variety of other areas. As a consequence of the Supreme Court's ruling in *McCulloch v. Maryland*, members of Congress "may lay out their money on roads and canals. . . . They may build universities, academies, and school houses for the poor." Under this ruling, they could create various national corporations "and rest in those companies a portion of their own funds in order to contribute to the general welfare." Then, in a spasm of hyperbole, because no one was even proposing this at the time, he warned:

> They may build churches, because it promotes the general welfare of the people, to resort to places of public worship, and they may support from the treasury those ministers of the gospel, whose tenets may in their opinion best advance the general welfare, that is conduce to the strength of the government.

He then added, "when consequences such as these are plainly deducible from the enlarged construction of the constitution, we must without hesitation pronounce that such construction is inadmissible." Nor did he accept Marshall's assertion in *McCulloch v. Maryland* that if Congress passed a law that overstepped the bounds of its power, " 'it would become the painful duty of that tribunal to say that an act of Congress was not the law of the land.' I apprehend this can hardly ever be the case, where the act is one which gives power to the federal government."[22]

Marshall was angered and alarmed by Amphictyon's essays. He was particularly concerned that the essays would be the beginning of a movement that would culminate in the Virginia legislature adopting resolutions similar to the ones it issued in 1798 and 1799, which Marshall believed would attack not only the Supreme Court but the Constitution and the union as well. Convinced that no one else was going to defend his decision, Marshall, in a truly singular act, decided to do so himself in a series of newspaper essays.

In doing so, Marshall did his best to remain anonymous. The only one in whom he confided was Bushrod Washington, who acted as a go-between. Not even Joseph Story knew about it, although he eventually figured out who authored the essays after they were finally published.[23] It is clear that Marshall's commitment to his decision in *McCulloch v. Maryland* was unusually strong. It is revealed in the care with which he prepared the decision for publication, for as Henry Wheaton, the official court reporter, observed, "he has evinced an unusual degree of solicitude on the subject of that argument by writing me several times to make some slight verbal alterations."[24] Marshall indicated his own strong feelings about the case when he explained to Washington why he was responding to the criticism of his decision in the *Richmond Enquirer*. "I find myself," he noted, "more stimulated on the subject than on any other because I believe the design to be to injure the Judges & impair the Constitution."[25] Wheaton also undoubtedly expressed Marshall's feeling on the dispute when he wrote, "It must by no means be left doubtful even for an instant whether the ground assumed by the court is to be maintained at all hazards."[26]

Getting his essays published turned out to be a much more difficult and frustrating experience than Marshall anticipated. He and Bushrod Washington selected the *Philadelphia Union*, edited by Enos Bronson, to publish two essays signed "A friend to the Union." They appeared in the April 24 and 28, 1819, issues, but they were badly mangled in the actual printing. As Marshall put it: "He [Bronson] has cut out the middle of the second number to be inserted in the first."[27] As a consequence, according to the chief justice, "the points & the arguments were so separated from each other & so strangely mixed as to constitute a labyrinth to which those only who understood the whole subject perfectly could find a clue."[28] Convinced that "this subject is not to drop," Marshall had Washington republish the essays in the *Gazette and Alexandria Daily Advertiser* in the May 15, 17, and 18, 1819, issues.[29]

Marshall focused on the two key issues raised by Amphictyon in his essays: the role of the state governments in the debate over the origins and nature of the union, and the meaning of the necessary and proper clause. In his first essay, he effectively took issue with the claim that the federal government came about as a consequence of the different state governments forming a compact granting specific and limited powers to the central government while retaining all of the remaining powers.

Marshall's response was that the Constitution was created by the people meeting in specially elected state conventions that were completely separate from the state governments. This was one of the essential differences between the Articles of Confederation, which explicitly indicated it was "a league of friendship" created by the existing state governments, and the U.S. Constitution that had been submitted for ratification to the people of the states. This is the way, Marshall asserted, Amphictyon's claim notwithstanding, that the term "people" had been used by the Court in *McCulloch v. Maryland,* and he absolutely denied that the Court meant by "the people" a single mass completely separated from state boundaries. Having made this point, Marshall reiterated his observation from his decision in *McCulloch v. Maryland* that "no political dreamer was ever wild enough to think of breaking down the lines which separate the states, and of compounding the American people into one mass." Marshall concluded his first number by expressing

> my regrets that a gentleman whose claims to our respect appear to be by no means inconsiderable should manifest such excessive hostility to the powers necessary for the preservation of the Union, as to arraign with such bitterness the opinion of the supreme court on an interesting constitutional question, either for doctrines not to be found in it, or on principles totally repugnant to the words of the constitution, and to the recorded facts respecting its adoption.[30]

In his second essay, Marshall took issue with Amphictyon's criticism of the Supreme Court's treatment of the necessary and proper clause. He argued that it had been misrepresented, cleverly asserting, "for the sake of accuracy I will observe that the Supreme Court has not said that the grant ought to be construed in a 'liberal sense' although it certainly denied that it ought to be construed in that 'restricted sense' for which Amphictyon contends."[31] The issues raised by the meaning of the term, Marshall went on to argue, are "of real importance to the People of the United States. If the rule contended for would not absolutely arrest the program of the government; it would certainly deny to those who administer it the means of executing its acknowledged power in the manner most advantageous to those for whose benefit they were conferred."[32] The interpretation of the necessary and proper clause promulgated by the Supreme Court, Marshall continued, did not enlarge the powers of Congress but only gave it the flexibility to adopt the best possible way to implement the powers already granted to it. On the other hand, a narrow or restricted approach to the clause "would essentially change the constitution, render the government of the Union incompetent to the objects for which it was instituted, and place all its power under the control of the state legislatures. It would, in a great measure, reinstate the old confederation."[33]

On another level, there also was a sharp difference between the tone of the Amphictyon essays and Marshall's response. At no point did Amphictyon attack Marshall personally in his essays; in fact the reverse was true, for at the beginning of his first essay he went out of his way to be respectful, describing the chief justice as "a man of gigantic powers." He also tended to be conciliatory for he observed that, under a system of government that distributed power between the states and a national government, "if the governments are to move on harmoniously, neither ought to attempt to pull down what the other has a right to build up, and this duty is as imperative on the government of the U. States, as it is on the several states." To this end, assurances were given that Virginia had no intention of moving directly against the 2BUS by taxing it or forcefully obstructing its operation.[34] Marshall's response, on the other hand, was hostile, condescending, and even smug. Privately, in a letter to Joseph Story, he indicated his contempt for the Amphictyon essays. He believed the Court's arguments had been "grossly misrepresented. . . . where its argument has been truly stated it has been met by principles one would think too palpably absurd for intelligent men."[35] Moreover, in his essays, the chief justice rarely lost an opportunity to personally attack his opponent. At one point he noted, "he is too little accustomed to political opposition, and is too confident of the prejudices he addresses, to be very attentive to the correctness of his positions, or to the accuracy of his reasoning."[36] In rejecting Amphictyon's arguments, he referred to them as "extraordinary, dogma" and accused him of trying to "create odious phantoms which may be very proper objects of detestation, but which bear no resemblance to anything that has proceeded from the court."[37] Even when Amphictyon made a valid point, Marshall would only grant "he has very gravely demonstrated what every body knows, & what no body denies."[38] Overall, Marshall suggested that Amphictyon's construction of the Constitution was "obviously erroneous" and that his interpretation of the Court's opinion involved "a palpable misrepresentation."[39] He then charged that Amphictyon's "strictures on the opinion of the supreme court are founded on a total and obvious perversion of the plain meaning of that opinion, as well as a misconstruction of the constitution," and suggested that "many laborious criticisms would be avoided if those who are disposed to condemn a paper, would take the trouble to read, with a disposition to understand it."[40]

In addition to having a sharp and even nasty edge to them, Marshall's "A friend to the Union" essays also had a defensive side, especially where the role of the Supreme Court was concerned. At the beginning of the essays, he complained:

[T]he bill for incorporating a bank of the United States had become a law, without a single murmur. The reason is obvious. Those who fill the legislative and executive departments are elected by the people, and are of course popular. In addition, they possess great power and great patronage. Had they been unjustly attacked, champions would have arisen on everyside, who would with equal zeal and ability have presented the truth to a publick not unwilling to perceive it. But the judges of the Supreme Court, separated from the people by the tenure of office, by age, and by the nature of their duties, are viewed with respect, unmingled with affection, or interest. They possess neither power nor patronage. They have no sops to give.[41]

Toward the end of his essays, Marshall asked: "Why then is Amphictyon so delicate on the constitutionality of the law, while he is so vehement and strenuous in his exertions to rouse the nation against the court?" Then, defending the Supreme Court's decision in *McCulloch v. Maryland*, he observed, "the court did not volunteer in this business. The question was brought before them, and they could not escape it."[42]

Here, Marshall was being disingenuous. The Supreme Court did not have to hear the case and certainly not with the speed that it did so, especially since it was clearly an arranged case and there was no record of it actually being heard by the Maryland Court of Appeals. Yet despite this, Marshall had signed off on the writ of certiori by which it came before the Supreme Court. Nor did he have to hand down his decision as quickly as he did. And it was not necessary for Marshall in his decision to have gone into the long discussion that he did in dealing with the origins and nature of the union and the meaning of the necessary and proper clause, particularly since the case involved the constitutionality of Maryland's tax and not the constitutionality of the 2BUS itself. Moreover, the evidence tilts strongly in the direction that the raising of these issues, which was done by Webster in his opening presentation to the Court, had been prearranged. While Marshall's relationship to this development is elusive, there is no question but that he enthusiastically embraced the opportunities it offered him to expound on these issues.

Shortly after he completed his "A friend to the Union" essays, Marshall learned "that some other essays written by a great man . . . will soon appear."[43] The author of these essays, as everyone involved in the controversy recognized, was Roane himself. Writing under the pseudonym "Hampden," he published four essays in the *Richmond Enquirer* of June 11, 15, 18, and 22, 1819. As with Amphictyon's pieces, they were introduced by Ritchie, who indicated, "we solemnly believe, that Hampden has refuted the opinion of the supreme court; and placed it in its proper light before the public."[44]

In his essays, Hampden, like Amphictyon, focused on what he believed were the ultranationalist implications of Marshall's view of the origins and nature of the union and his expansionist interpretation of the necessary and proper clause. Approaching the problem historically by looking in particular at the fears of the Antifederalists in 1787 and 1788 and the Republicans in 1798–1800, Hampden argued that the Supreme Court's decision in *McCulloch v. Maryland* needed to be viewed as part of a long-term campaign to overthrow the limitations on the powers of the federal government to be found in the Constitution. The ultimate purpose of this campaign, Hampden argued, was "to give a Carte Blanche to our federal rulers, and to obliterate the state governments, forever, from our political system." The driving force for this had come mainly from Congress, but it had always received strong support from the federal judiciary.[45]

Focusing his attention on the role of the U.S. Supreme Court, Hampden accused it of engaging in a

> judicial *coup de main*: to give a *general* letter of attorney to the future legislators of the union: and to tread under foot all those parts and articles of the constitution which had been, heretofore, deemed to set limits to the power of the federal legislature. That man must be a deplorable idiot who does not see that there is no earthly difference between an unlimited grant of power, and a grant limited in its terms but accompanied with *unlimited* means of carrying it into execution.[46]

What made the Supreme Court's opinion so objectionable and dangerous, Hampden argued, was that Marshall had rejected handing down a narrow decision to establish "a *general* and *abstract* doctrine whose effect was to adjudicate away the *reserved* rights of a sovereign member of the confederacy and vest them in the general government."[47] The union as created by the Constitution, according to Hampden, was federal in nature. This meant that the national government was one of carefully defined and limited powers, while the remaining powers were reserved to the states. To support this claim, he made reference to various assurances given by Madison during the Virginia Convention's ratifying debates, the Tenth Amendment, the Virginia Report of 1799 written by Madison, and statements by Vice President George Clinton, who had played a leading role in rejecting the bill to re-charter the 1BUS in 1811.

Hampden also examined the role of the U.S. Supreme Court under the Constitution. Accepting Marshall's view that the Constitution was formally adopted by the people of the states rather than the state governments, as Amphictyon had asserted, he turned the argument against the chief justice by averring that it was only the people and not the Court that had the power to alter or enlarge the power of the central government. Having rejected the practice of increasing the federal government's power "by construction," Hampden observed, "the people only are supreme. The Constitution is subordinate to them, and the departments of the government are subordinate to that Constitution." If changes were to be made to the Constitution, they could only be made by the people when "their opinion is greatly manifested, in the ample provisions it contains for its amendment."[48]

Toward the end of his essay, Hampden offered his own version of the complex history of the fight over the establishment of a national bank in the early republic, as well as the role of economic necessity in the creation of the 2BUS in 1816. It in certain ways does much more justice to the facts than does Marshall's one-sided claim at the beginning of his opinion in *McCulloch v. Maryland* that the constitutionality of the 2BUS had been settled by precedent:

I had intended Mr. Editor, to enter into a more detailed enquiry as to the constitutionality of the bank of the U.States. That however is but a single measure, and must probably be submitted to. With respect to it, the maximum factum valet [quod] fieri non debet [a fact/act which should not come to pass (nonetheless) stands/thrives] must, perhaps, apply. I would yield to it on the single principle, of giving up a part to save the whole. I principally make war against the declaratory decision of the supreme court, giving congress power to "bind us in all cases whatsoever"! That measure (the bank) has, perhaps, so entwined itself into the interests and transactions of our people, that it may not, without difficulty, be cast off. There is a great difference, too, between particular infractions of the constitution, and declaratory doctrines having the effect to change the constitution. . . . The old bank expired before the late war commenced, and the present one was only established since the peace; so that our country got along without it, through a bloody war, against a most powerful nation, and when a band of internal traitors was arrayed against it. After this, can a bank be said to be essential to the existence of the country? . . . While this institution is not necessary in relation to the government of the United States, its establishment cuts deep, on the other hand, into the rights of the several states. . . . It repeals a right before possessed by the states, to limit the number of banks within their territory. It inundates them with paper money, under pain of submitting to that evil, or breaking their faith with their own banks, previously established. If they should consent to this last alternative, as the lesser of two evils, it obliges them to refund from their treasuries, the premiums they have received therefor. . . . They exempt the persons of the stockholders from imprisonment for their bank debts, and the other property of the said stockholders from its liability to pay their said debts, in equal violations of justice, and the laws of the several states. They give exclusive privileges within the states, without any public services rendered to the states therefor . . . and they enable aliens and foreigners to hold lands, within the several states, in contravention of the general policy of their laws. —The supreme court were pleased to go out of the record, and to tell us, that some of our distinguished functionaries had changed their opinions, on this subject. They forgot, however, to inform us, that a motion was made and rejected, in the general convention, to give congress the power of erecting corporations. They also omitted to state, that Washington hesitated on the subject, and then decided against the majority of his cabinet, and particularly against the opinion of Mr. Jefferson[.] — As to the point of acquiescence . . . it is observed that only two bills have passed for establishing banks, while (that rejected by the casting vote of Mr. Clinton, and one rejected by Mr. Madison in the year 1814) two have been rejected. So that the account stands two and two. There was an interregnum, if I may so say, as to this institution. . . . There has been a chasm in the time of its continuance. It has not even that characteristic which is essential to the goodness of a custom, by the common law. It has not been *continued*. . . . There is no doubt that many who voted for the bank [in 1816], did it under what was supposed the peculiar pressure of the times. It was not adopted in relation to ordinary times, nor on the ground of its being a constitutional measure.[49]

Hampden concluded his essays by questioning the jurisdiction of the U.S. Supreme Court in cases involving federal-state relations. He pointed out that nowhere in the Constitution was the power explicitly provided, and its assumption by the High Court was leading to the usurpation of the reserved rights of the states. He also argued that the

Constitution had created a federal government or a "league as was the former confederation. The only difference is, that the powers of this government are much *extended*."[50] Under this system, the Supreme Court was a High Court of Appeals only in cases involving the different departments of the federal government, but was not a fair and competent tribunal in dealing with disputes involving the rights of the states, since it was a creature of the federal government.[51] Simply put: "the general government cannot decide this controversy and much less can one of its departments. They cannot do it unless we tread under foot the principle which forbids a party to decide its own cause."[52]

Marshall closely followed the publication of Roane's Hampden essays, and they angered him. Although Marshall began writing further essays as soon as he saw Roane's pieces, he requested that they not be published until after the last of the Hampden essays appeared.[53] He signed them "A friend to the Constitution," but tried to change it to "A Constitutionalist" because "A friend to the Constitution is so much like A Friend to the Union that it may lead to some suspicion of identity."[54] But the request came too late, and Marshall's nine short essays appeared by "A friend to the Constitution" in the *Gazette and Alexandria Daily Advertiser* between June 30 and July 15, 1819.

Marshall's response was vehement, even embittered. He asserted that Hampden had "grossly misrepresented" the Supreme Court's argument in *McCulloch v. Maryland* and that his essays were a "ranting declamation."[55] Opposition to the decision, Marshall claimed, had its roots in Virginia's strong Antifederalist tradition:

> The zealous and persevering hostility with which the Constitution was originally opposed cannot be forgotten. The deep rooted and vindictive hate, which grew out of unfounded jealousies, and was aggravated by defeat, though suspended for a time, seems never to have been appeased. The desire to strip the government of those effective powers, which enable it to accomplish the objects for which it was created; and by constriction, essentially to reinstate that miserable confederation, where incompetency to the preservation of our union, the short interval between the treaty of Paris [1783] and the meeting of

the general convention at Philadelphia, was sufficient to demonstrate, seems to have recovered all its activity.[56]

Marshall took particular umbrage at Hampden's assault on the role of the Supreme Court. "No rational friend of the Constitution," he wrote, could "view with indifference the systematic efforts which certain restless politicians of Virginia have been for sometime making to degrade that department in the estimation of the public."[57] Specifically, he directly challenged what he called "the unjust and insidious insinuation, that the Court had thrust itself into the controversy between the United States and the state of Maryland, and had unnecessarily volunteered its services." Instead, he argued, "the court proceeded in this business . . . because the question was brought regularly before it by those who had a right to demand, its decision."[58]

Marshall also lashed out against Hampden's claim that the U.S. Supreme Court did not have jurisdiction in cases between a state and the federal government, and certainly could not review the decisions handed down by state courts of appeal in such matters. This, of course, was the position taken by the Virginia Court of Appeals in *Hunter v. Fairfax*, but Marshall argued, quoting from the *Federalist* papers, that from this "nothing but contradiction and confusion can proceed."[59] He also pointed out that this interpretation had been reversed by the unanimous opinion of the U.S. Supreme Court in *Martin v. Hunter's Lessee.* Then he added that the Virginia position had

> been disapproved by every state court, and they are not a few, which had had occasion to act on the subject. The supreme court, as we perceive in the reports, has reversed the decisions of many state courts founded on laws supported by a good deal of state feeling. In every instance, except that of Hunter and Fairfax, the judgment of reversal has been acquiesced in, and the jurisdiction of the court has been recognized. If the most unequivocal indications of the public sentiment may be trusted, it is not hazarding much to say, that out of Virginia, there is probably not a single judge, nor a single lawyer of eminence, who does not dissent from the principle laid down by the court of appeals in Hunter and Fairfax.[60]

As he had in his response to Amphictyon, Marshall reiterated his denial that the decision in *McCulloch v. Maryland* undercut the sovereignty of the states or reduced their rights. He did, however, continue to reject the claim that the Constitution was a product of a compact between the states. Rather, Marshall asserted, "it is the act of a people, creating a government, without which they cannot exist as a people. The powers of a government are conferred for their own benefit, are essential to their own prosperity, and are to be exercised for their good, by persons chosen for that purpose by themselves."[61] He repeated this highly nationalist argument at another point in his essays by observing: "There is no agreement formed between the government of the United States and those of the states. Our Constitution is not a compact. It is the act of a single party. It is the act of the people of the United States, assembling in their respective states, and adopting a government for the whole nation."[62]

Marshall also turned Hampden's claims upside down by arguing that the real threat to the Constitution came from the advocates of states' rights who wanted to reduce the powers of the federal government rather than the other way around. "The people," he argued:

> are as much interested, their liberty is as deeply concerned in preventing encroachments on [the federal] government, in arresting the hands which would tear from it powers which its framers, and the American people, believed to be most conducive to the public happiness and to public liberty. The equipoise thus established is as much disturbed by taking weights out of this scale containing the powers of the government, as by putting weights into it.[63]

It was precisely this, Marshall believed, that was at the heart of the debate over whether the necessary and proper clause of the Constitution should be interpreted in a narrow and strict sense, as Hampden argued, or in a broad and flexible way as the Supreme Court had done in *McCulloch v. Maryland*. Should this be the case, its effect "would abridge, and almost annihilate the useful and necessary rights of the legislature to select its means."[64] More important, its overall impact would be to effectively overturn the U.S. Constitution itself. Marshall made this clear in the last paragraph of his essays:

I have been induced to review these essays the more in detail, because they are intended to produce a very serious effect; and because they advance principles which go, in my judgment, to the utter subversion of the Constitution. Let Hampden succeed, and that instrument will be radically changed. The government of the whole will be prostrated at the feet of its members; and that grand effort of wisdom, virtue and patriotism, which produced it, will be totally defeated.[65]

III

The debate in Virginia between Marshall and his critics did not focus very much on the actual role and legitimacy of the 2BUS and its branches. Moreover, while it dealt with important and enduring constitutional questions, it was abstract and theoretical and often tedious and convoluted. There is little to indicate that it attracted much popular interest, even among the state's political elite. In the legislature, there appears to have been a mixed reaction. What Marshall feared the most was that the Virginia General Assembly, which was to meet in December 1819, would "take up the subject & . . . pass resolutions not very unlike whose which were called forth by the alien & sedition laws in 1799."[66] Resolutions were indeed introduced recommending the creation of a special tribunal to deal with state versus federal issues and to instruct the state's senators and representatives to oppose "on every occasion" all legislation which was based on power not "expressly given" to the federal government under the Constitution. An amendment to the Constitution was also proposed that would limit Congress's power to incorporate a bank to the District of Columbia. Although adopted by the House of Delegates, the Virginia Senate declined to take up these proposals on the grounds it needed more time "to consider and digest them."[67]

But a short time afterward, a related issue emerged which had a much more concrete and direct impact on the state of Virginia. For while the proponents of states' rights in Virginia had not vociferously opposed the actual creation of the 2BUS and had adapted to their advantage the establishment of branches in the state, they were much more hostile to the general idea of national corporations. Their concerns surfaced in the U.S. Supreme Court case of *Cohens v. Virginia* (1821). Philip I. and Mendes Cohen had been tried and convicted in the quarter session court of the borough of Norfolk for selling lottery tickets in violation of a Virginia law prohibiting the sale of such tickets without authorization from the state. The Cohen brothers appealed the decision directly to the U.S. Supreme Court under section 25 of the Judiciary Act of 1789. They argued that their lottery had originally been organized in Washington, D.C., under an act of Congress, and therefore was a national lottery, not bound by state laws.[68]

The case quickly took on national significance when five prominent attorneys—William Pinkney of Maryland, Walter Jones of the District of Columbia, and David Ogden, Thomas Addis Emmet, and John Wells of New York—issued a public statement in support of the Cohen brothers' contention that national corporations were exempt from state restrictions. Their argument had profound nationalist implications:

> It would indeed, be a strange anomaly, if what Congress had created, or authorized to be created, in a valid manner . . . could be considered and treated by a state as the subject of a criminal traffic; . . . if a lottery ticket has a lawful origin under the Constitution of the Union, it is a lawful lottery ticket, wherever the powers of the union is [*sic*] acknowledged. The power of the union, constitutionally executed, knows no locality within the boundaries of the union, and can encounter no geographical impediments; its march is through the union, or it is nothing but a name. The states have no existence relative to the effect of the powers delegated to congress save only where their assent or instrumentality is required, or permitted by the constitution itself.[69]

In effect, *Cohens v. Virginia* raised once again many of the central constitutional issues that swirled around *Martin v. Hunter's Lessee* and *McCulloch v. Maryland*: the supremacy of federal over state law, the right of the U.S. Supreme Court to review acts of state legislatures and the decisions of state courts where the U.S. Constitution is concerned, and the right of Congress to create national corporations.

When Chief Justice Marshall issued a summons that "cited and admonished" the state to appear before the Supreme Court in *Cohens v. Virginia,* the governor of the Old Dominion, Thomas Mann Randolph, raised the matter in his annual address to the legislature in late 1820. The committee that responded to the address brought in a special report and a series of resolutions denying the U.S. Supreme Court's authority to hear the case. The report restated the principles laid down in the Kentucky and Virginia Resolutions and reiterated their belief, prevalent in the Old Dominion, that the federal and state governments represented separate and distinct sovereignties. "The word 'supreme'," it argued, "is descriptive of the federal tribunal, is relative, not absolute; and evidently implies that the supremacy bestowed upon the supreme court is over the inferior courts to be ordained and established by congress; and not over the state courts." Another resolution instructed the two lawyers for Virginia, Philip B. Barbour and Alexander Smyth, who were to represent the state before the U.S. Supreme Court, to limit their argument "alone to the question of jurisdiction, and if the jurisdiction of the Court should be sustained . . . they will consider their duties at an end."[70]

The case was heard in February 1821. Barbour and Smyth asserted Virginia's sovereignty and denied the authority of the Supreme Court to hear the case. They further claimed that the Eleventh Amendment prohibited the federal courts from taking jurisdiction in a case without the state's explicit permission. On behalf of the Cohen brothers, David B. Ogden and William Pinkney pointed to the precedent established in *Martin v. Hunter's Lessee,* that the people, not the states, had created the Constitution, and that federal judicial oversight over state decisions was vital to the continued existence of the union.[71]

Two weeks later, on March 3, 1821, Marshall handed down his decision for a unanimous Supreme Court. In it, the chief justice said little that was new; rather, his opinion was an eloquent restatement and elaboration of the principles of constitutional nationalism that had been enunciated by Story in *Martin v. Hunter's Lessee* and that he had articulated in *McCulloch v. Maryland*:

The American states as well as the American people, have believed a close and firm Union to be essential to their liberty and to their happiness. They have been taught by experience, that the Union cannot exist without a government for the whole: and they have been taught by the same experience that this government would be a mere shadow, that must disappoint all their hopes, unless invested with large portions of that sovereignty which belongs to independent states. Under the influence of this opinion and instructed by experience, the American people, in the conventions of their respective states adopted the present constitution. . . .

This is the authoritative language of the American people, and, if gentlemen please, of the American States. It marks, with lines too strong to be mistaken, the characteristic distinction between the government of the Union and those of the states. The general government, though limited as to its objects, is supreme with respect to those objects. This principle is a part of the Constitution, and if there be any who deny its necessity, none can deny its authority.[72]

Marshall next argued that jurisdiction of the U.S. Supreme Court depended on the nature of the case, not upon the particular forum in which it was heard on the local level, and included all cases of law and equity under the Constitution, federal laws, and treaties. The chief justice also rejected Virginia's claim that it was a sovereign entity and could not be sued without its permission. "America," he asserted:

has chosen to be, in many respects, and to many purposes, a nation; and for all these purposes, her government is complete; to all these objects it is competent. The people have declared, that in the exercise of all powers given for these objects it is supreme. It can, then, in effecting these objects legitimately control all individuals or governments within the American territory.[73]

In addition, Marshall took special aim at Virginia's claim that the federal and state courts were distinct and that no appeal existed from state court decisions to the U.S. Supreme Court on federal questions. Marshall warned that this would lead to chaos. He argued, "the necessity of uniformity, as well as correctness in expounding the constitution and laws of the United States, would suggest the propriety of vesting in some single tribunal the power of deciding, in the last resort, all cases in which they are involved."[74] Marshall also dismissed Virginia's claim that the Eleventh Amendment exempted the state from federal jurisdiction, by pointing out that the present action had been initiated by the state against individuals, not the other way around, and that therefore Virginia could not claim immunity under the Eleventh Amendment.[75]

Having used broad nationalist principles to justify the jurisdiction of the U.S. Supreme Court in *Cohens v. Virginia*, Marshall proceeded to decide the case on its merits. The central question was whether the act of Congress authorizing a lottery in the District of Columbia had created a truly national corporation empowered to operate within individual states without their permission. Marshall believed this raised two questions: the intent of Congress when it passed the law, and the law's constitutionality. Again, for a unanimous court, Marshall ruled that no evidence existed to indicate that Congress intended to create a national lottery or to authorize the sale of lottery tickets in states where they had been declared illegal. Although this part of the decision favored Virginia, it was not satisfactory to the proponents of states' rights. For Marshall had only ruled that the particular act under consideration had not created a national lottery. He did not deal with the more fundamental issue of whether Congress, using its powers to legislate for the District of Columbia, could create national corporations immune from state regulations, because at this point it was "merely speculative." The implication was clear, particularly at this point when the Supreme Court was in its most nationalist phase: carefully constructed legislation for the District of Columbia could be used to create national corporations. As Marshall observed, "The act incorporating the city of Washington is unquestionably of universal obligation; but the extent of the corporate powers conferred by that act, is to be determined by those considerations which belong to the case."[76]

Many Virginians denounced the decision, and again Roane took the lead. He published a series of essays in the *Richmond Enquirer* under the name of "Algernon Sydney."[77] In them, he argued that the *Cohens* decision "negatives the idea that the American states have a real existence, or are to be considered in any sense, sovereign and independent states."

He assailed federal judicial review of state court decisions and the doctrine of implied powers as undermining the concept of true federalism through the idea that the states were subordinate to the national government. He asserted that "if this power of decision is once conceded to either party, the equilibrium established by the Constitution is destroyed, and the compact exists thereafter but in name."[78]

This point of view received strong support from John Taylor of Caroline (a county in Virginia), who was coming to the end of a long life of opposition to the idea of a strong central government. He had opposed the adoption of the U.S. Constitution in 1787 and 1788, wrote several pamphlets during the 1790s condemning Hamilton's financial measures, and shepherded the resolutions Madison had anonymously written through the Virginia legislature in 1798–1799. He supported Jefferson in the election of 1800, but opposed Madison's succession in 1808 on the grounds that he was too inclined to compromise with the Federalist party's legacy. He also opposed the War of 1812 on the grounds that it would necessitate an increase in the power and activity of the central government.[79] In 1820, he published a treatise entitled *Construction Construed and Constitutions Vindicated*, which denounced *McCulloch v. Maryland* for dangerously expanding the powers of the national government. Two other treatises followed, *Tyranny Unmasked* (1822) and *New Views of the Constitution of the United States* (1823), which assaulted the economic program promulgated by the nationalist wing of the Jeffersonian Republican party: the protective tariff, the 2BUS, and a federal program of internal improvements. Taylor also denounced the Supreme Court: its decisions consolidated power in the hands of the national government, and by defending corporations and special privileges, it had aligned itself with a moneyed aristocracy. This was bad and dangerous, he argued, because

> [the] mass of evidence stands opposed to those constructions which are laboring to invest the federal government with powers to abridge the state right of taxation; to control states by a power to legislate for ten miles square; to expend the money belonging to the United States without control; to enrich a local capitalist interest at the expense of the people; to create

corporations for abridging state rights; to make roads and canals; and finally to empower a complete negative over state laws and judgments, and an affirmative power as to federal laws.[80]

Behind the scenes, Jefferson encouraged both Roane and Taylor. He had no sympathy for a strong and active federal judiciary, and he had a strong personal dislike for Marshall. As president, Jefferson had adopted a cautious and measured approach to the federal judiciary, in large part because he was determined to establish the precedent that, when the out party came into power (as the Republicans had as a consequence of the election of 1800), it would only mean a change in personnel and policies, but not a change in the government itself as it had in 1776 and 1788, for he understood that to go after the federal judiciary really also involved an attack on the Constitution. Besides, during Jefferson's presidency (1801–1809), the Supreme Court had not handed down any decisions that were especially controversial.[81] But following the High Court's decision in *McCulloch v. Maryland*, he began to privately excoriate the Supreme Court. He praised Roane's essays for containing "the true principles of 1800" and criticized the Supreme Court for "driving us into consolidation."[82] He also lavished praise on Taylor's *Construction Construed*, observing, "Colonel Taylor and myself have rarely, if ever, differed in any political principle of importance." He believed that the "judiciary of the United States is the subtle corps of sappers and miners constantly working underground to undermine the foundations of our confederated fabric. They are construing our constitution from a coordination of a general special government to a general and supreme one alone."[83] In addition, he criticized the Supreme Court's practice of handing down unanimous opinions in the form of one opinion for the entire Court as opposed to *seriatim* opinions (where each judge handed down his own opinion even if it were essentially a concurring one), the inclination of many members of Congress to favor expensive public projects that could only lead to higher taxes, and that the federal judiciary could not be made amenable to public opinion.[84]

As for Marshall, he believed that Jefferson, to whom he referred, because of his residence at Monticello, as "the great Lama of the

Mountains," was ultimately the central force behind the recent criticism of the Supreme Court.[85] The chief justice also characterized Jefferson as

> among the most ambitious & I suspect among the most unfor-
> giving of men. His great power is over the mass of the people &
> this power is chiefly acquired by professions of democracy. Every
> check on the wild impulse of the moment is a check on his own
> power, and he is unfriendly to the source from which it flows. He
> looks, of course with ill will at an independent judiciary.[86]

When Marshall learned that Jefferson had made an effort to arrange for the publication of Roane's Algernon Sydney essays along with the Supreme Court's decision in *Cohens v. Virginia* in a newly established publication in Philadelphia entitled the *Journal of American Jurisprudence*, he encouraged Joseph Story to prevent its publication mainly on the grounds that "the coarseness of its language, its personal and official abuse & its tedious prolixity constituted objections to the insertion of Algernon Sidney which were insuperable."[87] Marshall also denigrated two other anonymous critics of his *Cohens* decision, one as a disappointed litigant in the various cases involving the Fairfax estate that culminated in *Martin v. Hunter's Lessee*, and the other as a "hunter after office who hopes by his violent hostility to the Union which in Virginia assumes the name of regard for State Rights; & by his devotion to Algernon Sidney to obtain one."[88]

Perhaps most important, Marshall continued to lament that "in support of the sound principles of the constitution, & of the Union of the States, not a pen is drawn. In Virginia the tendency of things verges rapidly to the destruction of the government & the reestablishment of a league of Sove[reign] States. I look elsewhere for safety."[89] In arguing this, the chief justice was overreaching, for while the denunciation in Virginia of Marshall's decisions in *McCulloch v. Maryland* and *Cohens v. Virginia* was strident and aggressive in tone, it never threatened to go beyond the level of a pointed intellectual debate. No attempt was made to obstruct or forcibly resist the authority of the federal government. Concluding his assault on the Supreme Court's decision in *McCulloch v. Maryland*, Amphictyon stressed this dimension of Virginia's opposition: "When unconstitutional laws are passed, this state calmly passes her resolution to that effect, she endeavors to unite and combine the moral force of the states against usurpation, and she will never employ force to support her doctrine, till other means have entirely failed."[90] And at the beginning of his Algernon Sidney essays, which had spearheaded the attack on the *Cohens* decision, Roane indicated, "I want from you no insurrections, no rebellions, no revolutions, but what consists in the preservation of an excellent Constitution. I require from you no insurrection, but that of a frequent recurrence to fundamental principles."[91]

The central question raised in the extended debate between the proponents of states' rights in the Old Dominion and the Supreme Court was not the 2BUS and its branches, but the nationalist claim that the High Court should be the final arbiter in conflicts between the federal government and the states. In denying this authority to the U.S. Supreme Court, Brockenbrough, Roane, Taylor, Jefferson, and others raised a number of penetrating questions. Since the power was not explicitly provided for in the Constitution, where did it come from? Should the U.S. Supreme Court be allowed to claim this power for itself? How did the Supreme Court relate to the will of the people, especially since its members were appointed for life tenure during good behavior and were removable only by resignation, death, or impeachment? Was it proper for the Court to hold its discussions in secret and to hide internal dissent by handing down unanimous decisions? Even today, when for the most part a nationalist view of the origins and nature of the union, the meaning of the necessary and proper clause, and the role of the Supreme Court as final arbiter in federal-state controversies has been triumphant, these are difficult questions, not amenable to easy and straightforward answers, especially when one actually reads the U.S. Constitution carefully.

States' rights advocates doubted whether the U.S. Supreme Court could be a fair and balanced arbiter in disputes between the federal government and the states. As a creature of the Constitution and a part of the federal government, it increased its own powers whenever it increased the powers of the federal government. Amphictyon believed that, in creating the Constitution, the states could never "have committed an act of such egregious folly as to agree that their umpire should be appointed and paid by the other party."[92] In similar terms, Hampden argued that in federal-state disputes the Supreme Court could not be unbiased and asserted, "the general government cannot decide this controversy. . . . They cannot do it unless we tread under foot the principle which forbids a party to decide its own cause."[93]

Proponents of states' rights in Virginia responded in a number of different ways to the argument that a final arbiter was needed in disputes between the states and the federal government in order to ensure uniformity in the law. Some argued that the need for uniformity was exaggerated, that local differences were not necessarily bad. They believed that since both parties were committed to the union, conflicts between the states could be negotiated, or resolved through the amendment process. Instead, they stressed the danger involved in giving the power to resolve these disputes to the U.S. Supreme Court. As Justice Joseph Cabell remarked for the Virginia Court of Appeals in *Hunter v. Martin's Lessee*:

> It must have been forseen [*sic*] that controversies would sometimes arise as to the boundaries of the two jurisdictions. Yet the Constitution has provided no umpire, has erected no tribunal by which they shall be settled. The omission proceeded, probably from the belief, that such a tribunal would produce evils greater than those of the occasional collisions which it would be designed to remedy.[94]

It has been argued that Virginia's opposition to the Supreme Court was mainly a camouflage for the defense of slavery and that it laid the foundation for the disruption of the union in 1860–1861.[95] This is not the correct way to interpret Virginia's position in its struggle with the Supreme Court, for it makes a superficial and dubious connection between what are different and, in many ways, disconnected strains of states' rights thought. Virginia's opposition to a consolidated national government had its roots in its colonial and revolutionary experience, was legitimized by the failure of the framers of the U.S. Constitution to explicitly provide for some kind of final arbiter to constitutional disputes, and by the states' rights thrust of Jefferson's victory in the election of 1800. It was further fueled by the aggressive nationalism of the High Court and its national Republican allies during the latter part of the second decade of the nineteenth century. Virginia was not the only advocate of states' rights during this period. Strong support for this position could be found in northern, southern, and western states in the age of Jefferson.[96]

To be sure, the debate over the admission of Missouri, which did explicitly involve the slavery question, took place in the period between the Supreme Court's decisions in *McCulloch v. Maryland* (1819) and *Cohens v. Virginia* (1821), and critics of these decisions in Virginia and elsewhere generally opposed the attempt to force Missouri to become a free state.[97] But the assault on the High Court and the debate on the admission of Missouri were viewed by many spokesmen for the Old Dominion and elsewhere as different and essentially unrelated questions. Spencer Roane, for example, avoided all mention of the slavery issue in his criticism of the Supreme Court's decision in *McCulloch v. Maryland*. Privately, he justified this by observing, "the decision of the Supreme Court will be the principal object; as that claims a right to everything possessed by the states, whereas the Missouri question is but a particular measure."[98] William Brockenbrough in his Amphictyon essays also avoided all mention of the slavery issue. Further, during the debates in Congress over the status of slaves and free blacks in Missouri, a number of Virginia's representatives who had been severely critical of Marshall and the Supreme Court got up to argue that the judiciary and not Congress should rule on the issue.[99] And William Pinkney of Maryland, a leading nationalist where the powers of the federal judiciary were concerned and an advocate of national corporations, delivered a strong states' rights speech in opposition to Congress's attempt to restrict slavery in Missouri.[100] John Taylor was an exception for he made a small attempt to link the two debates in his *Construction Construed* treatise.[101] Jefferson, on the other hand, although concerned about the Court's decision and the Missouri debates, saw the two issues as distinctly separate.[102]

In the early 1820s, the proponents of states' rights tended to be an unfocused political force. In large part, this was because they could not come up with a common remedy for dealing with the Supreme Court. Some favored simply repealing section 25 of the Judiciary Act of 1789. Others supported amendments to the U.S. Constitution that would restrict the powers of the Supreme Court or give the power to resolve federal-state disputes to the U.S. Senate, which they believed could more fairly represent both the states and the federal government. None of these measures was adopted. Still, the debate that took place in Virginia over the Supreme Court was very significant, because it turned out to be the opening salvo of a movement in the mid-Atlantic, southern, western, and northern New England states in the 1820s that was to bring the question of the powers of the central government in general, and the federal judiciary in particular, to the forefront and that eventually led to a major constitutional revolution when the Jacksonians came to power in 1828.

SIX

OHIO AND THE BANK
OF THE UNITED STATES

The most intense confrontation between a state and the 2BUS took place in Ohio. The events were contradictory, involving both the use of force and a sustained and determined effort to vindicate the state's actions through the courts. The confrontation is particularly important because it laid bare in an unusually direct and clear manner the economic and constitutional forces that underlay the controversy between the states and the 2BUS. Indeed, so fundamental were the issues raised by developments in Ohio that the U.S. Supreme Court in the case of *Osborn et al. v. Bank of the United States* (1824) was forced, in effect, if not in name, to rehear many of the issues it had tried to settle in *McCulloch v. Maryland* (1819).[1]

I

The years following the end of the War of 1812 were a period of swift settlement and substantial economic growth in Ohio. The defeat of the Indians in the Old Northwest made the area safe, and this, combined with a federal land policy that facilitated the acquisition and settlement of land, led to a doubling of the state's population between 1800 and 1820. The immediate post-1815 period was one of economic expansion and prosperity as Europeans paid ever-higher prices for the wheat, flour, and meat products they imported from the United States, much of which was produced in the Ohio Valley. As a consequence, a spirit of enterprise permeated much of Ohio. It involved land speculation, urban development, a variety of transportation ventures, and the growth of commercial agriculture. These developments were fueled by a rapid increase in the number of banks, both chartered and unchartered. Before the War of 1812, Ohio had four banks. This number increased to twenty-one by 1816, with thirteen banks being chartered in that year. There also was an indeterminate number of unchartered banks that just sprang up. By issuing paper money and providing easy credit, these banks made available the medium of exchange needed to conduct business and contributed in a major way to the state's economic development, but along with these came an inflationary and unstable economy.[2]

It was in this context, in 1815 and 1816, that the governor of the state, Thomas Worthington, with the strong support of major figures in the business and more-established banking communities, moved to control local banking activities, and he did so in a way that would also produce a substantial amount of income for the state. In a series of laws, Ohio prohibited unchartered banks from issuing paper money and levied a 4 percent tax on all dividends paid by the banks. An additional act, known as the Bonus Law, adopted in early 1816, required that a twenty-fifth of all stock issued by a bank be given to the state and that the dividends on this stock were to be used for the purchase of future shares until the state owned one-sixth of the total stock of the bank, following which the dividends from the stock would be paid directly to the state. In return, the charters of the existing banks, most of which were to expire in 1818, were extended to 1843, and the banks were to be exempted from any future taxation. Other provisions required that at least one-half of the purchase price of a bank's stock be paid in specie, that the amount of debt incurred by these banks be limited to three times the amount of paid-up stock, that records of these banks be open to regular inspection by the state, and that the banks' directors be personally liable for infractions of any of these regulations. In this fashion, Ohio asserted its control over the activities of the various banks operating within its boundaries. In addition, it provided the state with an important alternative source of revenue to a tax on land, which impacted the less affluent and more numerous agricultural population.[3]

The creation of the 2BUS in 1816 was welcomed by most people in Ohio as a major source of additional banking capital, and the business communities of both Cincinnati and Chillicothe engaged in a fierce competition to obtain a branch office. The matter was finally resolved when branches were established in both places in 1817. In late December of that year, the legislature turned its attention to finding a way to raise revenue from the operation of the 2BUS in Ohio. Unsure of exactly how to proceed, the legislature appointed a committee consisting of members of both houses to investigate the constitutionality and expediency of laying some kind of tax.

The report was delivered in late December 1817, and both it and its reception by the legislature revealed the uncertainty and confusion that existed on the right of the state to levy a tax on the branches of the 2BUS in Ohio. In the report, the committee observed, "there are so many important principles connected, and intricate questions involved," and it tried to present both sides of the issue. Among other things, it noted that the 2BUS was not merely a government instrument:

> In this our eyes are deceived, and judgments misled: for when
> we raise the curtain we find it composed of an association of
> members, half encircling the globe, each contributing to the
> mighty storehouse of its wealth, where the funds of the stranger,
> the alien and American, are mingled in one common mass.[4]

The committee further pointed out that the 2BUS is a privately controlled and profit-making corporation, and that corporations, like individuals, are subject to taxation wherever they reside. The branches therefore were "as subject to a tax as any corporate body could be, if acting under the authority of the state."[5] In fact, not to tax the branches of the 2BUS in Ohio would be ruinous, for to indicate that the state did not have the power to tax would encourage other corporations led by "wily capitalists" to find ways to "put your power of taxing them at defiance."[6] Banks, the committee went on, had become a major source of revenue for the state, which would soon be equal to the ordinary expenses of the government. "Dry up this important source of your revenue," the committee observed, "and you must supply it by a tax on the faithful laborious husbandman, whilst the greater proportion of the funds, thus prevented from reaching your treasury, is carried beyond the state, to increase the wealth of strangers and foreigners."[7]

On the other hand, the committee also indicated that the state's constitution stated that "no ex post facto law, nor any law impairing the validity of contracts shall ever be made," and that the law creating the 2BUS was a contract and should be considered the supreme law of the land. It recognized the constitutionality of the creation of the 2BUS and noted, "it would be a very unreasonable construction to say that they [the states] had still reserved to themselves sufficient power to prevent the enjoyment of those privileges, or the exercise of that power." Finally, the committee indicated that even if the constitutionality of the 2BUS were questioned, "it would still be impolitic for the legislature of the state, being one of the youngest, and most highly favored in the Union, to be among the first to contravene the acts of the general government." The committee concluded by resolving "that it is inexpedient to tax the office of discount and deposit of the bank of the United States, that are or may be established in the state."[8]

The Ohio House of Representatives, however, refused to adopt the report. Instead, it approved a new report which called for the actual taxing of the branches of the 2BUS in Ohio. This report reiterated the earlier report's insistence that the 2BUS was essentially a privately controlled institution, and its main thrust was the assertion of Ohio's right to tax the branches in Ohio. To do otherwise, it argued, would have "consequences . . . derogatory to the state sovereignties and destructive of the equal rights of the citizens." It would provide an unfair advantage for holders of 2BUS stock over those who had invested in the stock of state-chartered banks, which were subject to state taxation. This would also encourage other businesses to obtain national charters, for "capital is ever in search of special privileges" in order to claim exemption from local revenue laws.[9] The new report vigorously denied the claim of the 2BUS that it was exempt from state taxation:

This exception from taxation is not among the privileges purchased by the company. It is no part of the contract stipulated
in the charter; it is based on no constitutional provision; it is
founded upon no combination of general provisions, or general
principles. But it is an unreasonable, unequal, unjust and
unconstitutional pretension.[10]

Questioned also was the value of the establishment of the branches of
the 2BUS in Ohio. These branches, it was argued, had adversely affected the business of the state banks and placed the control and the profits derived from the money circulating in Ohio into the hands of "the
stock jobbers of the Atlantic cities and Europe."[11]

The Ohio House then voted 48–12 to support the report's recommendation that it would be constitutional to tax the branches of the
2BUS and, by a much closer vote of 33–27, that it was expedient to
immediately levy such a tax. The next day, a bill was presented which
levied a 4 percent tax on the sum of the dividends paid by the Ohio
branches. Since this was precisely the same sum levied on state-chartered
banks, it indicated that the purpose of the tax was to raise revenue and
not to destroy the branches.[12]

Opposition to the proposed law was led by Duncan McArthur, the
Speaker of the Ohio House of Representatives. He described the measure as an attack upon "the peace of the country and the sovereignty of
the U. States." He also warned, in a particularly prophetic statement,
that there would be serious consequences if the state levied such a tax,
for among other things it would jeopardize future aid from the federal
government for Ohio's program of internal improvements and for its
public education system. This, along with the lobbying of a number of
the directors of the Chillicothe branch of the 2BUS, proved successful,
for when the bill was read for the third time on January 24, 1818, a final
vote was postponed until December 1818.[13]

II

Criticism of the 2BUS turned to open hostility during the summer and
fall of 1818, as the economic downturn later associated with the Panic
of 1819 began. Commodity prices declined, and real estate values

plummeted. Also at this time, the 2BUS was required to make a substantial specie payment to England on behalf of the government of the United States to retire the bond issue for the Louisiana Purchase, and it responded by instituting a severe policy of credit contraction. In particular, it required its branches in Ohio, which had accumulated substantial amounts of state bank paper, to extinguish this debt and remit it to the mother bank in Philadelphia at the rate of 20 percent per month. This in turn forced the state chartered banks to suspend their own loans and demand payment for them in specie. The ensuing distress and ruin was widespread throughout the state, but was especially intense in Cincinnati, where business expansion in the immediate post–War of 1812 period, based on borrowed money, had been greatest.

The coming of hard times changed the nature of the debate over the role of the branches of the 2BUS in Ohio. What had begun as a debate in the legislature over the constitutionality and expediency of taxing its branches now became a major public issue. Amid widespread complaints of hard times, numerous Ohio newspapers excoriated the policies of the 2BUS, and public meetings were held to denounce its policy of credit contraction. In many people's minds, the 2BUS had gone from being alien, intrusive, and aggressive to being coercive and dangerous; indeed, many believed it had become the cause of the state's economic difficulties.

Popular hostility to the 2BUS strongly manifested itself in Ohio's fall 1818 elections, which in many ways was a referendum on the bank. Moreover, it turned out to be a total victory for those who were opposed to the 2BUS and wanted it driven from the state. Duncan McArthur, Speaker of the General Assembly and a supporter of the bank, was defeated in his bid to be reelected to the legislature. In fact, the entire legislature was now in the control of people hostile to the 2BUS. As a consequence, Thomas Worthington, who stepped down from the governorship in December 1818, who owed the bank money, who had played a determinative role in obtaining the branch of the 2BUS for Chillicothe, and who had opposed the taxing of the branches, was defeated in his bid to be elected to the U.S. Senate. As Secretary of the Treasury William H. Crawford noted, he had become a "victim of the paroxysm which has convulsed the western country in relation to the U.S.B."[14]

The newly elected governor of the state, Ethan Allen Brown, was particularly hostile to the 2BUS. In his opening address to the Ohio legislature, he pointed out that it had "without asking leave," and in disregard of the laws of the state against unauthorized banking companies, created two branches that were "corporations enacted within our sovereignty; over whose character, and over whose conduct of whose offices we have no control; whose course of proceeding, the state banks loudly complain, . . . and diminishes the profits of the latter, as well as impairs the state revenues arising from those sources." Brown did not make any specific recommendations, however, for fear that it would produce a confrontation with the federal government and "hazard the reputation of the state."[15]

The legislature, however, did not share the governor's reservations about taking some kind of action against the 2BUS. There, the leading figure among the antibank forces was Charles Hammond, a man who defies any easy kind of political classification. Born near Baltimore, Maryland, in 1799 and raised in the western part of Virginia, he trained to be a lawyer, but spent much of his life as a journalist in which capacity he was a fierce and, at times, a vicious proponent of the causes he advocated. Very intelligent, with an acute and agile mind, he was also a skillful lawyer with a profound understanding of constitutional issues. In 1810, he settled in St. Clairsville in Belmont County in southeastern Ohio. A great admirer of George Washington, Hammond quickly became a leading member of Ohio's Federalist party and vigorously denounced James Madison and opposed the War of 1812.[16]

Despite the fact that he was a Federalist and later became a critic of Andrew Jackson, Hammond's political thinking had a strong egalitarian strain to it. At the time of his death in 1840, James Wilson, a grandfather of Woodrow Wilson who had engaged in frequent editorial controversies with Hammond, observed, "although calling himself a Federalist, I soon discovered he was a better Democrat than many of those who bawled [howled?] democracy the loudest." He also added:

[H]is powerful intellect, deep research, and the natural goodness of his heart, secured to him great influence among his fellow members [in the legislature]—which was checked in no other way but by consenting to be called a Federalist whilst in reality his manners, opinions and principles were strictly democratic.[17]

From the very beginning of the 2BUS's operations in Ohio, Hammond had been critical of the bank. He first became alarmed in early 1817 over the pressure it was placing on local banks in the West for an immediate resumption of specie payments, which he believed would lead to a major drain of what little specie existed in the West to the East. The 2BUS, he believed, controlled over $1 million of western paper, was not subject to any kind of local control, and was not sensitive to western needs. "The more I reflect upon it," he observed:

and the more facts are developed the stronger are my convictions that the Bank of the United States is about to be a most potent engine for the controlling of all the pecuniary concerns of the country. I regard it as a most melancholy circumstance that this places all our best interests at the mercy of stockjobbers and Brokers, mostly foreign agents without moral or social feelings of any kind whatever which can induce them to assimilate with us in the great concerns which they may, and I am fearful will, controul [sic].[18]

In January 1819, the lower house of the Ohio legislature, under the leadership of Hammond, issued yet another report on "the subject of levying a tax on the capital of the United States Bank employed in Ohio." It stressed that the 2BUS had established branches without permission of the state and in violation of state law. In the report, it was asserted that the 2BUS had sent people as cashiers of the branches who were ignorant and insensitive to local needs and who had displayed an "undisguised hostility" toward the state banks. The branches had adopted policies that had forced the state banks to suspend specie payments, reduced the circulating medium, and caused a drain of specie eastward, all of which had intensified Ohio's economic problems. The report further indicated that Ohio had been victimized by the 2BUS, and it had to be driven from the state. To this end, it was recommended that a tax of $50,000 be levied on each branch of the 2BUS.[19]

It took less than a month for the legislature to levy the tax. Although the law was applicable to all unauthorized banks, the preamble to the law specifically targeted the 2BUS, which was given until September 15, 1819, to make payment. If it did not, the auditor of Ohio was authorized to appoint someone to forcibly collect the tax from the assets of the bank's branches. The law declared:

> [I]f the person appointed to execute such a warrant . . . cannot find any money, bank notes, goods, chattels, or other property of said banks . . . to satisfy the tax . . . it shall and may be lawful, and it is hereby made the duty of such persons to go into each and any other room, or vault of such banking house to open and search; and any money, bank notes, or other goods and chattels [are to be appropriated to pay the tax].

The funds collected were to be deposited in the state treasury, except for a 2 percent commission that went to the individuals collecting the tax. The law's explicit provision formally endorsing the use of force to collect the tax led to it being known as the "crowbar law."[20]

Almost immediately after the adoption of the crowbar law, the Ohio legislature adjourned, which was just before the U.S. Supreme Court rendered its opinion in *McCulloch v. Maryland*. When news of the decision arrived in Ohio, it met with widespread criticism and was denounced for prostrating the rights of the states before the national government. The U.S. Supreme Court was now added to the 2BUS as an alien and intrusive institution, which was beyond the control of the state and not subject to the will of the people and therefore had to be resisted by local authorities. In a public letter, Hammond indicated that he hoped "the freemen of Ohio feel enough of the spirit of independence to afford the Judges [of the U.S. Supreme Court] an opportunity of reviewing their opinion." "It is time enough," he added, taking a swipe at the feigned and contrived nature of *McCulloch v. Maryland*, "to succumb, when the western states have been heard, and when their rights have been decided upon in a case where they are themselves parties."[21]

During the summer and fall of 1819, the Ohio branches of the 2BUS ignored the crowbar law because after the U.S. Supreme Court's decision in *McCulloch v. Maryland*, as William Creighton, the president of the Chillicothe branch, put it, "we never imagined that the Auditor of the state of Ohio would attempt to execute the state law imposing a tax of fifty thousand dollars on each of the offices in the state."[22] The state authorities, on the other hand, refused to recognize the U.S. Supreme Court's authority in the matter and were determined to enforce the crowbar law. Governor Brown was unwilling to call a special session of the state legislature to discuss the implications of the High Court's decision in *McCulloch v. Maryland* because he believed "that Ohio should take a lead in all lawful resistance to any violation of the reserved state sovereignty . . . which whether effected by direct acts, or by judicial construction, would be a death blow to our Union; or to our free government, or both."[23]

As the September 15 date designated by the crowbar law for the forceful collection of the taxes levied on the two branches approached, the state auditor, Ralph Osborn, was faced with a difficult decision. The U.S. Supreme Court had said one thing while the state had instructed him to do the exact opposite. As a state official, he decided to implement the state law, but, recognizing that it involved an "important and delicate affair," he first consulted with Governor Brown, who instructed him to proceed with the collection of the tax.[24] Meanwhile, when the officers of the Chillicothe branch of the 2BUS got word that Osborn was actually going to implement the crowbar law and collect the tax, they, on September 14, hurriedly made an application to the judges of the Seventh Circuit Court of the United States for an injunction enjoining the auditor from collecting the tax. The bank and its branches, they argued, had been established under both the Constitution and a law of Congress, while the purpose of the Ohio law was "to deprive them of their goods, despoil them of their monies and effects and completely check the existence and operation of the two . . . offices established." On September 15, they presented what they believed was the injunction to Osborn along with a subpoena for him to appear before the federal circuit court on the first Monday in January 1820 to respond to the petition.[25] As it turned out, what they served Osborn was the petition for the injunction and not the writ of injunction itself, which the circuit court had issued prohibiting the collection of the tax. Unsure what all this meant, Osborn requested advice from the Ohio secretary of state who, upon the advice of legal counsel, responded that Osborn should proceed to collect the tax since he had not been served with an enforceable legal injunction. Osborn then issued a warrant to John L. Harper who with two others, James McCollister and Thomas Orr, went to collect the tax.[26]

On September 17, 1819, shortly after noon, Harper arrived at the branch of the 2BUS in Chillicothe along with the two other men, who upon entering the bank "in a ruffian-like manner, jumped over the counter, took and held forcible possession of the vault." Harper then "intruded himself" behind the counter, and demanded of Creighton and A. G. Claypoole, the cashier of the branch, and J. Walker, a teller, all of whom were present, whether they intended to pay the tax. When Claypoole answered in the negative, read them the injunction, and reminded them of the U.S. Supreme Court's decision in *McCulloch v. Maryland*, they proceeded to remove from the bank specie and notes totaling $120,425, which they loaded into a wagon that was waiting outside and deposited overnight in the Bank of Chillicothe. The next day, the money was reloaded into the wagon and taken to the state capital in Columbus. On the way, Harper was served with another injunction issued by the federal circuit court, ordering him to return the money, but he ignored it and proceeded to deliver the money to the state treasurer, who deposited it in the Franklin Bank of Columbus. Osborn also received an injunction, but he indicated that the matter was now out of his hands and under the authority of the state treasurer. Harper received a $2,000 fee for his services, and the state retained $98,000. When it was discovered that too much money had been taken, the balance was returned to the Chillicothe branch of the 2BUS.[27]

The reaction was immediate. An injunction, quite valid this time, was issued by the federal circuit court prohibiting Osborn, the treasurer of Ohio, and the president of the Franklin Bank from making any disposition of the funds that had been collected. Later, this injunction was replaced by another issued by Chief Justice John Marshall on November 23, 1819. The 2BUS also filed suit against Osborn and Harper and his two assistants to recover the money. Harper and one of his assistants, Thomas Orr, were also arrested for trespassing, and imprisoned. Further, Osborn and Harper were ordered to appear before the federal circuit court to explain why they had ignored the injunctions issued after they had collected the tax.[28]

Langdon Cheves, the new president of the 2BUS, was enraged when he learned what had happened. He sent Claypoole's account to Secretary of the Treasury Crawford, remarking, "the outrage which it narrates can be rarely paralleled under a Government of laws, and if sanctioned by the higher authorities of the State, strikes at the vitals of the Constitution."[29] Henry Wheaton, the reporter for the Supreme Court, similarly noted, "the authors of this outrage must be punished with exemplary severity, or our government is an empty name."[30]

This point of view was shared by all of the most important newspapers in the country, especially those in the East, where support for the 2BUS was strongest. Buying into the view, based on the opinion in *McCulloch v. Maryland*, that the 2BUS was an agency of the national government, they condemned Ohio for turning its opposition to the 2BUS into a confrontation between the states and the central government, and they argued that Ohio's actions were a form of rebellion and treason that, if allowed to stand, would lead to the destruction of the union. The *National Intelligencer*, the semi-official organ of the Monroe administration, expressed the hope that "this drama which has commenced as a farce may not have a *tragical end.* . . . the authors and abettors of it *have much to answer for.*"[31] Even *Niles' Weekly Register*, long an outspoken critic of the constitutionality of the 2BUS and the Supreme Court's opinion in *McCulloch v. Maryland*, made it clear that it "regrets this act of Ohio." Hezekiah Niles also added: "It is not for any of the states much less individuals to oppose force to the operation of the law, as settled by the authorities of the United States, however zealous we may be to bring about a different construction of it."[32] In some quarters, there was even talk of using force against Ohio. Gorham Worth, who had recently stepped down as cashier of the Cincinnati branch of the 2BUS, was in Baltimore and reported a conversation he had about what had happened in Chillicothe with someone who commented that he "considered Ohio as dam'd for keeping the Bank money, said the Govern[ment] would take it back by *force*; that the State was in rebellion, etc. etc."[33]

On the other hand, within Ohio, those opposed to the 2BUS remained obdurate and in complete control. The state continued to be racked by hard times, and the successful candidates in the fall 1819 elections for the state legislature continued to focus on the activities of the branches. Joseph Kerr, for example, stressing the need for Ohio to protect its sovereignty, argued, "if the rights of the state are to be encroached upon, that it be from necessity: not to establish a monied aristocracy, administered by swindlers, over whom the state authorities, nor indeed the authorities of the United States have no control."[34] Two other candidates issued a "Declaration of Independence" against the 2BUS, which they charged with "having quartered large bodies of armed brokers among them," and then went on to proclaim "that all connection between the people of Ohio and the branch banks ought to be dissolved, and that as a free and independent state, we have full power to levy a tax upon all banks within our jurisdiction of whatsoever denomination and by whomsoever established."[35] Even William Henry Harrison, a major hero of the battle of Tippecanoe in the War of 1812 and a future president of the United States, found himself in serious political trouble as a candidate for the Ohio Senate because he had been a director of the branch bank in Cincinnati. He won a close election only after he published a long letter disingenuously claiming that he was "the enemy of banks in general, and especially the Bank of the United States," which he described as "an immense political engine to strengthen the arm of the general government."[36] Sweeping the elections, the antibank forces continued to dominate the legislature and governorship.

III

The strongly polarized confrontation between Ohio and the 2BUS was a source of concern among a number of important people who tried to defuse the situation through some kind of compromise. Worthington had remained one of the few supporters of the 2BUS in Ohio. In a letter to its new president, Cheves, he denounced the forced removal of the tax, commenting that he viewed "this transaction in the most odious light, and from my very soul I detest it. . . . I am ashamed it has happened in Ohio."[37] Nonetheless, he favored some kind of compromise. In particular, he believed the state should disown the action of its officers and return the money they had taken, while the 2BUS should drop all legal charges, because it was important to remember "that Ohio is a sovereign, independent state," not to be easily trifled with.[38] Important support for this kind of approach came from Henry Clay who, as an attorney, represented the interests of the 2BUS in Kentucky and Ohio. He too condemned Ohio's action in using force to collect the tax, but warned Cheves to be cautious. He asked:

[H]ow is the state to be coerced? It is all important I think that the General Government should not move in the affair without it most clearly has the Constitution in its support. It is to be regretted I think also that any intemperance should have been manifested towards the *State* of Ohio on your side of the mountains. . . . Should it not disown the conduct of its officers it will stand condemned by every thinking & considerate man. It would then be clearly in the wrong.[39]

But nothing could be worked out between Ohio and the 2BUS, so there was no compromise.

Despite this, two key members of the anti-2BUS forces in Ohio, concerned about the state's increasing isolation, also tried to moderate the crisis. In this case, it was the unlikely duo of Hammond and James Wilson, who was a doctrinaire Jeffersonian and who had received his editorial training working for the Philadelphia *Aurora*, owned by William Duane, a frequent critic of Presidents Jefferson and Madison for their not taking a more aggressive stance against the vestiges of Federalism in the post-1800 era. He also was a newspaper editor and a member of the Ohio legislature.[40] Hammond had opposed the War of 1812 while Wilson vigorously supported it, and they had frequently criticized each other in their editorial columns. Although both had been critical of the 2BUS's activities in Ohio and of the *McCulloch v. Maryland* opinion, neither of them had been involved in the actual collection of the state-imposed tax. What they wanted to do was to tone down any kind of provocative political rhetoric and avoid any further use of force. As an alternative, they were determined to channel Ohio's opposition into constitutional and legal channels.

They started by attempting to respond to the harsh criticism that had been directed at Ohio's forcible collection of the tax. They stressed the political and constitutional issues involved in the controversy and pictured Ohio as a victim of an arbitrary decision by the U.S. Supreme Court. To this end, Hammond convinced Niles to back off from his earlier harsh criticism of Ohio's actions and to publish pieces explaining the controversy from the state's point of view.[41] Niles started by reprinting an editorial from Wilson's *Steubenville Herald*. In it, Wilson had stressed the inadequacies of the *McCulloch* decision. He pointed out:

> [It] was a case prepared and submitted to the supreme court of the U.States by voluntary consent of the parties. The doctrines set up by the court, on that occasion, are such as the people of this state, so long as they determine to preserve their rights cannot recognize as correct. If a case decided—an agreed case—in which the state is not a party can be considered as binding upon this state—if such a decision is to suspend the force and operation of our laws, legally, regularly and constitutionally enacted, what are our boasted privileges?

Wilson then went on:

> [W]e complain that, in the case of McCulloch v. Maryland matters have been conceded by the latter, or rather many of the strongest grounds were relinquished or not brought into view, on which the state meant to reply. The state of Ohio does not admit that a case between the two parties, collusively or ignorantly agreed upon, is or ought to be *binding on any other party*.[42]

As for Hammond, in a letter to Niles which was anonymously published, he made it clear that Ohio was not going to accept the High Court's decision in *McCulloch v. Maryland*, and he demanded that the case be reargued. "We know," he claimed:

> there have been cases of individual controversy in which the parties did not acquiesce in the decision of that court, and escaped both the imputation of folly and rebellion; and we believe that cases may be found, in which the Supreme court of the United States have changed their opinion. We consider the subject as open for us to litigate; and in proceeding to execute our law [the collection of the tax on September 17], we give an

occasion to test the doctrines of the supreme court by a practical application to a real case—and of this we conceive that no man has a right to complain.[43]

Both Hammond and Wilson also tried to put a positive spin on the actual collection of the tax by arguing that it was legal. Hammond pointed out that "the solicitors of the bank made a blunder . . . in serving the injunction, and as a consequence the warrant was issued and the money collected." Wilson argued that the tax "was collected in pursuance of an act of the general assembly of the state of Ohio, enacted previous to the *agreed case* between the U.S. bank and the state of Maryland."[44]

Hammond's and Wilson's sharpest criticism was directed not at the Supreme Court but at the 2BUS, which they believed had acted in an arrogant and high-handed manner. Wilson argued: "The law levying a tax on those branches has been in existence for nine months past—the bank cannot plead ignorance of it—it was in their option to avoid paying the tax by removing the branches—they made their choice—and the tax has been paid into the treasury agreeably to the laws."[45] Hammond similarly pointed out:

> [U]pon a subject of so much delicacy and of so much importance, a little respect for state pride, and a little deference for state opinions, might very properly have been manifested. . . . By suspending their operations and founding an appeal to the moral sense of the state legislature, upon decision of the supreme court, a repeal of the tax might have been effected. Instead of this they preferred to attempt dragging the state before the federal court; and it would seem as if they were more intent upon triumphing over the state sovereignties, than they were upon continuing their business or protecting their property.

Both Wilson and Hammond indicated that if the 2BUS removed its branches from Ohio, the state would be willing to return the money that had been collected.[46]

Both men argued that it was absolutely essential that the 2BUS should recognize it was not above state law. They did not accept

Marshall's claim that it was a federal agency; they believed that since 80 percent of its stock was held by private interests, it was essentially a private profit-making institution. Hammond argued: "there is nothing in the character of the bank of the United States to distinguish its pretensions from those of other citizens. We are not willing that it shall be exempted from the operation of our laws, until we know *why* and *wherefore*."[47]

Although neither Hammond nor Wilson had backed down on their opposition to the branches of the 2BUS in Ohio nor in their criticism of *McCulloch v. Maryland*, their messages also had a conciliatory dimension. Above all, what they wanted was a rehearing of the issues that had been dealt with in *McCulloch*, only this time Ohio would make the argument as to why a state had a right to tax the branches that had been established within it without the consent of the state. If this occurred, then Ohio would accept the decision handed down by the U.S. Supreme Court. Hammond made this explicit in the last paragraph of his letter: "we propose not force but judicial decisions before competent tribunals where we are parties. When you obtain the judgment of a federal court against us, we will pay you the money back: until then we will keep it." He pointed out that Ohio did not intend to back down in exercising its sovereign rights for it knew

> well the ground they stand upon. They make no case for the opinion of the supreme court. They deny the power of the federal courts to enjoin the officers of the state in executing the state laws; they are prepared to resist the exercise of that power until, in a case fairly forced before them, the supreme court of the United States shall sustain it. They believe this never will be done. But if it is effected they are prepared to submit. They deny that the federal court can proceed against them for the collection of the tax; they are prepared to contest every inch of ground: but when the case is decided against them they will attempt no resistance by force. They deny that congress can authorise the bank of the United States to sue in the federal court—if this point is decided against them they acquiesce. In short, they know that the bank, like an individual, must seek redress at law—at law they are prepared to meet it; and when

the case is adjudged against them, upon all the points they raise,
they know that submission is the duty of honest men and good
citizens. The public should understand that this is nothing but
a legal controversy and must terminate like all other legal controversies. It involves no question of bloodshed or revolution.[48]

IV

From this point on, the dispute between Ohio and the 2BUS was pursued exclusively in legal and constitutional terms. An early skirmish
occurred in the Ohio Court of Common Pleas in early November 1819,
when the state made application for a writ of habeas corpus to obtain the
release of Harper and his assistant Thomas Orr, who had been arrested
because of a suit instituted against them for the restitution of the collected money. Because their bail had been set at $200,000 each, twice the
amount of the collected money, and they could not meet it, they
remained incarcerated. The application was turned down by Judge John
Thompson, in large part on the grounds that the Supreme Court's decision in *McCulloch v. Maryland* had settled the matter by ruling that the
branches of the 2BUS could not be taxed.[49] The two men were eventually freed in January 1820 on technical grounds, because the arresting
officer had not been properly sworn in.[50]

Among other things, this development allowed Hammond and his
associates to portray the 2BUS as vindictive and malicious, since neither Harper nor Orr had possession of the collected money any longer,
and the state, which did have the money, should have been the object of
the suit.[51] Actually, Hammond had had major reservations about going
into a state court to ask for a writ of habeas corpus since the suit had
originated in a federal court. As he put it, in endorsing the strong
demarcation between the state and federal courts that had been elaborated on at length by the Virginia Court of Appeals in the series of cases
that culminated in *Martin v. Hunter's Lessee*, "I do not think the state
judges can enjoin a judgment in the Federal Courts. I do not believe in
the intermingling of jurisdictions."[52] Hammond undoubtedly was more
pleased by a suit that had been initiated in the federal circuit court by
the 2BUS against Osborn and Harper for refusing to return the money

to the bank after they had been ordered to do so by the court. This is because, under states' rights theory, to which Hammond and his allies were adhering at this time, this would allow an eventual and legitimate appeal to the U.S. Supreme Court, and therefore give them an opportunity to force a reconsideration of the issues that had been decided in *McCulloch v. Maryland.*

The case of *Bank of the United States v. Ralph Osborn, Auditor of the State of Ohio, and John L. Harper* was heard by the federal circuit court in January 1820. Osborn and Harper were represented by John C. Wright, a close political ally and friend of Hammond. Wright was a former U.S. district attorney in Ohio and soon to be a member of the U.S. House of Representatives, as well as a very good lawyer. He also was an outspoken critic of the 2BUS, having expressed doubts about its constitutionality and arguing that it could not establish branches outside of the District of Columbia.[53]

In defending the actions of the officers of the state, Wright raised a number of important questions for the federal circuit court's consideration. He argued that the 2BUS's suit was really against the state of Ohio, over which the court had no jurisdiction since the Eleventh Amendment provided that a sovereign state could not be sued without its permission. He also argued that the papers served on Osborn and Harper had been irregularly obtained and therefore did not constitute a legal injunction, and that Harper had not intentionally ignored the injunction and for that reason could not be held in contempt. Recognizing that "important legal and constitutional enquiries" had been made, the federal circuit court ruled that the case would be taken under "advisement until September term."[54]

When the federal circuit court reconvened, it handed down a ruling that completely rejected Wright's arguments. It ruled that "a suit against an officer of a state is not necessarily a suit against a state." Although it recognized that there were irregularities in the procedures used to obtain the second injunction of September 18, 1819, it decided that it had been "sufficient" because Ohio could not tax the branches of the ·2BUS within its borders and that Osborn and Harper were in contempt of court; and it issued a writ of attachment against Osborn. It also granted an injunction prohibiting the state treasurer from spending the collected money and allowed the 2BUS to file an amended and supplemental bill making the state treasurer a defendant. Finally, the court indicated that its injunction prohibited the collection of any taxes from the 2BUS as well. It then concluded by observing, "we think the whole proceeding shows a manifest intention to proceed in levying the tax or penalty imposed by the law of Ohio; and that the grounds set up are mere contrivances and pretexts, to elude and evade the effects of the process of this court."[55]

When the Ohio legislature reconvened in December 1820, it remained under the control of the anti-2BUS forces, and it quickly made it clear that it was not ready to back down. That month, a joint committee of both houses of the Ohio legislature issued a report in response to the actions taken by the 2BUS against the various officers of the state. The report demanded attention because it was the fullest and most precisely argued justification, in constitutional terms, of Ohio's dispute with the 2BUS and its unwillingness to abide by *McCulloch v. Maryland*. It was mainly written by Hammond, who was now the undisputed manager of the Ohio side of the controversy.[56]

The committee report began by responding to the various charges that had been leveled against Osborn and those of his associates for failing to obey the federal circuit court's order to return the money. It argued that the suit should not be against Osborn and the various individuals who aided him, but against the state of Ohio, whom they represented and on whose behalf they had performed official acts. This distinction was significant because it went to the very core of Ohio's constitutional position that its very sovereignty was at stake in its dispute with the 2BUS. In the report, the committee pointed out that, in all cases involving a state, under the original Constitution, the Supreme Court had original jurisdiction. Therefore, the federal circuit court did not have the power to issue an injunction. In fact, no federal court had jurisdiction any more because the Eleventh Amendment explicitly provided that the judicial power of the United States did not extend to suits against a state by citizens of another state.

The committee, in addition, took sharp issue with the claim that the U.S. Supreme Court was the exclusive and final arbiter of constitutional questions. "To this doctrine, in the latitude contended for," it asserted, "they can never give their assent." As an alternative, they endorsed the Kentucky and Virginia Resolutions of 1798–1799, which argued that the union was a compact of the states and that the states had a right to declare acts of the federal government to be unconstitutional. Moreover, since these principles had been central to Jefferson's successful bid for the presidency in 1800, they had clearly "been recognized and adopted by a majority of the American people."[57]

The committee also dismissed the Supreme Court's decision in *McCulloch v. Maryland*, especially the claim that it was in any way binding on Ohio, noting, "the committee have considered this position, and are not satisfied that it is a correct one." The case had come about as a consequence of "the management of a party, and through the inadvertence or connivance of a State," and because it involved "important and interesting questions of State power and State authority, upon no just principle ought the State to be concluded by any decision had upon such a case."[58] Instead, it characterized *McCulloch v. Maryland* as an "agreed case" that was hurriedly "manufactured" in the summer of 1818. The committee observed that the case was "passed through the county court of Baltimore county and the court of appeals of the State of Maryland in the same session, so as to be got on the docket of the Supreme Court of the United States for adjudication at their February term." It then averred, "it is only by the management and concurrence of the parties that causes can be this expeditiously brought to a final hearing in the Supreme Court."[59]

The purpose of *McCulloch v. Maryland*, the committee went on, was to save the 2BUS, which at the end of 1818, as a consequence of "the extravagant and fraudulent speculations of those intrusted [*sic*] with conducting the concerns of the bank . . . stood . . . upon the very brink of destruction." The effect of the decision was to prop up the bank's reputation and sinking credit even though it "inflicted a dangerous wound upon the authority of the states." In addition, the decision was particularly alarming because it demonstrated how the power of a corporation could undermine the "vital interests of the States." Under these circumstances, the committee asserted in its report, the refusal to obey a decision of the U.S. Supreme Court was a long-standing tradition. This had been the case in *Marbury v. Madison* and *Fletcher v. Peck*, for it was generally recognized "that in great questions of political rights and political powers a decision of the Supreme Court of the United States is not conclusive of the rights decided by it."[60] The Supreme Court's decision in *McCulloch v. Maryland* had to be resisted, the committee argued, because "it asserts a supremacy nowhere recognized in the Constitution." If allowed to stand, "there must soon be an end to the state governments." If it remained unchallenged, "the Government of the Union may and undoubtedly will, progressively draw all the powers of government into the vortex of its own authority. Against these doctrines . . . it is the duty of the states to enter their most solemn protest."[61]

The committee did not deny the constitutionality of the 2BUS, but did argue at length that it was essentially a privately controlled, profit-making institution. "Banking," it noted, "where the capital is owned by an association of individuals, is a private trade, carried on by individuals constituting the company for their own profit. A mercantile company trade[s] in produce and merchandise; a banking company trade[s] in money, promissory notes, and bills of exchange."[62] Although it performed certain functions for the U.S. government, it was not an agency of the federal government. It was not analogous to the mint or the post office, as Marshall had claimed in *McCulloch v. Maryland*, but like the private contractors who provided supplies to the federal government or carried the mail. To illustrate its argument, the committee pointed out that the various officers of the mint and post office—the director, engraver, chief coiner, assayer, melter, treasurer, postmaster general, and various deputy postmasters—were not allowed to hold their positions and serve in Congress at the same time. On the other hand, the stockholders, the president and directors, even the government-appointed directors of the 2BUS, were not prohibited from serving in Congress, because they were not considered public officers.[63]

The committee noted that, since the 2BUS was essentially a private, profit-making corporation, the states had every right to tax it like other private corporations within their jurisdiction. The 2BUS, it pointed out, had not been "clothed with the supreme authority to conduct its business without respect to the existing laws of the States, and free from any apprehension of those that may be enacted." For if Congress had intended to exempt the 2BUS from the taxing power of the states, such a provision would have been included in the original charter. The committee argued that what the U.S. Supreme Court had done in *McCulloch v. Maryland* was to espouse "a new doctrine as applied to corporations" that was "as dangerous as it is novel." The committee insisted that the branches of the 2BUS were part of "a private corporation of trade, the capital and business of which may be legally taxed in any State where they may be found."[64]

Having vigorously rejected the claims of the 2BUS and the Supreme Court's reasoning in *McCulloch v. Maryland*, the joint committee urged that the state try to effect come sort of compromise to the controversy. If the bank would abandon its suit against Osborn and his associates and withdraw its branches, Ohio would return the money collected for the tax without interest. Failing this, however, the constitutional confrontation had to continue, for the state's reputation had to be vindicated and the contested issues brought to the attention of the other states. Therefore, should the proffered compromise be rejected, Ohio would withdraw all legal protection from the branches, forcing the bank to exclusively rely on the federal government for protection, which would allow the issues that had been raised to be "fairly, peaceably, and constitutionally tested."[65]

The committee summarized and concluded its report by recommending a series of resolutions to be adopted by the legislature. It declared that the state should approve the doctrines of the Kentucky and Virginia Resolutions, which had been "recognized and adopted by a majority of the American people." Other resolutions rejected the authority of the federal circuit court as maintained in its proceedings against the officers of the state "as being in direct violation of the eleventh amendment to the Constitution of the United States." An additional resolution declared the 2BUS to be a private corporation "which may be legally taxed." A further resolution rejected "the doctrine that the political rights of the separate States that compose the American Union, and their powers as sovereign states, may be settled as determined in the Supreme Court of the United States." The committee also recommended that the report be transmitted to the governors of the several states with the hope that they be presented to their respective legislatures and that these legislatures would express their opinion on the issues that had been raised. Finally, the committee urged that its report and resolutions also be sent to the president, the president of the Senate, and the Speaker of the House of Representatives of the United States to be submitted to their respective houses of Congress in order that "the principles upon which this State has, and does proceed, may be fairly and distinctly understood."[66]

The Ohio legislature overwhelmingly approved these resolutions. The legislature also adopted the strategy recommended in the report and passed a law on January 29, 1821, outlawing the 2BUS by denying it the use of the state's legal system. Under the law, judges and justices of the peace were prohibited from providing any kind of legal process to the 2BUS, nor could anyone who committed theft, burglary, or arson against the bank be incarcerated in a state jail, and monetary penalties were to be levied against any legal officers, including sheriffs, notary publics, and recorders, who violated the law. However, the law also provided that if the 2BUS agreed to pay a 4 percent annual tax on dividends (which was the amount levied on state-chartered banks) and dropped the case it had instituted against Osborn and other state officials or withdrew entirely from Ohio, the law which was to go into effect on September 1, 1821, would be suspended. A few days later, the legislature adopted another law that repealed the $50,000 tax on each branch of the 2BUS in Ohio, replacing it with the 4 percent yearly tax and a lump sum payment of $2,500 until the dividends were declared. And once again the state declared its willingness to compromise, by offering to return $98,000 of the money it had forcibly collected in return for the bank agreeing to drop the suits it had initiated and for withdrawing its branches or agreeing to pay the tax that had just been levied.[67] The state, it is clear, was not simply interested in forcing the 2BUS to withdraw from Ohio, but to establish its right to tax it.

The 2BUS, on the advice of Henry Clay, who had recently resigned his seat in Congress in order to return full time to private practice in the hope of straightening out his personal finances, which had been devastated by the Panic of 1819, rejected the compromise. Instead, he was determined to pursue the matter in the federal courts.[68] But shortly before *Osborn et al. v. the Bank of the United States* came for trial in the federal circuit court on September 6, 1821, Hammond and Clay struck a deal. On September 5, they agreed that the court would issue an order to the state treasurer requiring the return to the 2BUS of the $98,000 tax collected plus interest on the $19,830 in specie, which had been part of the $98,000 collected, taken from the vault in Chillicothe by September 6. They also agreed that Harper's collection fee of $2,000, along with any additional interest sought and court costs, would be appealed to the U.S. Supreme Court. In addition, the circuit court also issued a permanent injunction against any future collection of a state-imposed tax on the 2BUS until the matter had been settled by the U.S. Supreme Court.[69] In effect, Hammond had gotten his way, for many of the issues raised in *McCulloch v. Maryland* would now be reheard by the U.S. Supreme Court.

A complication and delay occurred when the newly appointed state treasurer, Samuel Sullivan, who had replaced Hiram Curry, refused to release the money on the grounds that it required a formal warrant from the state treasurer. A writ was therefore issued holding Sullivan in contempt and placing him under arrest, and another writ of sequestration against his personal property was also issued. As a consequence, Sullivan was taken into custody by a federal marshal, who took his keys and entered the vault where the original $98,000 that had been taken from the Chillicothe branch was being kept, separated from other state funds. This money was then taken to the federal circuit court, where it was picked up by officials of the 2BUS. Although the procedure was condemned by a few newspapers, it did not create a public furor and there was no official protest. Most likely, the whole thing had probably been prearranged and staged so the state of Ohio could not be charged with capitulating to the authority of the federal circuit court, whose jurisdiction in the case it had previously denied.[70]

SEVEN

OHIO AND GEORGIA BEFORE THE U.S. SUPREME COURT

The U.S. Supreme Court began hearing the case of *Osborn et al. v. the Bank of the United States* in early 1823. By this time Brockholst Livingston, who was suffering from a fatal illness, had resigned his position on the Court. He was replaced by a fellow New Yorker and relative, Smith Thompson, who did not take his seat until 1824. Eventually, Thompson was to go his own way, opposing some of the more nationalist decisions of Marshall and Story, but as a freshman member of the Supreme Court he went along with the chief justice's rulings.[1]

On its main points, the *Osborn* case dealt with issues very similar to the ones that had been decided by *McCulloch v. Maryland*: the right of a state to tax the 2BUS and the extent to which the bank was an agency of the federal government. But there were also some important differences. Instead of the relevancy of the Tenth Amendment, which Marshall had quickly dismissed in 1819, the Eleventh Amendment was now being used as a defense by Osborn's attorneys. In addition, there were a variety of technical questions that had to be decided in connection with the various injunctions that had been issued by the lower federal courts. *Osborn et al. v. the Bank of the United States* also differed from *McCulloch v. Maryland* in that it also dealt with the extent of the jurisdiction of the federal courts in hearing cases involving the 2BUS. At the same time, the *Bank of the United States v. the Planters' Bank of Georgia* came up before the Supreme Court, which involved in a somewhat different way the relationship of the states to the 2BUS and which led to a decision in which Marshall appears to have recognized that his claim that the 2BUS was primarily a federal agency really did not do justice to the reality of the situation.

I

Hammond opened the proceedings of *Osborn et al. v. the Bank of the United States* by raising a number of technical objections in opposition to the U.S. Circuit Court's decree that the $100,000 along with interest on the $19,830 in specie that had been forcibly removed be returned to the 2BUS. The main thrust of his argument, however, focused on the lower court's finding, based on the decision of the Supreme Court in *McCulloch v. Maryland*, that the tax laid on the 2BUS was unconstitutional. This, he claimed, was "the most important point in the case," and he proceeded to "ask the court to reconsider so much of their opinion in *McCulloch v. Maryland*, as decides that the states have no rightful power to tax the Bank of the United States."[2] In making this request, Hammond asserted: "It is not the argument of the opinion in *McCulloch v. Maryland* but the premises upon which that argument is founded, that we ask the court now to reexamine and reconsider."[3] Hammond's key point was that the 2BUS was not a government agency but

> a private concern; the capital is private property; the business a
> private and individual trade; the convenience and profit of pri-
> vate men the end and object. Such is the true character of a
> bank constituted by individual stockholders. Its rights and priv-
> ileges, its liabilities and disabilities are all the rights, privileges,
> liabilities and disabilities of private persons.[4]

Hammond recognized that this was his key point, and he elaborated and fleshed it out at great length in order to make it as effective as possible. He denied the claim that, because the 2BUS performed certain financial services for the federal government, this made it a government agency. Instead, he argued that the federal government had sold or contracted this privilege to the 2BUS "for a large sum of money," meaning the bonus it had agreed to pay of $1.5 million. Hammond took particular issue with Chief Justice Marshall's claim in *McCulloch v. Maryland* that the bank was analogous to the mint or the post office. These were government agencies, Hammond argued, and as such they could at any time be "amended, altered, or even abolished, at the discretion of the national legislature," since this was true of all public agencies. They had been "created purely for public purposes" and therefore "may at any time be modified in such manner as the public interest may require. This was also true of public corporations such as towns, cities, parishes, and counties."[5] Public corporations, Hammond continued, "are such only as founded by the government for public purposes, where the whole interest belongs also to the government." For a bank to be a public corporation, it would have to be created by the government for its own uses, and its stock would have to be "exclusively owned by the government." On the other hand, "a bank whose stock is owned by private persons, is a private corporation, although it is erected by the government, and its objects and operations partake of a public nature." In other words, the 2BUS was analogous to various "insurance, canal, bridge and turnpike companies." The 2BUS was "a private association, the proprietors and conductors of a private trade, bound by contract, for a consideration paid, to perform certain employments for the government."[6] It followed from this, Hammond believed, that not only was the 2BUS a private corporation, but that it also was subject to state taxation. He did not challenge the constitutionality of the 2BUS, but argued that the national legislature's power to create a private corporation was "not a general but a special power," and it "does not include or imply a power to exercise discretion in conferring privileges. If this be attempted it is open for inquiry, whether such privilege be compatible with the constitution."[7]

Specifically, Hammond argued that an act creating a privately controlled national corporation did not in itself exempt it from state law and especially not from state taxation. To do this, "an extraordinary provision must be inserted in the charter." Such a privilege or "immunity is not incident to a corporation; the power to create one does not include the power to confer such immunity upon it. It is not essential to its creation or existence." Moreover, even if the national legislature could confer an exemption from state taxation, it could not be implied, but would have to be done in "express terms," and it did not apply to the 2BUS since its charter had not contained such a provision.[8]

Hammond also directly disputed Marshall's claim in *McCulloch v. Maryland* that the 2BUS was in any way analogous to "the post-office, or the mint, or the custom house or the process of the federal courts." Elaborating on this, Hammond pointed out that the post office was "a public institution." The people who worked for it are public officers, and no one has the right to acquire any property in it, and the compensation of the people who work for it are paid out of the national treasury, and the payments the post office receives for performing its services are "public property." This was fundamentally different from the people who owned stock in the 2BUS, "who trade upon their own capital, for their own profit, and who have paid the government a million and a half dollars for a legal charter and name, in which to conduct their trade."[9]

To be sure, Hammond pointed out, the post office contracted out for many of the services it needed. These contractors provided "horses, carriages, and whatever else is necessary for the transportation of the mails upon their own account." Yet while the horses, carriages, and drivers of the contractor were now in public service, it did not alter their character, for they were private property before the contract was made and remain private property after the contract was let, and therefore they are liable to be taxed. The reason for this was clear, Hammond argued: "the contractor is employing his own means to promote his own private profit, and the tax collected is from the individual though assessed upon the means he uses to perform the public service."[10]

Hammond agreed that "to tax the transportation of the mails as such, would be taxing the operations of the government," which could not be allowed. On the other hand, to tax the means of transportation of the mails was acceptable because "the fact that an individual employs his private means in the service of the government, attaches to them no immunity whatever."[11] The 2BUS, Hammond went on, is not analogous to the post office per se, but to the contractors who serve the post office. The 2BUS is a contractor of the federal government. It receives the public money upon deposit, and pays it out when ordered to do so by authorized members of the government. It handles the government's money in the same way that it handles the deposits of individuals using the money to make loans that pay interest. It is one of the means by which the 2BUS makes its profit. Any other individuals or moneyed corporations could be safely employed. As such, they would "be an instrument used by the government; a means of executing its powers. Yet it has never supposed that such employment constituted a public office, or that the person employed was thereby invested with official character."[12] The contract between the 2BUS and the federal government was made for the purpose of making a profit. From this, it followed that the 2BUS was subject to local law, which protected it "and, therefore, cannot be exempt from its exactions."[13]

If anything, Hammond pointed out, the contractors carrying the mail had a better claim to exemption from local taxation because carrying mail was the main reason for which the carriages and horses were hired, while the transportation of passengers and baggage was only incidental. On the other hand:

> in the case of the bank, the private trade of the company is the great object of pursuit, and the end of their exertions; the public business is subordinate and incidental, and is, in reality, a very essential means of promoting that private gain, which is the principal, if not the sole object of the corporation.[14]

Another difference between the contractor who carried the mail and the 2BUS was that the former received a fixed sum and took "upon himself a burthensome and hazardous employment." The 2BUS, on the other hand, received "a substantial pecuniary advantage" through its control of the government's money, which resulted "in the augmentation of the private individual wealth of the stockholders," who had purchased stock in the 2BUS "not for the public account, but for private use."[15]

Hammond continued by arguing that Marshall's claim in *McCulloch v. Maryland* that the 2BUS was analogous to "the mint, the custom house, the process of the federal court" was even more specious. They are clearly public agencies which are run by public employees and are not engaged in private business. For them, Marshall's claim in *McCulloch v. Maryland* that "exemption from state taxation is attached, as an incident essential to their very existence" is correct. But this, Hammond argued, cannot be extended to the 2BUS, "unless its character, end, and object are the same," which it is not possible to do, for it is clear "that the persons who compose it are not public officers; that the business it pursues is not a public business, and that its agency for the government is that of a private individual; from none of which it can derive any exemption not common to private corporations."[16]

Hammond concluded his argument before the U.S. Supreme Court by rejecting the idea that an exemption from state taxation could in any way be incidental or implied in an act of incorporation by Congress. He added that, if it were necessary for either the existence or effective operation of the corporation, "it must obtain it by a special grant; it must be specifically inserted." He then indicated that it was by no means clear that Congress had the power to make such a grant to a private corporation by observing "an inquiry, how far Congress have constitutional power to do this, were they to attempt it, would still further elucidate the erroneous character of the position, that it is an incident of the charter, independent of special grant."[17] Significantly, also, in his argument before the Supreme Court on behalf of Osborn and his fellow appellants, Hammond did not question the constitutionality of the law that created the 2BUS in 1816.

II

In an unusually brief presentation, given the complexity and significance of the issues involved, Clay, on behalf of the 2BUS, began by making it clear that he was not going to take on Hammond's formidable arguments about the essentially private nature of the bank and the right of Ohio to tax it. He simply pointed out that he was "considering it as finally determined by the former decision of the court [*McCulloch v. Maryland*], which was supported by irresistible arguments, for which [he] could add no further illustration."[18]

Instead, Clay focused on the law that Ohio had adopted in February 1819, which he pointed out "was not, like the law of Maryland, a case of taxation." Its purpose was to force the 2BUS to withdraw its branches from Ohio. This was not a tax but "a bill of pains and penalties" that involved amounts greater even than the dividends the branches paid. "It was a confiscation and not a tax," Clay asserted. Ohio could not be allowed to get away with this, for "if one state could, in this manner, expel one of the offices of discount and deposit from its territory, every state might do the same thing." Moreover, he added: "if one state may expel a branch, another state may expel the parent bank itself, and thus this great institution of the national government would be extirpated and destroyed by the local governments, within whose territory it was established."[19]

Clay's point was well taken, for the purpose of the Ohio law of 1819 was, indeed, to force the 2BUS to withdraw its branches; however, he gave no indication that the state itself had repealed this law in 1821 and had substituted a much more reasonable tax in its place, one that was similar to the tax it had levied on its own local banks. Further, in making this argument, Clay clearly admitted that the Maryland tax and the Ohio tax of 1819 were fundamentally different in their purposes, and that Marshall had used his decision in *McCulloch v. Maryland* to deal with what was happening in states like Ohio and Kentucky.

Clay then proceeded to take on the assortment of jurisdictional and procedural questions that had been raised in various ways in connection with the case. He denied the claim that the case should not be heard because it violated the Eleventh Amendment, which prohibited the suing of a sovereign state without its permission, since Ohio was not "a formal party on the record" for "although the interests of a state may be ultimately affected by the decision as a cause, yet if an effectual remedy can be had, without making the state a defendant to the suit, the courts of the United States are bound to exercise jurisdiction."[20] Finally, Clay also defended the use of the injunction that had been issued by the U.S. Circuit Court on behalf of the 2BUS and, more significantly, the general jurisdiction of the federal courts over the case since it was "a case arising under the constitution and laws of the union."[21]

John C. Wright, on behalf of Ohio, followed Clay. He reiterated the argument that the case was in essence an action against the state by a citizen of another state (the 2BUS) and that such an action was barred by the Eleventh Amendment. Suddenly at this point, the Supreme Court "indicated a wish that the case should be re-argued [at the next term] upon the point of the constitutionality and effect of the provision in the charter of the bank, which authorizes it to sue in the circuit courts of the Union," because a similar case was coming up in that term.

When the High Court reconvened on March 11, 1824, the 2BUS was represented by Clay, Daniel Webster, and Thomas Sergeant, the bank's general counsel, while Wright, former governor Ethan A. Brown, who was now a U.S. senator, and Robert G. Harper, a former U.S. senator and a frequent pleader before the Supreme Court, presented the case for Osborn and Ohio. Hammond was not present at the rehearing because he stayed home to be at the side of his ill wife and because of pecuniary considerations.[22]

Once again, the arguments at the rehearing focused on the jurisdiction question. The lawyers for the bank argued that its right to sue in the federal courts "was expressly and unequivocally conferred" by section 7 of the 1816 act creating the 2BUS. This had not been provided for in the act creating the 1BUS in 1791. It was to correct this defect that Congress had explicitly granted this right to the 2BUS. The authority to grant this power, they argued, came from the U.S. Constitution, which authorized the federal courts to hear "a case arising under the Constitution and laws of the United States."[23]

The lawyers for the 2BUS then spelled out the strong nationalist implications of their argument. "The question here," they asserted, "is about the exercise of a sovereign power, given for great national purposes. Those who framed the constitution intended to establish a government complete for its own purposes, supreme within its sphere and capable of acting by its own proper powers." The Constitution had created three coordinate branches, the legislative, executive, and judicial, and from this it followed that "the judicial authority . . . must be coextensive with the legislative power." It was as unreasonable to leave the execution of the laws of the federal government to the governors of the states as it would be to leave their exposition and enforcement to the state courts. "The great object," they asserted, ". . . of the constitutional provision respecting the judiciary must make it co-extensive with the power of legislation, and to associate them inseparably, so that where one went, the other might go along with it."[24]

The attorneys for the 2BUS also promulgated the view that it was essentially an instrument of the national government. It was necessary "for the fiscal purpose of the Union. It is established not for the benefit of the stockholders, but for the benefit of the nation." The 2BUS had been created in order to facilitate the fiscal operation of the national government. In doing this, it performed a crucial public service as "the collection and administration of the public revenue is, of all others, the most important branch of the public service."[25]

In making their argument for the right of the 2BUS to use the federal courts in all cases whatsoever, its attorneys denigrated both the fairness and reliability of the state courts. Denying that there existed "no unreasonable jealousy of the state judiciaries," they pointed out that "the Constitution itself supposes" that the state courts "may not always be worthy of confidence, where the rights and interests of the national government are drawn in question." In addition, it was essential that the application of the laws and treaties of the national government should be uniform, which would not necessarily occur if most decisions were left in the hands of local court systems. Further, the concern over leaving the administration of "national justice to local tribunals" was not simply a theoretical one. In Ohio, the 2BUS had actually been outlawed, "and if it cannot seek redress in the federal tribunals, it can find it nowhere. Where is the power of coercion in the national government? What is to become of the national revenue while it is going on?"[26]

It is to deal with these questions, the bank's lawyers pointed out, that section 25 had been included in the Judiciary Act of 1789. In doing so, the federal government had acted in a cautious and restrained fashion, they argued. Congress had not given original and exclusive jurisdiction to the federal courts in all cases arising under the laws and treaties of the United States, but had "contented itself with giving an appellate jurisdiction [to the U.S. Supreme Court], to correct the errors of the state courts." At the heart of the jurisdiction issue, the attorneys for the 2BUS argued, was "whether the government of the United

States can execute one of its own laws, through the process of its own courts. The right of the bank to sue in the national courts, is one of its essential faculties. If that can be taken away, it is deprived of a part of its being."[27]

The lawyers for Osborn and his fellow appellants vigorously denied that the federal courts had jurisdiction in the case. They denied that there was any real difference between the First and Second Banks of the United States or that Congress had the power to grant such a power to the 2BUS. The 2BUS simply could not go into the federal courts on a case involving "a breach of contract or a trespass on its property." The 2BUS had to use the state courts "for neither its character as a party, nor the nature of the controversy can give the court jurisdiction. The case does not arise under its charter. It arises under the general or local law of contract, and may be determined without opening the statute book of the United States."[28]

III

Marshall delivered the Supreme Court's decision on March 19, 1824. He began by focusing on the jurisdiction issue. He viewed this as "of such vital importance as to induce the court to request that it might be particularly spoken to."[29] As was his inclination in constitutional matters, Marshall, who wrote the opinion for the majority of the Court, proceeded to interpret the powers of the federal government very broadly. In doing this, he rejected the appellant's claim that the U.S. Circuit Court did not have the power to hear the case. This power, he argued, had been specifically granted by the bank's charter in 1816 and could not be "made plainer by explanation."[30] To this, he added the claim that, under "the arising under clause" of Article III of the U.S. Constitution, the federal courts were empowered to hear all cases involving the 2BUS, since it had been brought into being by federal law; it did not matter that this particular case did not involve a federal statute nor that it could have also been settled by Ohio law. The underlying assumption behind Marshall's extremely nationalist interpretation of the jurisdiction question in *Osborn et al. v. Bank of the United States* was "that the legislative, executive, and judicial powers of every well-constructed government, are co-extensive with each other."[31]

Having ruled "that the clause in the act of incorporation enabling the bank to sue in the courts of the United States, is consistent with the constitution, and to be obeyed in all courts," Marshall turned his attention to the various technical issues that had been raised by Ohio's opposition to the U.S. Circuit Court's decision against Osborn and his fellow appellants. These involved a variety of issues, such as the form the original suit had taken, the adequacy of the evidence presented, the appropriateness of the injunctions that had been issued, and the fairness of the decision that had been rendered. Marshall proceeded to reject, at some length, all of the arguments that were presented on their behalf.[32]

Marshall also denied the claim that, under the Eleventh Amendment, the case should never have been heard because the amendment prohibited a suit against a state without its permission, and the 2BUS had tried to get around this by suing the agents of the state rather than the state itself. Marshall ruled that, for the Eleventh Amendment to apply, it was not enough for a state to be affected by the outcome of the decision, but it must be specifically named in the record. By this ruling, Marshall continued on the course that he had initiated in *Cohens v. Virginia* of sharply limiting the Eleventh Amendment's scope as an instrument for defending the rights of the states.[33]

Marshall next turned his attention to the request that the Supreme Court's decision in *McCulloch v. Maryland* be revised in light of the formidable argument Hammond had presented during the previous term that the 2BUS was a private, profit-making corporation and not an agency of the federal government. There is no question but that Marshall recognized that Hammond's presentation had been unusually impressive, for later that year (1823) Hammond had published it as a separate pamphlet, which he sent to the chief justice. Marshall had graciously responded by noting, "I have read the argument with that pleasure which I always feel in reading or hearing one in which the subject is discussed with real ability, whether I concur or not in opinion with the person who makes it."[34]

Despite this, the chief justice's response to this important issue was basically perfunctory, indicating he was more interested in asserting than he was in persuading. To this end, Marshall simply reiterated the argument in *McCulloch v. Maryland* that the 2BUS was essentially a public corporation, "a necessary and proper" instrument for managing the federal government's fiscal operations. "The bank is not," he argued, "considered as a private corporation, whose principal object is in individual trade and individual profit; but as a public corporation created for public and national purposes." The private functions of the bank were necessary for it to perform its legitimate operations for the government. To deny the bank its private operations would be to make it "a very defective instrument when considered . . . for the purposes of the government." He concluded that, therefore, "the act of the state of Ohio, which is certainly much more objectionable than that of the state of Maryland, is repugnant to a law of the United States, made in pursuance of the constitution, and, therefore, void."[35]

In further defense of his position, Marshall might also have pointed out that the private ownership and functions of the 2BUS were absolutely necessary since the federal government was broke in 1816, and it could not have created a national bank without handing over control of it to the private sector. But then Marshall would also have had to recognize that, in the boom period that followed its inception, from 1816 to mid-1818, the 2BUS followed policies that were meant to increase the dividends it paid and to raise the value of its stock, and during the hard times that followed the summer of 1818, under the leadership of Jones, the 2BUS adopted policies whose purpose was to save itself, and it did nothing to help the U.S. government to alleviate the impact of the Panic of 1819. The only point Marshall granted to Osborn and the other appellants was to reverse the U.S. Circuit Court's decision that interest be paid on the money that the state's official had taken and held, on the grounds that they had not been allowed to use the money in any fashion.[36]

Justice William Johnson, a Jefferson appointee from South Carolina, dissented, although he was not an advocate of states' rights, nor was he sympathetic in any way to Ohio's decision to tax the 2BUS. He fully appreciated the value of the bank as the federal government's fiscal agent and the role it played in controlling the activities of state-chartered banks and in stabilizing the economy. He also believed that "a state of things has now grown up, in some of the states, which renders all the protection necessary that the general government can give to the bank."[37] Nonetheless, Johnson took sharp issue with Marshall's decision on the grounds that it expanded the jurisdiction of the federal courts and that it completely stripped the state courts of their common law jurisdiction in any case in which the federal government might have an interest even if it did not involve a federal statute. This, he believed, had dangerous consolidationist tendencies. He was especially concerned about a "chain of implied powers" and warned that "no one branch of the general government can new-model the constitutional structure of the other."[38]

IV

The U.S. Supreme Court's decision in the *Osborn* case ended Ohio's opposition, which had gone as far as it could go in legal channels. The levy of a $50,000 tax on each branch (already repealed before the decision was handed down), the forcible collection of the tax in September 1819, and the outlawing of the bank had been both the most extreme and the weakest parts of its case, and the state's leadership was no longer willing to act in an openly defiant and coercive manner, which was the only course left to Ohio after the Supreme Court had made its final ruling.

There were many reasons for this. To begin with, popular feeling was no longer on the side of open resistance in 1824. To a considerable extent, the intensity of feeling that had existed between 1819 and 1821 had been alleviated by a series of relief measures adopted by the federal government to allow purchasers of land in Ohio, which was part of the national domain, to break their original contracts by retaining that portion of their land for which they had already paid and returning the rest. During this time, the 2BUS had curtailed most of its operations in Ohio and was keeping a very low profile. Moreover, the struggle with the 2BUS had generally been crowded out of the public's attention by the wild and complex struggle that was to characterize the presidential election of 1824. In the election, there were five candidates for the office: William H. Crawford, John Quincy Adams, Henry Clay, John C. Calhoun, and Andrew Jackson. Despite the fact that Hammond and Clay were on opposite sides of the struggle over the 2BUS in Ohio,

Hammond, who hated Jackson, supported Clay's presidential ambitions, which undoubtedly encouraged him to accept the finality of Marshall's decision.

The long lapse that existed between the actual collection of the tax in September 1819 and the final decision of the U.S. Supreme Court four and a half years later had clearly worked to the advantage of the 2BUS. Henry Clay, who was probably not as good a lawyer as Hammond but was a much more astute politician, recognized this as early as September 1821 when, in a letter to Langdon Cheves, he indicated that he had adopted a moderate course against Osborn and his associates by not pushing for their imprisonment because it would "produce excitement in the public mind" and would not really accomplish anything. He then added: "Our moderation has done us no harm; and the current of public sentiment, already turning and turning in our favor, is now impetuously directing itself against those, by whose councils, the State is brought into its present predicament."[39]

By 1822–1823, Hammond was also having political problems. He ran for a seat in the U.S. House of Representatives in 1822 but was defeated. Soon after that, the Ohio legislature rejected him for a seat on the state's supreme court. The cause Hammond espoused was losing its popularity and becoming increasingly costly. A minority report issued in early 1821 opposing the outlawing of the 2BUS had correctly stressed the dangers involved in Ohio's actions. The struggle, it argued, had gotten out of hand to the point where it was "extraordinary and alarming." It went on: "the character of the state, has already suffered much. . . . this is no longer a controversy with a simple corporation, but with the constituted authorities of the general government." The authors of the report pointed out that the 2BUS had not been all bad. It had, after all, brought order to the chaos, fraud, and dishonesty created by various poorly managed state banks. In addition, the controversy with the 2BUS was beginning to "endanger the safety of our political union," and this could not be allowed to happen. It was inevitable, they argued, that the state would eventually lose the struggle and that the state's taxpayers would pay the cost for this "unprofitable contest."[40]

The leaders of the anti-2BUS forces in Ohio also had to contend with other difficulties. Although they received some private letters of support for their cause, most notably from Thomas Jefferson and DeWitt Clinton, no formal endorsement of their cause was forthcoming. Especially disappointing was the failure of the Virginia House of Delegates to adopt resolutions that proposed a set of amendments to the U.S. Constitution that could have made clear its support for Ohio. On the other hand, Ohio's actions were severely condemned by the legislature of Massachusetts, which did pass a set of resolutions that upheld Congress's power to create a national bank, that denied any state the right to prevent the operation of a federal law, that explicitly denounced Ohio's actions, that asserted that the federal courts had the power to adjudicate disputes between the states and the federal government, and that made clear its belief that Ohio's rights under the Eleventh Amendment had not been violated by the federal courts.[41]

Meanwhile, the Ohio congressional delegation in Washington also was running into problems. Neither President Monroe nor Congress took a formal position in the dispute between Ohio, on one side, and the 2BUS and the U.S. Supreme Court, on the other, but there was very real indirect pressure. The state's supporters found themselves shunned and passed over for federal offices. Also, the state's attempt to get federal aid for the development of a canal system linking the southwestern part of Ohio to the Great Lakes, which would facilitate trade with the eastern states and provide employment to construction workers, was "discountenanced" because, as Governor Brown complained, the state "has suffered much obloquery [obloquy], and misrepresentation in the other states, for having resisted certain pretensions of the Bank of the U.S." He then added that if Ohio did not get the support of other states, "or if, the Supreme Court, on a hearing, shall decide the suits pending against her, I trust there is no evidence of her indisposition to respect the decisions in her subsequent conduct."[42]

Hammond expressed disappointment over the Supreme Court's decision in *Osborn et al. v. the Bank of the United States* and cynically expressed the belief "that it is a great folly for a man to confide in the force of argument."[43] And Wright expressed the opinion that "a few more such decisions and good-bye to the state sovereignties."[44] True to their word, however, Hammond and Wright, as well as the other proponents of Ohio's opposition to the 2BUS, accepted the finality of the

Supreme Court's decision, abandoned their cause, and turned their attention to other issues. Most notable of these was the presidential election of 1824, where Hammond took over the management of Clay's candidacy in Ohio. It is therefore especially ironic that Clay's leading opponent in that contest was Andrew Jackson, whom Hammond both loathed and feared, and who in less than a decade was to lead a much more powerful, effective, and successful campaign against the 2BUS, using the very arguments Hammond had developed.

V

The other case decided at the 1824 term of the U.S. Supreme Court, which involved both the jurisdiction of the federal courts and the 2BUS, originated in Georgia, which had a long-standing tradition of opposition to and criticism of the High Court's rulings. This had begun in 1793, in the case of *Chisholm v. Georgia*, which led to the adoption of the Eleventh Amendment. The Supreme Court had also declared the state's rescinding of the Yazoo land sales to be a violation of the contract clause of the U.S. Constitution, and therefore unconstitutional, even though by the time this occurred, the lands involved had been ceded to the federal government.[45]

In addition, Georgia had engaged in a major confrontation with the 1BUS. It had to do with an 1805 tax that the state had levied on the Savannah branch, and when the 1BUS refused to pay, it had been forcibly collected by the local sheriff. The 1BUS sued for the return of the money. Believing it would get a fairer hearing in the federal courts, as opposed to those of the state, the 1BUS initiated its suit in the U.S. Circuit Court under the diversity clause of Article III of the U.S. Constitution by claiming that it was a citizen of Pennsylvania, where it was headquartered. In response, the attorneys for Georgia on behalf of Peter Deveaux, the sheriff, and Thomas Robertson, who actually collected the tax, denied that the federal courts had jurisdiction in the case. Supreme Court associate justice William Johnson, riding circuit, ruled in favor of Deveaux and Robertson, denying that as a corporation the 1BUS had adequate diversity of citizenship to give the federal courts jurisdiction. But he also recognized that it was doubtful whether the 1BUS could get a fair hearing from the state courts, and he therefore welcomed a review of his decision by the U.S. Supreme Court.[46]

The case came before the High Court as *Bank of the United States v. Deveaux et al.* in 1809. Marshall, on behalf of the Supreme Court, supported the view that a corporation usually could not be considered a citizen in the traditional sense, and therefore could not be allowed to initiate suits in federal courts unless specifically granted that right in its charter (which was what occurred when the 2BUS was chartered in 1816). But he did find enough diversity of citizenship in the 1BUS to remand the case back to the lower court for trial. This, however, did not occur since "the confiscation was dissolved and the action died."[47] Among other things, this meant that neither the circuit court nor the Supreme Court ended up considering the constitutionality of the Georgia tax.[48]

When, a decade later, the U.S. Supreme Court in *McCulloch v. Maryland* ruled against the states, the decision received some pointed criticism in Georgia. One perceptive writer drew a sharp distinction between the point of view of the role of the 2BUS presented in Marshall's decision and the one that emerged from reading the charter that had created it in 1816, for if people only read the decision, "they would be led to believe that it was perfectly a political institution, having for its object the greatest governmental advantages." The charter, on the other hand, made it clear that "it has no other *end* or *design* but to associate together certain individuals, for the purpose of enlarging their credit, employing their capital, advancing mercantile dealings, and thereby promoting large and extensive speculations." The 2BUS was, in short, a privately controlled corporation whose purpose was to make a profit. The crucial question, according to this writer, was whether because it performed certain services for the federal government, it "derives greater powers than belongs to common corporations." This was particularly true where the branches were concerned for "would an act of Congress be binding that should designate by name a certain number of citizens within a given state, and declare that their property should be free from the taxes in that state?"[49]

Many members of the Georgia legislature also were dissatisfied with the High Court's decision in *McCulloch v. Maryland*. Later that year, one writer predicted that it "would tax the Branch Bank of the United

States in Savannah, in the same ratio as the state banks are taxed in this state. This, they think, they have a right to do; and that it is constitutional—although it is diametrically opposite the opinion given by chief justice Marshall." He then added, "The bank we are informed, tends to resist the tax. I trust that we shall not witness the same scene lately played off by our sister state, Ohio."[50] But such a tax never was adopted, and Georgia never directly challenged the U.S. Supreme Court's decision in *McCulloch v. Maryland*.

The Georgia legislature also chose to maintain a moderate and restrained course in dealing with the constitutional issues raised by the relationship of the branches of the 2BUS to the governments of the states in which they were established. This was clearly manifested in Georgia's response to Pennsylvania's proposed amendment to the U.S. Constitution, which would have limited the operation of a national bank to the District of Columbia. Georgia rejected it on the grounds that it was not

> expedient to deny absolutely to the general government, the power to establish a bank beyond the District of Columbia, although they are impressed with the belief, that the original grant of such power should be accompanied with a restriction, requiring the assent of each and every state to the location of said bank or any branch . . . within the limits of such state.[51]

Both more equivocal and extreme was Georgia's response to developments in Ohio. The Ohio Resolutions justifying the state's collection of a $50,000 tax on each of the branches of the 2BUS in Cincinnati and Chillicothe, as well as its unwillingness to accept the Supreme Court's decision in *McCulloch v. Maryland*, had been transmitted to the Georgia legislature by the state's governor in November 1821. A short time later, the Georgia Senate issued a manifesto which attracted national attention:

> In the conflict between federal and state authorities, the state of Georgia will not enlist her self on either side. She regards the federal union of these states as their best safe-guard against intestine discord, and the injuries of foreign powers. She is disposed to preserve to the federal and the state governments,

respectively, those powers which are intrusted [*sic*] to the former, or reserved by the latter, in the federal constitution.

However, in addition to this, the manifesto also contained a sharp diatribe against both the legitimacy and operations of the 2BUS and its Savannah branch. It questioned its constitutionality: "It is in vain that we have defined and written constitutions, if, by a latitude of construction, they may be made to embrace every power thought convenient to the temporary policy of those who administer the government." It protested the establishment of the Savannah branch "on the territory of Georgia without her consent" and called it "a usurpation of her sovereign power." It denounced the economic policies of the 2BUS as adversely affecting the welfare of the state by forcing the local banks to "curtail their business. Georgia beholds her revenue dwindling, and her various public interests threatened with ruin, by the operations of this hostile bank." It went on to ask: "Can the obligations to manage the revenue of the United States, imply a right to establish within any state a bank, which shall be protected, for its own profit, in waging a constant and ruinous war against the institutions of the state?" It expressed concern that once the 2BUS had crushed the state banks, "it shall exert all the monied influence of the country, where can its power be resisted? It will have *a direct influence over the government. . . . How many elections may it not control? How many officers of government may it not bias?*" It concluded with the warning:

> Georgia anxious to pursue a moderate course, still withholds her hand, under the hope that the parent bank will take the solemn warning, and withdraw her branch from the state. But, shall Georgia exercise eternal forebearance [*sic*] towards an institution which usurps her sovereignty; which invades her territory; which impoverishes her citizens; which exhaust[s] her revenue; which arrests her improvements, and which threatens the federal republic with dishonor and ruin?[52]

Georgia's ambivalent and even contradictory responses to the resolutions from Pennsylvania and Ohio probably came about as a consequence of an attempt to reconcile the essentially irreconcilable points of view of the state's two leading political factions. Ever since the 1790s, when the Yazoo scandals occurred, the state's politics had been dominated by a series of sharp political struggles between the Clarkites and the Troupites. The former were led by John Clark, who captured the governorship in 1819 and again in 1821. The latter were led by George M. Troup, a close political ally of fellow Georgian William H. Crawford, the secretary of the treasury and the leading candidate to succeed Monroe to the U.S. presidency in 1824. Personal feuds and animosities and the desire to control patronage as well as the pursuit of power and prominence explain much of the differences between them. But on certain issues, there were also real differences, especially regarding the 2BUS during the years 1819–1821. The Clarkites were generally hostile to the 2BUS and the operation of its branch in Savannah, as well as banks in general, which they viewed as at best a necessary evil, and they therefore wanted the states to limit and control them. The Troupites, on the other hand, had favored the expansion of state banking activities during the prosperous years that followed the end of the War of 1812, and they also favored a more moderate course on the 2BUS because of their support for Crawford, who had been a strong advocate of its creation and a defender of many of its policies, and whose chances for the presidency they did not want to jeopardize by now taking too extreme a position of opposition.[53]

Much more serious was the confrontation that occurred between some of Georgia's state-chartered banks and the Savannah branch of the 2BUS, for it went beyond mere rhetoric and actually led to a case before the U.S. Supreme Court. The Savannah branch had accumulated large amounts of state paper, especially the notes of the Bank of the State of Georgia, the Planters' Bank, and the Bank of Darien, primarily from customs duties and the sale of western lands in Alabama, where no branch of the 2BUS existed. During good times, the Savannah branch recirculated much of this money when it made loans. But in hard times, and following instructions from the home office in Philadelphia, it stopped making any kind of loans. Moreover, it now demanded that the state banks redeem their notes in specie, often on a daily basis. This in turn exacerbated existing economic difficulties, by forcing the local banks to curtail their own loans and limiting the amount of money in circulation.[54]

Because the state owned a substantial amount of stock in the state banks, and it appeared they might fail, Governor John Clark requested an investigation of the situation. In his address to the legislature, he pointed out that the operations of the 2BUS had led to "the injury and embarrassment" of the state banks and asserted that the measures of the 2BUS "seem to have been taken with a view to universal monopoly, and to have been prosecuted with a singular hostility against state corporations." Its relentless demand for specie, he argued, "has practiced towards us a course of conduct, if not illegal, at least oppressive, and palpably illiberal" and was the cause of the state's economic difficulties.[55]

Meanwhile, tensions between the local banks in Georgia and the 2BUS continued to heat up. An attempt at a compromise was made whereby the Savannah branch of the 2BUS consented to weekly settlements instead of daily ones and agreed to hold $1 million of state bank notes, but would receive 6 percent interest and specie payment on the remaining balances of state bank paper in its possession. But this only lasted a short time, and by June 1821 the Planters' Bank and the Bank of the State of Georgia had stopped paying on any of its notes presented by the Savannah branch. The state then passed a law that made it virtually impossible for the 2BUS to use the state courts against the local banks, whereupon the 2BUS initiated a suit in the U.S. Circuit Court, with U.S. Supreme Court justice William Johnson presiding, to compel the Planters' Bank to make payment.[56]

The central issue was one of jurisdiction, or the right of the federal courts to hear the case. Presumably, the 2BUS believed it could use the federal courts because it was granted the right to do so in its charter. The attorney for the Planters' Bank of Georgia, on the other hand, argued the necessity "to look behind the charter of the bank defendant, in order to determine the individual characters of the corporators defendants also." In connection with this, the attorneys for the Planters' Bank of Georgia made two main points "against the jurisdiction of the circuit court." The first was that, because many of the stockholders in the 2BUS were from Georgia as were the stockholders of the Planters' Bank, it was a matter of the citizens of one state suing the citizens of the same state, and therefore it was essentially a local dispute to be settled by the Georgia courts. The other and more significant point was that the state of Georgia had both incorporated and owned stock in the Planters' Bank, and the bank therefore "was exempt from suit under the 11th amendment." Making repeated references to the Supreme Court's earlier opinion in the case of *Bank of the United States v. Deveaux*, which Johnson presumed was "one of the canons of this court," he precluded the U.S. Circuit Court from hearing the case. Johnson also upheld the claim that, since the state of Georgia was a stockholder in the Planters' Bank, that bank was exempt under the Eleventh Amendment, pointing out, "I would ask in what other capacity can a state appear or even exist? In every possible form or shape, it is a sovereign state, or it is nothing." But district court judge Jeremiah Cutler refused to support the ruling, and so a pro forma division was agreed to so that the question could go to the U.S. Supreme Court where "it might undergo the fullest investigation and give time for the maturest reflection."[57]

There, Marshall, writing the majority opinion, with Johnson dissenting, found for the 2BUS. He upheld the right of the 2BUS to sue a state bank in the federal circuit courts, even if some of its stockholders were citizens of the same state. He pointed out that this right had been explicitly conferred in the charter of the 2BUS and that, since "there is probably not a commercial state in the Union, some of whose citizens are not members of the Bank of the United States," to decide otherwise would be to totally undermine this right. He concluded therefore, "Such a construction can not be the correct one."[58]

Marshall also narrowed the meaning of the Eleventh Amendment by rejecting the Planters' Bank's claim of sovereign immunity. This is hardly surprising since he had already done so in his *Osborn* decision during that same term. But what was surprising was the argument he used to do it, for in many ways it was similar to the argument that Maryland and Ohio had used in the *McCulloch* and *Osborn* cases, when they claimed the 2BUS was not an instrument of the federal government, and which Marshall and the High Court had rejected and generally ignored. For Marshall now asserted:

> It is, we think, a sound principle, that when a government becomes a partner in any trading company, it divests itself, so far as concerns the transactions of that company, of its sovereign character, and takes that of a private citizen. Instead of communicating to the company its privileges and its prerogatives, it descends to a level with those with whom it associates

itself, and takes the character which belongs to its associates, and to the business which is to be transacted. Thus, many states of this Union who have an interest in banks, are not suable even in their own courts; yet they never exempt the corporation from being sued. The state of Georgia, by giving to the bank the capacity to sue and be sued, voluntarily strips itself of its sovereign character, so far as respects the transactions of the bank, and waives all the privileges of that character. As a member of a corporation, a government never exercises its sovereignty. It acts merely as a corporator, and exercises no other power in the management of the affairs of the corporation, than are expressly given by the incorporating act.[59]

Marshall's *Planters' Bank* decision did not receive any attention or analysis in the newspapers, probably because the country was absorbed in the debate over a protective tariff and preoccupied with the upcoming and hotly debated presidential election of 1824. For its part, Georgia accepted the decision and proceeded to quietly repeal its anti-2BUS legislation and let the matter die.[60]

EIGHT

CODA

The opposition to the U.S. Supreme Court's decision in *McCulloch v. Maryland* in each of the four states most concerned about the issue was distinct and self-contained. Maryland did not challenge either the constitutionality of the 2BUS or its right to establish a branch in Baltimore. The object of its tax was to raise revenue while the main purpose of the legal dispute it engendered was to clarify a contested constitutional point and, perhaps more important, to facilitate getting a case before the Supreme Court as quickly as possible. In Virginia, while many people were wary of the constitutionality of the 2BUS, they nonetheless accepted it, and even embraced it, turning it to their own advantage, and the state never taxed its branches. Opposition in the Old Dominion was directed more at the U.S. Supreme Court than at the 2BUS and focused almost exclusively on the first part of Marshall's decision, which dealt with such recurring issues as the origins and nature of the union, the meaning of the necessary and proper clause of the Constitution, and the constitutionality of section 25 of the Judiciary Act of 1789. Although some of these issues were touched on in Ohio,

Virginia's grounds of opposition to *McCulloch v. Maryland* was for the most part different from that of the other states. In Ohio, where the opposition to the decision manifested itself in its most extreme form, it dealt mainly with the second part of the decision, which focused on such issues as the private nature of the 2BUS, the power of it to arbitrarily create branches without the permission of the states where they were to be located, the right of a state to levy a tax on the branches, and the legitimacy and binding quality of the *McCulloch v. Maryland* decision. Georgia took a much more moderate position, denouncing the 2BUS and its Savannah branch, but taking no real action and in the end accepting a Supreme Court decision that supported the 2BUS.

I

Opposition to the 2BUS and its branches also existed in other states. In Tennessee, the $50,000 per year tax on the proposed branch in Nashville had prevented its establishment, and so when the U.S. Supreme Court handed down its decision in *McCulloch v. Maryland*, there was nothing for the state to do except to endorse Pennsylvania's proposed amendment limiting operation of a national bank to the District of Columbia, which it did. Indiana, Illinois, Missouri, Alabama, and Mississippi also did not contain a branch of the 2BUS and consequently did not take any action, although Indiana and Illinois supported the Pennsylvania proposal. Much more serious was the hostility to the 2BUS that existed in the states of North Carolina, Pennsylvania, and Kentucky, although in the end their opposition never went beyond failed resolutions and proposals in their legislatures and a spate of bitter denunciations in speeches, the press, and private letters.

North Carolina was one of the least commercially developed and poorest states in the union, but it too had undergone significant economic development in the immediate post–War of 1812 years. As a result, it had increased the operating capital of its existing branch banks and requested the establishment of a branch of the 2BUS, which opened for business in Fayetteville in 1817. Hostility toward the operations of the 2BUS, however, quickly developed. It began when the Fayetteville branch demanded that the federal funds that had been deposited in the state banks before it had been created be transferred to it, and that the payments be made in specie. This created all kinds of difficulties for the state banks. Among other things, it forced them to decrease their discounts and the amount of notes they issued which, in turn, reduced their profits and the state's circulating medium. When the Panic of 1819 hit, the 2BUS further intensified its pressure for specie payments. And when the North Carolina legislature imposed a $5,000 tax on the Fayetteville branch to be collected by the end of October 1819, the 2BUS refused to pay it, pointing out that the tax had been declared unconstitutional by the U.S. Supreme Court's decision in *McCulloch v. Maryland*.[1]

Between 1818 and 1821, hostility toward the 2BUS increased further. Archibald D. Murphey, a leading lawyer, was one of the most economically forward-looking members of the state legislature, who sponsored various pieces of legislation to develop inland waterways and to create a statewide educational system. Murphey reflected the fear and concern over the power of the 2BUS when he requested the help of a friend to transfer his loans from the 2BUS to a state bank so that he would not "be sacrificed" because he intended to write a pamphlet addressed to the people of North Carolina condemning the activities of the Fayetteville branch. According to Murphey: "I am convinced that the Branch of the U.S. Bank at Fayetteville . . . is the greatest Curse that has befallen us . . . and that the local Banks as well as Individuals will continue to be pressed, if not ruined, unless we get rid of it. We can't bank in this State, with this Monster feeding upon our Vitals."[2]

But getting the legislature to take some kind of action proved elusive. For example, a resolution was introduced in the North Carolina Senate in December 1820 condemning the "illiberal policy" of the Fayetteville branch of the 2BUS for "running on the State Banks . . . for specie," a policy which it claimed would lead to the "injury and destruction of said Banks." It then called for the removal of the 2BUS from the state on the grounds that "the dictates of common sense and sound policy forbid the destruction of institutions owned by the citizens thereof, exclusively for the advancement and benefit for one owned principally by foreigners," but the resolution was indefinitely postponed.[3]

The following year, an attempt was made to get around the *McCulloch* decision by levying a tax upon "every tenement upon which any Banking operations shall be located" which had not been chartered by the state. In reality, this meant the Fayetteville branch, since it was the only bank operating in North Carolina that had not been chartered by the state.[4] But it too failed to be adopted. In the end, North Carolina took no action at all; it did not even endorse Pennsylvania's proposed amendment. As a result, the Fayetteville branch, despite the opposition to it, continued to dominate the banking scene in North Carolina.[5]

Although the 2BUS was headquartered in Philadelphia, where it had many supporters, especially in the business community, there also existed widespread hostility toward it throughout the state. Southwestern Pennsylvania was the fastest growing area, and most people initially welcomed the establishment of a branch office in Pittsburgh, expecting it to be an important source of investment capital. But they quickly became disillusioned and hostile to the 2BUS when it adopted its stringent policy of demanding specie whenever it redeemed the notes of local banks to the point where it threatened their very existence and wrought havoc on the local economy. At the same time, in Philadelphia, a series of essays were published under the pen name "Brutus" in the Philadelphia *Aurora*, edited by William Duane, a long-time critic of most Jeffersonian nationalist policies and of the spread of banking after the War of 1812. Brutus turned out to be Stephen Simpson, a former employee of the 2BUS and the son of George Simpson, chief cashier of the well-respected Girard Bank, which had assumed what was left of the 1BUS after its demise. Brutus's essays, which ran throughout most of 1818, represented an unusually well-informed and blistering attack on the machinations that had led to the control of the board of directors of the 2BUS under Jones's presidency by speculators and stockjobbers whose primary interest was quick profits through high dividends and rising stock prices, rather than running the 2BUS according to sound banking practices.[6]

By March 1818, hostility to the 2BUS in Pennsylvania was widespread enough for the state legislature, about to adjourn, to agree to take the matter up at its next session, at which time, according to several sources, "there is very little doubt it will be severely taxed."[7] On

December 7, 1818, the legislature scheduled March 10, 1819, for a full discussion of the question. But when the U.S. Supreme Court handed down its decision in *McCulloch v. Maryland* on March 6, 1819, it abandoned the idea of a tax.[8] Instead, opponents of the 2BUS now talked of going directly to the people as a way of circumscribing the decision. For a while, there was even vague talk of trying to call a national constitutional convention, but this came to nothing. In the end, the opponents of the 2BUS and the U.S. Supreme Court's decision in the *McCulloch* case settled for proposing an amendment to the U.S. Constitution that would have limited the activities of a national bank to the District of Columbia. But this never really led to anything, since it only received the support of a scant four other states.[9]

In the press, there was much criticism of Marshall's decision in *McCulloch v. Maryland*. Again, Brutus led the assault, arguing that it undermined the rights of the states and had helped to prop up the "moneyed aristocracy" that controlled the 2BUS. Supporters of the 2BUS, on the other hand, praised the outcome of the case, but were more cautious about fully endorsing the decision. One writer in the *Franklin Gazette*, a newspaper that had consistently supported the 2BUS since its origins in 1816, defended it against the attacks launched by Brutus; the findings of the Spencer Committee, which accused it of all kinds of questionable activities; and the charges leveled against it by local banks and claimed that the U.S. Supreme Court's decision was an important victory for the 2BUS because "it now possesses the conjoined sanction of the highest legislative and the highest judicial decision in its favor, as a corporation which the Congress had a right to establish, and may continue to support." Yet at the same time, the writer distanced himself from the *McCulloch* decision by noting that the 2BUS was not under the control of the government, but under the control of its stockholders. "This is," he wrote, "a corporation managed for the benefit of those who furnish the capital, by agents or directors chosen by the stockholders, and in no other way." As for the U.S. government, it chose only a limited number of directors "to represent the share which the public has in the institution."[10]

Kentucky is the most difficult state to explain why nothing really happened in response to *McCulloch v. Maryland* because, of all the states, it had levied the heaviest tax upon the branches of the 2BUS that had been located, at the invitation of the state, at Lexington and Louisville in 1817. Although welcomed at first, by early 1818, disillusionment and hostility had become widespread. The branches' policy of demanding specie in payment for the notes of state-chartered banks not only threatened the existence of unsound and mismanaged smaller local banks, but also the Bank of Kentucky, which had branches throughout the state and which was a sound and well-managed institution. So desperate was the situation by the late summer of 1818 that one of the managers at a branch of the Bank of Kentucky observed, "I think it would be proper for all the other Banks in the union to unite, if possible, and assist each other in opposing the illiberal and oppressive, nay ruinous *policy* of that mammoth Bank and her branches."[11]

In early 1818, the Kentucky legislature levied an annual tax of $5,000 on each branch of the 2BUS located within the state. The small amount of the tax indicates that its purpose was mainly to raise revenue, although in the debate over the measure the constitutional issue of the right of a state to levy such a tax was raised. The 2BUS, however, refused to pay the tax, and when the hard times unleashed by the Panic of 1819 swept across the state, many people blamed them on the policies of the 2BUS. There followed widespread agitation for some kind of action. As a consequence, when the legislature reconvened in late 1818, it appointed a special committee to reconsider the tax. It recommended a $5,000 per month (or $60,000 per year) tax on each branch and made it clear that its purpose was to drive the branches from the state. The resulting law also authorized the forcible collection of the tax if the branches refused to pay. It stipulated, in particular, that the state's agent was to have the power "to break and enter any outerdoor, or inside door . . . or any vault, drawer, chest or box, in which money, goods, chattels, rights, credits . . . or other property or effects may be deposited or concealed," as well as to sell the property of the branches to satisfy the tax. It also provided that the tax would not be collected if the 2BUS declared that the branches would be withdrawn within six months.[12]

The 2BUS responded by obtaining an injunction from the U.S. Circuit Court for Kentucky to prevent the state from collecting the tax, and as a result, no attempt was made to collect the tax. Although denounced as an assault upon the sovereign power of the state, it nonetheless was obeyed. When the U.S. Supreme Court handed down its decision in *McCulloch v. Maryland* a short time later, it too came under sharp attack in the newspapers. But the Kentucky Court of Appeals, the highest court in the state, in December 1, 1819, hearing an appeal from a local court that had ruled in favor of the 2BUS's claim that the $5,000 revenue tax adopted in early 1818 was unconstitutional, handed down a lengthy decision in which it argued for the sovereign right of the state to tax the national bank. Nonetheless, by a 2–1 vote, it affirmed the lower court's ruling on the grounds that the U.S. Supreme Court's decision "is decisive of the question in this case, and binding upon this court." It then went on to explain:

> To preserve an uniformity in the operation of the constitution and laws of the United States in every part of the nation it is essential that there should be vested in one tribunal the power of ultimately deciding all question[s] involving their validity or effect, and understanding the supreme court to be vested with that power, and that it has, under the constitution and laws of the United States, appellate jurisdiction in this case, they conceive themselves concluded by its decision.[13]

The dissenting vote was cast by John Rowan, a strong states' rights man and future Jacksonian, who believed in legislative supremacy. He regretted that his fellow judges had not united with him to reverse the lower court's opinion for, in a passionate argument that fully revealed the tension that existed between the state and the U.S. Supreme Court, he indicated it would have

> truly afforded to the appellate court of the nation [the U.S. Supreme Court] an opportunity of reconsidering this very important question. He is unwilling to surrender any portion of the sovereign power of his state upon the first summons. Indeed he is not prepared to say that he should feel himself bound by the repeated decisions of that tribunal to make the surrender. If the nation can, through the agency of congress, usurp the sovereign power of the states, and by its judiciary affirm the

usurpation, the states it would seem to him, ought to be indulged in the remnant privilege of withholding their consent, and thereby indicating that they had some little regard for the sovereignty of which they were disrobed. A prompt acquiescence on their part would seem to invite the nation to repeat and extend its encroachments to the utter annihilation of their sovereignties—but he can not believe that they are under any obligation to become accessories to their own destruction; for he insists that the principles asserted in that decision may be extended to the entire prostration of state power; and therefore protests against its binding influence upon this court. It may be said that an acquiescence in the decisions of the supreme court of the nation, conduces to uniformity of decision and promotes the harmony of the union. That the binding force of the opinions of the appellate tribunal of the nation upon that of the state, in cases like the present, is to be deduced from those beneficial results. He acknowledges the mighty influence which considerations of the sort should have upon the tribunals of both the powers; but he denies that it should actuate either to surrender to the other any essential part of the sovereignty of the government whose functionary it is, and with whose power it has been intrusted [*sic*]. He thinks it can not be surrendered by either to the other—nor can either consent to the diminution or demolition of any of the essential vital function of its government. The taxing power in the sovereign is, in political economy, analogous to the vital fluid in the economy of nature, and is a substance too precious to be so disposed of. It may be said that if a confliction between the state and national governments be continued by the protracted resistance of the judiciary of the former to encroachments of the latter, the consequences may be serious and unpleasant. He replies, let the nation see to that, and retrace its steps. The worst that can happen to the state, in the event of protracted resistance, is, the loss of its sovereignty; and if that is to happen, let it be deferred as long as possible, and be produced by any other than its own agency—let it be wrested from the state, not surrendered by its functionaries.[14]

A few days later, Governor Gabriel Slaughter, a hard-money man, delivered a ringing rallying cry against *McCulloch v. Maryland* and the 2BUS:

I am aware that the supreme court of the nation have declared the law creating this bank constitutional, and have denied to the states the power of taxing it. But much as we reverence the institutions of the national government and respect their incumbents, is it not due to the character of sovereignty, that the states who possess it . . . should assert their right to exercise it, and relinquish it only upon the most thorough conviction, that it has been surrendered by the states to the nation? . . . How far is it compatible with the dignity of the supreme power of the state to be manacled, restrained, or propelled by persons clad with authority to the nation. . . . For if one department of the national government may usurp the sovereignty of the states, and another department consecrate the usurpation by pronouncing it constitutional—then is the tenure of sovereignty by the states a fit subject for derision. The principle that any portion of supreme power must be tamely surrendered by a state, in obedience to a decree made by the usurper . . . can never, it would seem to me, be conceded by a rational people.[15]

Yet in the end, nothing happened. A few laws were passed to help obstruct the operations of the Lexington and Louisville branches by making it difficult for them to collect debts or to use the federal courts for this purpose. But these were quickly reversed by the Kentucky Court of Appeals.[16] Moreover, the Kentucky legislature did not endorse Pennsylvania's proposed amendment to the U.S. Constitution nor the Ohio Resolutions of 1821. As a consequence, the branches of the 2BUS at Lexington and Louisville continued to operate without any effective opposition.

There were probably several reasons that Kentucky did not become, despite its early actions and the heated rhetoric that emanated from the state, a major player in the opposition to *McCulloch v. Maryland*. To begin with, Henry Clay, the state's most influential national politician and a strong supporter of the 2BUS, worked effectively behind the scenes, most likely with John C. Crittenden, his leading protégé in Kentucky at that time, on the local level, to moderate the state's opposition to the decision and to make sure that the state operated only in legal channels. Supporting this approach were the many people who recognized that, if the state were successful in forcing the branches of the 2BUS to shut down, it would have the immediate effect of further aggravating the state's economic difficulties by creating even more pressure for the payment of outstanding debts to the 2BUS while it prepared for removal.[17] According to one observer in Louisville:

> [I]f this office shall be withdrawn and the debtors for public lands shall be required to make payment in currency they cannot obtain, it would work a forfeiture of their Homes and firesides and alienate the affections of the west from and destroy the confidence in their rulers—and might in the end produce insurrections.[18]

There is also a strong possibility that Kentucky chose not to take any kind of extreme action against the U.S. Supreme Court and its *McCulloch* decision because the state had its own case coming up before the High Court which involved issues even more vital to the state's well-being. At stake in *Green v. Biddle* (1821) were the land titles to almost half of the land in Kentucky. The dispute was with Virginia and involved various provisions in the act of separation between the two states. Since the U.S. Constitution in Article III explicitly granted the U.S. Supreme Court original jurisdiction in cases involving two states, it was not possible to deny its authority as had been done with cases coming up under section 25 of the Judiciary Act of 1789, and it simply did not make sense to violate the decision handed down in *McCulloch v. Maryland* and alienate the High Court. Although all of this proved to no avail since the High Court found for Virginia.[19]

The fragmented, uncoordinated, and unfocused nature of the opposition to the 2BUS and *McCulloch v. Maryland*, as well as local circumstances, explains more than anything else why the opposition to the decision did not mount a more effective counterattack during the 1819–1822 years. As a consequence, the decision had a more important impact than might normally have been the case. In particular, it benefited the 2BUS in two very important ways. First, coming as it did when the bank was teetering on the edge of economic collapse because of mismanagement; when it had just been revealed to have violated the provisions of its own charter; when popular opinion had turned sharply against it; and when the underhanded, fraudulent, dishonest, and larcenous operation of the 2BUS in Baltimore under the leadership of its board of directors was about to be revealed, Marshall's decision in *McCulloch v. Maryland* helped to prop up the 2BUS and gave it a degree of respectability that both led to an increase in the value of its stock and contributed in an important way to its survival.[20]

Second, the U.S. Supreme Court's ruling in *McCulloch v. Maryland* set a very important precedent for the lower federal and state courts to follow. For while some state judges criticized the decision, no court, even in Ohio where the most extreme opposition to *McCulloch v. Maryland* took place, attempted to deny its binding quality. Official opposition to *McCulloch v. Maryland* came exclusively from the legislative and executive branches. Moreover, in the important states of Pennsylvania and Kentucky, the effect of *McCulloch v. Maryland* was to short-circuit any direct opposition to the branches of the 2BUS and to force the opposition to adopt less direct methods, which turned out to be ineffective.

II

As the 1820s wore on, other developments helped to alleviate some of the tensions over the 2BUS that had been uncovered by the difficulties associated with the Panic of 1819. In 1823, Nicholas Biddle replaced Langdon Cheves as president of the 2BUS. Cheves had been unremitting in his demands for specie without any regard for its impact on the operations of the state banks or the pressure it placed on people who had to repay their bank loans. Biddle, who had the luxury of taking over just as the hard times were bottoming out, generally softened the policies of the 2BUS and worked hard to conciliate the state banking interests. Also, after 1823, other issues such as a protective tariff, the election of 1824, and the Jacksonian campaign to capture the presidency in 1828, which began in 1825, overshadowed the role of the 2BUS and the U.S. Supreme

Court. It also helped that, during the latter half of the 1820s, the Supreme Court did not hand down any truly controversial decisions and that two of its most vociferous critics, Spencer Roane and John Taylor, died in 1822.

Criticism of the 2BUS may have ameliorated somewhat in the late 1820s, but there is nothing to indicate that most of the people opposed to *McCulloch v. Maryland* were in any sense reconciled to the various principles enunciated by Marshall, for states' rights thought continued to be on the rise throughout the decade. During this time, various unsuccessful attempts were made in Congress to reduce the powers of the federal judiciary and to make sure that states, rather than the U.S. Supreme Court, would be the final arbiter in disputes between the states and the federal government. There was a movement to repeal section 25 of the Judiciary Act of 1789, to increase the size of the Supreme Court, and to require that more than a bare majority decision by the High Court would be needed to declare a state law unconstitutional. In addition, an amendment to the U.S. Constitution was proposed to make the U.S. Senate, whose members were elected by state legislatures at that time, a final court of appeals to determine disputes between the states and the nation.[21]

Then, in 1828, Jackson was elected president. Jackson's popularity at this time stemmed mainly from his fame as a successful military leader who had defeated the Creeks in the Old Southwest, the British in the Battle of New Orleans, and the Seminoles in Florida. Although Jackson's stand on most issues was vague and unclear in 1828, his opponent, incumbent president John Quincy Adams, was an extreme nationalist who had vigorously supported the nationalist decisions of the Supreme Court, the rights of Indians as opposed to the states in which they resided, and a federal program of internal improvements without an amendment to the U.S. Constitution. This alienated the advocates of states' rights, who flocked to Jackson's banner. As Thomas Ritchie put it in 1827: "the coming election will be the crisis of our Constitution. Principles will then be fixed which will cast their shadows, or their lights, upon years to come."[22]

As President Jackson argued, the will of the people, majority rule, a strict interpretation of the Constitution, and states' rights were inextricably intertwined. His objective was to dismantle the program of the nationalist wing of the Jeffersonian Republicans, which became known as the American system. He and his supporters effectively opposed a federal program of internal improvements on constitutional and policy grounds, eventually lowered the tariff, and abandoned any commitment to protection. Jackson also opposed nullification not because he was a nationalist but because it converted states' rights into a doctrine to protect minority interests and threatened the future of the union by legitimizing the concept of secession. Because of his belief in majority rule and states' rights, Jackson was wary of the Supreme Court, whose members held their offices for life tenure during good behavior. He also refused to recognize the U.S. Supreme Court as either the exclusive or final arbiter in constitutional disputes that took place over national legislation or in disputes between the federal government and the states. Jackson's greatest influence on the role of the U.S. Supreme Court occurred as a consequence of his appointment power, which included more members of the High Court than any president since George Washington. All of them were unsympathetic to the broad constructionist and nationalist decisions of the Marshall Court, and during the next several decades they helped to shift the Supreme Court in a strong states' rights direction.[23]

III

It was on the question of the 2BUS that Jackson's states' rights beliefs manifested themselves with particular clarity. The 2BUS was coming up for rechartering in 1836; Jackson refused to support it, and he articulated his opposition in terms that found their roots in the arguments used by the opponents of *McCulloch v. Maryland*. At bottom, the struggle was a constitutional one, and it pitted the greatest decision of our greatest chief justice against what is arguably the most important veto ever issued by a president of the United States.

At the beginning of his second term as president of the United States, Jackson had noted, "Everyone that knows me does know, that I have always been opposed to the United States Bank, Nay all Banks."[24] Jackson's hostility toward banks stemmed from several sources: from his own business dealings during the 1790s when he accepted a promissory note from a merchant who went bankrupt, causing him to have to work for years to make good on the debts that ensued; from his hostility toward the growth of irresponsible banking institutions, which proliferated during the second decade of the nineteenth century; and from his opposition to various paper money relief measures that were proposed in Tennessee during the depression that followed the Panic of 1819. To be sure, Jackson was not against people making money, but he believed they should earn it through hard work and frugality. Because bank profits came from interest earned on loans, Jackson believed that banks benefited unnaturally from the industry of others. Further, by their liberal loan policies, banks encouraged speculation, extravagance, and the pursuit of luxury. When numerous banks failed or got into trouble like the 2BUS during the Panic of 1819, various investigations revealed the political machinations and corrupt activities that had led to the granting and implementation of their charters, as well as the unfair and exploitative manner in which many banks had been managed. Thus, when numerous banks suspended specie payments on their notes during the Panic of 1819, the notes depreciated sharply, leaving those holding them to deal with the losses, while at the same time the same banks foreclosed on the property of debtors; paid dividends to stockholders; gave special dispensations to their officers, members of their boards of directors, and political allies who owed them money; and bought up their own notes at sharply discounted prices.[25]

For Jackson, the 2BUS was the largest, most powerful, and most dangerous of all banks. He believed, in addition, that the 2BUS had used its great influence to oppose him during the election of 1828 by supporting his opponents financially. Shortly after Jackson assumed the presidency, word went out that he would oppose the rechartering of the 2BUS, at least in its current form, but not all of Jackson's political advisors shared his feelings about the 2BUS. They emphasized, in particular, the services the bank provided as the government's fiscal agent in maintaining a sound and uniform currency and in checking the instability of many state banks. Some also believed that it would be politically risky for the president to engage in a confrontation with the 2BUS.[26]

This opposition forced Jackson to be cautious. Moreover, he also seemed to recognize that, by the time of his inauguration in 1829, the 2BUS had, under the leadership of Nicholas Biddle, shed much of the unpopularity it had acquired from its role in the Panic of 1819. In fact, under Biddle's leadership, it had become well respected and even popular in some quarters. None of this convinced Jackson to abandon his objections, but it did make him wary about launching a frontal assault on the bank. Nonetheless, he was determined to bring the issue before Congress, so in his first annual address he indicated:

> The charter of the Bank of the United States expires in 1836, and its stockholders will most probably apply for a renewal of their privileges. In order to avoid the evils resulting from precipitancy in a measure involving such important principles and such deep pecuniary interest, I feel that I cannot in justice to the parties interested, too soon present it to the deliberate consideration of the Legislature and the people. Both the constitutionality and the expediency of the law creating this bank are well questioned by a large portion of our fellow citizens. . . . if such an institution is deemed essential to the fiscal operations of the Government, I submit to the wisdom of the Legislature whether a national one, founded upon the credit of the Government and its revenue might not be devised which would avoid all constitutional difficulties, and at the same time secure all the advantages to the Government and the country that were expected to result from the present bank.[27]

At least at the beginning of his presidency, Jackson recognized that a direct assault on the 2BUS could be very divisive. He also seemed to recognize that, if he managed to destroy the bank, he would have to replace it with some other kind of institution or risk financial disorder and other serious economic consequences. Jackson, therefore, in the early years of his first term appears to have been willing to accept some kind of national institution if it could be made to be constitutionally acceptable. Therefore, most of his private remarks on the bank in 1829, 1830, and 1831 did not deal with the social, moral, and economic issues associated with the 2BUS and banking in general, but on the more focused issues of its constitutionality and political acceptability. Alarmed by Jackson's hostility toward the 2BUS, Biddle visited Jackson to discuss the problem. At that meeting, Jackson indicated that he understood the value of the bank, but then significantly added: "I think it right to be perfectly frank with you. I do not think that the power of Congress extends to charter a Bank out of the ten mile square [the District of Columbia]. . . . I have read the opinion of John Marshall [in *McCulloch v. Maryland*] . . . and could not agree with him."[28]

It is hard to say for sure exactly what kind of national bank Jackson would have found constitutionally acceptable, for he probably never fully made up his mind on the subject. Basically, he wanted a bank located only in the District of Columbia and under the exclusive control of the Treasury Department, acting only as the federal government's fiscal agent. The problem with this, however, was that it would not be as useful as a national bank that had branches throughout the country. Moreover, Jackson never fully came to grips with the complicated constitutional question of what kind of control the states would have over branches within their boundaries and whether the states could be required to accept a branch if they did not want one, although he probably favored the rights of the states. In addition, he wanted control of the bank and its profits to be entirely in the hands of the federal government, and he opposed having stock in the bank sold to private investors. Further, he believed it should be a bank of deposit, which would hold and transfer the government's money, but not one which would make loans and investments, sell stock, or pay dividends. Nor did he believe a national bank should create money, except in emergency situations such as a war.[29]

In his second annual message to Congress in December 1830, Jackson publicly expressed his feelings on the 2BUS:

> Nothing has occurred to lessen in any degree the dangers which many of our citizens apprehend from the institution as at present organized. In the spirit of improvement and compromise which distinguishes our country and its institutions it becomes us to inquire whether it be not possible to secure the advantages afforded by the present bank through the agency of a Bank of the United States so modified in its principles and structures as to obviate Constitutional and other objections.

It is thought practicable to organize such a bank with the necessary officers as a branch of the Treasury Department, based on the public and individual deposits, without power to make loans or purchase property, which shall remit the funds of the Government, and the expense of which may be paid, if thought advisable, by allowing its officers to sell bills of exchange to private individuals at a moderate premium. Not being a corporate body, having no stockholders, debtors or property, and but few officers, it would not be obnoxious to the constitutional objections which are urged against the present bank; and having no means to operate on the hopes, fears, or interests of large masses of the community, it would be shorn of the influence which makes that bank formidable. The States would be strengthened by having in their hands the means of furnishing the local paper currency through their own banks, while the Bank of the United States, though issuing no paper, would check the issues of the State banks by taking their notes in deposit and for exchange only so long as they continue to be redeemed with specie. In times of public emergency the capacities of such an institution might be enlarged by legislative provision.[30]

Although Jackson clearly had strong feelings about the 2BUS, he also realized that he might not be able to get his way on it. When he introduced his remarks on the 2BUS in December 1830, he referred to "the spirit of improvement and compromise which distinguishes our country," and he concluded his remarks by observing:

These suggestions are made not so much as a recommendation as with a view of calling the attention of Congress to the possible modifications of a system which cannot continue to exist in its present form without occasional collisions with the local authorities and perpetual apprehensions and discontents on the part of the States and the people.[31]

At this point, Jackson seems to have been torn between his antipathy to the 2BUS and his recognition that, under Biddle's leadership, it was running smoothly and performing valuable and indispensable services for the federal government. He undoubtedly was aware that the United States had suffered financial chaos between 1811 and 1816, when there had been no national bank, and that state banks had proliferated and many had acted irresponsibly during those years. Jackson did not like banks, but he understood that they were here to stay and that some kind of national bank was needed to control and regulate their existence.

Biddle recognized that Jackson's advisors were split on the bank. As he saw it, Jackson's formal cabinet, the one he appointed in 1831, was favorably disposed to rechartering the 2BUS, while his informal advisors were against it. All of this confused Biddle and made him very nervous. "What I have always dreaded about this new cabinet," Biddle observed, "was that the kitchen would predominate over the parlor." He was essentially correct, for privately Jackson denied he "had changed [his] views of the Bank of the United States" and continued to view it as unconstitutional and inexpedient. Jackson also wrote that support for the bank from within the cabinet "springs from convictions much more favorable than mine of the general character and conduct of this institution." Jackson may have been willing to accept a national bank of some kind, but it would have to be stripped "of the constitutional objections by the Executive."[32] This probably meant he would refuse to give his assent to one where private interests held stock and that made private loans, and he would have required that it only have branches with the permission of the states where they were to be located. These were substantial changes, and any one of them would have drastically altered the 2BUS as it then existed.

On the other hand, in 1831, Jackson was eager to have the national debt paid off by early 1833. He hoped to be able to announce this accomplishment either on the anniversary of his famous victory at New Orleans on January 8, 1833, or failing this, in time for his second inauguration on March 4, 1833. To do this, he would need the cooperation of the 2BUS. Moreover, by this time, it was clear that Jackson had decided to seek reelection, and he wanted to keep the bank issue out of the campaign. Therefore, once again, he backed off from an open fight with the 2BUS.

At this point, Biddle made an understandable but fateful decision. He decided to openly ally the bank with Henry Clay and Daniel

Webster, two of Jackson's most important political enemies. Clay was going to be Jackson's opponent in the upcoming presidential election and was willing to make rechartering the bank a major issue; therefore, he and Webster favored an early rechartering. Their strategy was simple. They expected to have no trouble getting Congress to approve a bill extending the charter of the 2BUS, and since Jackson was concerned about the effect of the issue on his reelection bid, there even existed a small chance that he might sign it. If not, as seemed probable, and if he chose to veto it, then it would be made a major issue in the election. There was also an expectation that the issue would have an impact on the congressional election in such a way as to ensure the bank a two-thirds majority to override the veto at the following session.[33]

This development infuriated Jackson. When Congress passed a bill rechartering the 2BUS, with only minor modifications, Jackson vetoed it on July 10, 1832. The message, written by Amos Kendall and Roger Brooke Taney, is one of the most important in the history of the presidency. It was directed not only at Congress, but also at the people of the United States. In it, Jackson emphasized that the 2BUS was essentially a privately controlled, profit-making institution. He argued that the bill granted various special privileges and a monopoly in the handling of the federal government's money to an institution dominated by stockholders from the private sector of the economy. The substantial earnings that resulted from this "special favor of the government" went to people whom Jackson variously described as "opulent citizens," "chiefly of the richest class," "a designated and favored class of men," and "a privileged order." The 2BUS was, according to the president, "an interest separate from that of the people" and created "a concentration of power in the hands of a few men" beyond the control of the people or the government. He admitted that it provided important services for the federal government, but once it received its charter, it was no longer a part of the government.[34]

For the most part, Jackson's message stressed constitutional considerations, and the arguments he used were clearly meant to be a response to the Supreme Court's decision in *McCulloch v. Maryland*, and they had their roots in the various criticisms that the decision had provoked. He began his veto message by indicating that he was "deeply

impressed with the belief that some of the powers and privileges possessed by the existing bank are unauthorized by the Constitution, sub-
versive of the rights of the states, and dangerous to the liberties of the
people." He was vetoing the bill to recharter the 2BUS because its provisions were not adequate "in my opinion to make it compatible with
justice, with sound policy, or with the Constitution of our country."[35] In
confronting the constitutionality of the 2BUS, Jackson rejected the idea
that the matter had been settled either by precedent or the Supreme
Court. "Mere precedent," he asserted, "is a dangerous source of authority, and should not be regarded as deciding questions of constitutional
power except where the acquiescences of the people and the states can
be considered well settled." While it was true that Congress had passed
laws in favor of a national bank in 1791 and 1816, he pointed out that
bank bills had failed to pass in 1811 and 1815.[36]

As for the U.S. Supreme Court, Jackson forcefully argued against
the claim of judicial supremacy, made by nationalists, which asserted
that the High Court was the final arbiter of constitutional disputes:

> If the opinion of the Supreme Court covered the whole ground
> of this act, it ought not to control the coordinate authorities of
> this Government. The Congress, the Executive, and the Court
> must each for itself be guided by its own opinion of the
> Constitution. Each public officer who takes an oath to support
> the Constitution swears that he will support it as he understands
> it, and not as it is understood by others. It is as much the duty
> of the House of Representatives, of the Senate, and of the
> President to decide upon the constitutionality of any bill or res-
> olution which may be presented to them for passage or approval
> as it is of the Supreme Judges when it may be brought before
> them for judicial decision. The opinion of the judges has no
> more authority over Congress than the opinion of Congress has
> over the judges, and on that point the President is independent
> of both. The authority of the Supreme Court must not, there-
> fore, be permitted to control the Congress or the Executive
> when acting in their legislative capacities, but to only have such
> influence as the force of their reasoning may deserve.[37]

In other parts of his veto message, Jackson focused on additional aspects of the constitutional issues that had been raised in *McCulloch v. Maryland*. He opposed a liberal interpretation of the Constitution and the misuse of the necessary and proper clause as "a palpable attempt to amend the Constitution by an act of legislation." He criticized the new bill rechartering the 2BUS for granting it the power to establish up to two branches in any state regardless of whether the state wanted a branch or not, as well as the denial, on the part of the 2BUS, of the right of the states to tax the activities of its branches, even at the same rate they taxed their own banks. To buttress his argument Jackson pointed out that although the U.S. Constitution granted the federal government the power to purchase lands for the purpose of erecting "forts, magazines, arsenals, dockyards, and other needful buildings," it required the "consent of the legislature of the state in which they were to be constructed." But that the 2BUS was not required to do this, thereby indicating it has even greater power than the federal government. In the course of making these points, he reiterated the widely held belief that the 2BUS was not a government institution, but essentially a private one, operated for profit and controlled by private interests, that at best performed certain useful functions for the federal government.[38]

Jackson linked all of this to his basic social and political philosophy:

It is to be regretted that the rich and powerful too often bend the acts of government to their selfish purposes. Distinctions in society will always exist under every just government. Equality of talents, of education, or of wealth cannot be produced by human institutions. In the full enjoyment of the gifts of Heaven and the fruits of superior industry, economy and virtue, every man is equally entitled to protection by the law; but when the laws undertake to add to these natural and just advantages artificial distinctions, to grant titles, gratuities, and exclusive privileges, to make the rich richer and the potent more powerful, the humble members of society—the farmers, mechanics and laborers—who have neither the time nor the means of securing like favors to themselves, have a right to complain of the injustice of their

Government. There are no necessary evils in government. Its evils exist only in its abuses. If it would confine itself to equal protection, and, as Heaven does it[s] rains, shower its favors alike on the high and low, the rich and the poor, it would be an unqualified blessing. In the act before me there seems to be a wide and unnecessary departure from these just principles.[39]

Having made these important points, Jackson returned to the constitutional issues involved in his decision to veto the rechartering of the 2BUS:

Nor is our Government to be maintained or our Union preserved by invasions of the rights and powers of the several states. In thus attempting to make our General Government strong we make it weak. Its true strength consists in leaving individuals and states as much as possible to themselves—in making itself felt, not in its power, but in its beneficence; not in its control, but in its protection; not in binding the states more closely to the center, but leaving each to move unobstructed in its proper orbit.[40]

Jackson's veto of the rechartering of the 2BUS became the central issue in the election of 1832. His attack on the bank, his opponents claimed, would wreck the economy and destabilize the currency. Henry Clay led the opposition and, with the underwriting of the 2BUS, distributed copies of the veto message which, they argued, revealed Jackson's numerous prejudices and limitations in dealing with economic issues. But this turned out to be a serious mistake, for Jackson's veto message was an extremely popular and effective campaign document for the president. The result of the election was an unambiguous victory for Jackson as he carried a clear majority of both the popular and electoral votes. The president interpreted his decisive victory as a popular mandate to move immediately against the 2BUS rather than wait until its charter expired in 1836. He resolved to sever all ties between the federal government and the 2BUS, by not depositing any more government funds in it and spending what government funds it continued to hold, using in its place a number of carefully selected state-chartered institutions, which became known as "pet banks." While this policy was controversial and problematic, it soon became clear that the 2BUS was finished. It received a charter from the state of Pennsylvania in 1836, and, while it continued to do business until 1841, it came to an ignominious end when it went bankrupt as a result of the Panic of 1837 and the hard times that followed.[41]

The Jacksonians not only destroyed the 2BUS, but they also effectively killed off the American system, which the nationalist wing of the Jeffersonian coalition had initiated in 1816 and which the Whig party unsuccessfully strived to revive in the 1830s and 1840s.

Other important aspects of Marshall's opinion in the *McCulloch* and *Osborn* cases have also not fared well in the overall legal and constitutional development of the United States. National, privately controlled, profit-making corporations have not been the rule. Almost all private profit-making corporations have been state based. The only exceptions—Fannie Mae, Freddie Mac, and Sallie Mae—were not created until well into the twentieth century, and then only because they serviced specific programs of the federal government. The establishment of the Federal Reserve Bank in 1913 created a central bank, but it is not under private control nor does it sell stock or pay dividends. (Ironically, the U.S. Supreme Court cited *McCulloch* to uphold its constitutionality.) Further, Marshall's attempt to limit the meaning of the Eleventh Amendment by limiting it only to states if they were part of the record has also been overturned.

IV

Why then has *McCulloch v. Maryland* been a case of such enduring significance, especially since so much of Marshall's opinion, as we have seen, was not relevant to the real issues involved in the case? The answer lies in the broad principles laid down in his long *obiter dicta*. The opinion has served as a beacon for those who believe in a strong and active federal government by providing a broad interpretation of the powers granted, especially to Congress, by the U.S. Constitution, and by circumscribing the meaning of the Tenth Amendment's reserving to the states those powers not specifically granted to the federal government.

In short, it has served as a rationale for the development of a jurisprudence of nationalism by the U.S. Supreme Court. Particularly important in this regard was Marshall's claim that the U.S. Constitution emanated not from the states but from the sovereign people, a concept that is the central tenet of constitutional nationalism. Equally significant is the sharp distinction Marshall drew between a constitution which has to contain broad generalizations so that it can be adaptable to the various exigencies with which a nation will have to deal if it is going to adapt and survive as opposed to a law or code, which should be more narrowly interpreted. Marshall's assertion that "we must never forget that it is a constitution we are expounding," Justice Felix Frankfurter asserted over a hundred years later, "bears repeating because it is, I believe, the single most significant utterance in the literature of constitutional law—most important because most comprehensive and comprehending." Finally, Marshall's decision asserted in no uncertain terms the supremacy of federal law over state law. These are among the most enduring principles of American constitutional law, and it has mattered not that they were applied to the wrong case.[42]

Yet the dominance of these principles has not come easily. The states' rights revolution wrought by Jackson's election to the presidency in 1828 was continued by his successors—Martin Van Buren, James K. Polk, Franklin Pierce, and James Buchanan—who dominated the presidency right up to the eve of the Civil War. At the same time, starting in the late 1820s, there emerged a new strain of states' rights thought, one that stressed the protection of minority rights and the doctrine of secession and that was at the heart of the defense of slavery during the middle of the nineteenth century.

The election of Abraham Lincoln in 1860 and the fighting of the Civil War had a major centralizing effect on American constitutional thought. This was further buttressed by the passage of the Thirteenth, Fourteenth, and Fifteenth amendments. Nonetheless, the concept of federalism was embedded in the U.S. Constitution and remained a source of continued controversy. Moreover, the growth of big business and finance capitalism and the spread of interstate commerce, which had deep roots in the antebellum period, now began to dominate the country's economic existence. This in turn raised a broad variety of political, constitutional, and ideological considerations. Increasingly, different interests participating in the ever-accelerating national economy lobbied for uniform laws that would override the diversity of legal rules on the local level and eliminate state-based attempts to regulate their activities. At the same time, various attempts were made to regulate the economy through national legislation. The major division was between those who were advocates of laissez-faire and those who favored asserting some kind of governmental control—state and federal— over the activities of big business. On most economic issues, the U.S. Supreme Court sided with big business against labor unions, consumers, and farmers, often, though not always, basing its rulings on states' rights considerations, which were made acceptable to many because this concept no longer implied a threat to the union. During this same time, the U.S. Supreme Court adopted a states' rights, or "dual federalism," posture that allowed whites in the South to deny blacks their civil rights.

All of this changed with the coming of the New Deal. The hard times and mood of desperation that characterized the Great Depression that began in 1929 created a broad-based demand for action on the part of the national government. Following Franklin Delano Roosevelt's election to the presidency in 1932, the federal government, in a seismic assumption of power, created a broad variety of regulatory agencies and instituted a number of social programs. At first, this was resisted by the U.S. Supreme Court, which declared much of this activity to be unconstitutional, but following widespread popular clamor and Roosevelt's threat to increase the size of the Supreme Court and to pack it with justices sympathetic to his New Deal programs, the High Court reversed itself and allowed the legislation to stand. History at this point, it seems, was on John Marshall's side, and his opinion in *McCulloch v. Maryland*, along with his expansive definition of the commerce clause in *Gibbons v. Ogden* (1824), became the key precedents for a vigorous and active federal government. This trend was strengthened even further by the centralizing tendencies of World War II and the civil rights cases and enforcement legislation of the 1950s and 1960s, which, among other things, placed under federal scrutiny various institutions that had traditionally been local concerns. Basically, it is changing social and political realities combined with altered ideological views of the legitimate role of the federal government's authority that have given many of the arguments contained in *McCulloch v. Maryland* an appeal and legitimacy that they did not have when the decision was handed down in 1819.

Yet the constitutional revolution that took place during the era of the New Deal has not been able to permanently minimize the rights of the states under the U.S. Constitution. In more recent years, the Burger and Rehnquist courts have moved to curtail the powers of the central government that had been so greatly expanded in the 1933–1970 period. The swing in the pendulum back in the direction of states' rights in part is to be explained by the belief that it is simply more efficient to administer various programs on the local level, but it is also clear that while the compact theory of the origins and nature of the union and the concept of secession have been permanently rejected, the state governments remain a separate, integral, and permanent part of the American system of government. Since the distribution of power between the national and state governments is not clearly defined in the U.S. Constitution, it continues to remain a lively and constant source of contention, subject to the changing ideological and political realities of the times when it becomes an issue. John Adams, writing in 1808, probably got it right when he noted, "I have always called our Constitution a game at leapfrog."[43]

NOTES

INTRODUCTION

1. Jacob E. Cooke (ed.), *The Federalist* (Middleton, Conn., 1961), 257. For other treatments of state power under the U.S. Constitution, see also *Federalist*, Nos. 45 and 46.

2. The best general treatments of the U.S. Supreme Court are Charles Warren, *The Supreme Court in United States History*, 2 vols. (Boston, 1926); Charles G. Haines, *The Role of the Supreme Court in American Government and Politics, 1789–1835* (New York, 1960); G. Edward White (with Gerald Gunther), *The Marshall Court and Cultural Change, 1815–1835* (New York, 1988).

   Standard biographies of John Marshall are Albert Beveridge, *The Life of John Marshall*, 4 vols. (Boston, 1916–1919); Jean Edward Smith, *John Marshall: Definer of a Nation* (New York, 1996); Charles Hobson, *The Great Chief Justice: John Marshall and the Rule of Law* (Lawrence, Kans., 1996); Herbert A. Johnson, *The Chief Justiceship of John Marshall, 1801–1835* (Columbia, S.C., 1997); R. Kent Newmyer, *John Marshall and the Heroic Age of the Supreme Court* (Baton Rouge, La., 2001).

   For a recent treatment of the case, see Daniel A. Farber, "The Story of McCulloch: Banking on National Power," in Michael C. Dorf (ed.), *Foundation Press: Constitutional Law Stories* (New York, 2004), 34–67.

3. Important exceptions here are Harold J. Plous and Gordon E. Baker, "McCulloch v. Maryland: Right Principle, Wrong Case," *Stanford Law Review* 9 (1957), 710–39; George Dangerfield, *The Awakening of American Nationalism, 1815–1828* (New York, 1965), 89–96. Also of considerable value is Gerald Gunther (ed.), *John Marshall's Defense of McCulloch v. Maryland* (Palo Alto, Calif., 1969).

4. For example, see Bray Hammond, "The Bank Cases," in John A. Garraty (ed.), *Quarrels That Shaped the Constitution* (New York, 1962), 30–48.

5. The path-breaking work is Charles Sellers, *The Market Revolution: Jacksonian America, 1815–1846* (New York, 1991). See also Harry

L. Watson, *Liberty and Power: The Politics of Jacksonian America* (New York, 1990); Richard E. Ellis, "The Market Revolution and the Transformation of American Politics, 1801–1837," in Melvyn Stokes and Stephen Conway (eds.), *The Market Revolution in America* (Charlottesville, Va., 1996), 149–76. For an intemperate critique of the concept, see William E. Gienapp, "The Myth of Class in Jacksonian America," *Journal of Policy History* 6 (1994), 232–59.

6. Marvin Meyers, *The Jacksonian Persuasion: Politics and Belief* (Palo Alto, Calif., 1960), 13.

CHAPTER 1

1. Donald R. Hickey, *The War of 1812: A Forgotten Conflict* (Urbana, Ill., 1989); J. C. A. Stagg, *Mr. Madison's War: Politics, Diplomacy, and Warfare in the Early American Republic, 1783–1820* (Princeton, N.J., 1983); Richard Buel, Jr., *America on the Brink: How the Political Struggle over the War of 1812 Almost Destroyed the Young Republic* (New York, 2005); Henry Adams, *A History of the United States of America during the Administrations of Thomas Jefferson and James Madison*, 2 vols. (New York, 1986), 2:446–1184.

2. Albert Gallatin to Matthew Lyon, 7 May 1816, in Henry Adams (ed.), *The Writings of Albert Gallatin*, 3 vols. (Philadelphia, 1879), 1:700.

3. Joseph Story to Nathaniel Williams, 22 February 1815, in W. W. Story (ed.), *Life and Letters of Joseph Story*, 2 vols. (Boston, 1851), 1:254.

4. Charles Warren, "New Light on the History of the Federal Judiciary Act of 1789," *Harvard Law Review* 37 (1923), 49–132; Wythe Holt, "To Establish Justice: Politics, the Judiciary Act of 1789 and the Invention of the Federal Courts," *Duke Law Journal* (1989), 1422–1531; Wilfred J. Ritz (Wythe Holt and L. H. LaRue [eds.]), *Rewriting the History of the Judiciary Act of 1789: Exposing Myths, Challenging Premises, and Using New Evidence* (Norman, Okla., 1990); Maeva Marcus (ed.), *Origins of the Federal Judiciary: Essays on the Judiciary Act of 1789* (New York, 1992).

5. Max Farrand (ed.), *The Records of the Federal Convention of 1787*, 4 vols. (New Haven, Conn., 1937), 1:21; Charles Hobson, "The Negative on State Laws: James Madison, the Constitution, and the Crisis of Republican Government," *William and Mary Quarterly* 36 (April 1979), 215–35.

6. *Statutes at Large of the United States of America, 1789–1873*, 17 vols. (Washington, D.C., 1850–1873), 1:85–87.

7. Doyle Mathis, "*Chisholm v. Georgia*: Background and Settlement," *Journal of American History* 54 (1967), 19–29; William R. Casto, *The Supreme*

Court in the Early Republic: The Chief Justiceships of John Jay and Oliver Ellsworth (Columbia, Mo., 1995), 188–202.

8. Casto, *The Supreme Court in the Early Republic*, 98–101.

9. The best treatment of Antifederalism is still Jackson T. Main, *The Antifederalists: Critics of the Constitution, 1781–88* (Chapel Hill, N.C., 1961), and Main, *Political Parties before the United States Constitution* (Chapel Hill, N.C., 1973). More recent works on the Antifederalists include Saul Cornell, *The Other Founders: Anti-Federalism and the Dissenting Tradition in America, 1788–1828* (Chapel Hill, N.C., 1999); David J. Siemers, *Ratifying the Republic: Antifederalists and Federalists in Constitutional Time* (Stanford, Calif., 2002).

10. I have examined this dimension of states' rights more fully in Ellis, *The Union at Risk: Jacksonian Democracy, States' Rights and the Nullification Crisis* (New York, 1987).

11. Helen E. Veit et al., *Creating the Bill of Rights: The Documentary Record from the First Federal Congress* (Baltimore, Md., 1991), 11–28.

12. Ibid.

13. Ibid., 55–213. See also Kenneth Bowling, "'A Tub to the Whale': The Founding Fathers and the Adoption of the Federal Bill of Rights," *Journal of the Early Republic* 8 (1988), 223–51; Richard E. Ellis, "The Persistence of Antifederalism after 1789," in Richard Beeman et al. (eds.), *Beyond Confederation: Origins of the Constitution and American National Identity* (Chapel Hill, N.C., 1987), 295–314.

14. William W. Hening, *The Statutes at Large; Being a Collection of All the Laws of Virginia from the First Session of the Legislature, in Year 1619*, 13 vols. (1819–1823; reprint edition, Charlottesville, Va., 1969), 13:234–39; Herman V. Ames (ed.), *State Documents on Federal Relations: The States and the United States* (1900–1906; reprint edition, New York, 1970), 4–7.

15. William Watkins, Jr., *Reclaiming the American Revolution: The Kentucky and Virginia Resolutions and Their Legacy* (New York, 2004); Adrienne Koch and Harry Ammon, "The Virginia and Kentucky Resolutions: An Episode in Jefferson's and Madison's Defense of Civil Liberties," *William and Mary Quarterly* 5 (1948), 145–76. For an excellent treatment of politics during the 1790s, see J. Roger Sharp, *American Politics in the Early Republic: The New Nation in Crisis* (New Haven, Conn., 1993); also useful is Stanley Elkins and Eric McKitrick, *The Age of Federalism: The Early American Republic, 1788–1800* (New York, 2003).

16. Watkins, *Reclaiming the American Revolution*, 165–77.

17. On the election of 1800, see Susan Dunn, *Jefferson's Second Revolution: The Election Crisis of 1800 and the Triumph of Republicanism* (Boston, 2004); John Ferling, *Adams vs. Jefferson: The Tumultuous Election of 1800* (New York, 2004); Bernard A. Weisberger, *America Afire: Jefferson, Adams and the Revolutionary Election of 1800* (New York, 2000); H. Jefferson Powell, "The Principles of '98: An Essay in Historical Retrieval," *Virginia Law Review* 80 (April 1994), 689–743.

18. Richard E. Ellis, *The Jeffersonian Crisis: Courts and Politics in the Young Republic* (New York, 1971), 19–95; Richard Hofstadter, *The Idea of a Party System: The Rise of Legitimate Opposition in the United States, 1780–1840* (Berkeley, Calif., 1969), 122–69.

19. Ellis, *The Jeffersonian Crisis*, 53–68; William E. Nelson, *Marbury v. Madison: The Origins and Legacy of Judicial Review* (Lawrence, Kans., 2000).

20. Richard E. Ellis, "The Impeachment of Samuel Chase," in Michael R. Belknap (ed.), *American Political Trials* (Westport, Conn., 1994), 52–76; Dumas Malone, *Jefferson the President: The Second Term, 1805–1809* (Boston, 1974), 291–371.

21. Harry Ammon, "James Monroe and the Election of 1808 in Virginia," *William and Mary Quarterly* 20 (1963), 33–56.

22. M. Ruth Kelly, *The Olmstead Case: Privateers, Property, and Politics in Pennsylvania, 1778–1810* (Cranbury, Pa., 2005), chapters 1 and 2; Henry J. Bourguignon, *The First Federal Appellate Prize Court of the American Revolution, 1775–1787* (Philadelphia, 1977), 101–34; Kenneth W. Treacy, "The Olmstead Case, 1778–1809," *Western Political Quarterly* 10 (1957), 675–91; Gary D. Rose, "Constitutionalism in the Streets," *University of Southern California Law Review* 78 (2005), 401–56.

23. Dwight Wiley Jessup, *Reaction and Accommodation: The Supreme Court and Political Conflict, 1809–1835* (New York, 1987), 140–48; Kelly, *The Olmstead Case*, chapters 3 and 4; Sanford Higginbotham, *The Keystone in the Democratic Arch, 1800–1816* (Harrisburg, Pa., 1952), 177–204.

24. 5 Cranch 136.

25. Simon Snyder to James Madison, 6 April 1809, in Robert A. Rutland et al. (eds.), *The Papers of James Madison: Presidential Series*, 4 vols. (Charlottesville, Va., 1984–), 1:105; James Madison to Simon Snyder, 13 April 1809, in ibid., 114.

26. Kelly, *The Olmstead Case*, chapter 5.

27. C. Peter Magrath, *Yazoo: Law and Politics in the New Republic: The Case of Fletcher v. Peck* (Providence, R.I., 1966), 1–49; Ellis, *The Jeffersonian Crisis*, 83–95.

28. *Fletcher v. Peck*, 6 Cranch 87 (1810); Magrath, *Yazoo*, 85–101.

29. Jessup, *Reaction and Accommodation*, 156–59.

30. F. Thornton Miller, *Juries and Judges versus the Law: Virginia's Provincial Legal Perspective, 1783–1828* (Charlottesville, Va., 1994), 74–86; John A. Treon, "Martin v. Hunter's Lessee: A Case Study" (Ph.D. diss., University of Virginia, 1970).

31. "Editorial Note on Fairfax Lands," in Charles Cullen and Herbert A. Johnson (eds.), *The Papers of John Marshall* (Chapel Hill, 1977), 2:140–49; "Articles of Agreement," 1 February 1793, in ibid., 149–56.

32. 1 Munford 218 (1809).

33. 7 Cranch 602 (1813).

34. *Hunter v. Martin, Devisees of Fairfax*, 4 Munford 1 (1814).

35. Ibid., 26.

36. Joseph Story to George Ticknor, 22 January 1831, in Story (ed.), *Life and Letters of Joseph Story*, 2:48–49.

37. 1 Wheaton 304 (1816).

CHAPTER 2

1. Bray Hammond, *Banks and Politics in America from the Revolution to the Civil War* (Princeton, N.J., 1957), 114–43; John Thom Holdsworth, *The First Bank of the United States* (Washington, D.C., 1910). Because of a paucity of information, treatments of the 1BUS have tended to lack real substance.

2. Charlene Bangs Bickford et al. (eds.), *Documentary History of the First Federal Congress of the United States of America, 4 March 1789—3 March 1791*, 17 vols. (Baltimore, Md., 1983–2004), 14:365–75, 378–81, 471–77; David P. Currie, *The Constitution in Congress: The Federalist Period, 1789–1801* (Chicago, 1977), 78–80.

3. "Opinion on the Constitutionality of the Bill for Establishing a National Bank," in Julian P. Boyd (ed.), *The Papers of Thomas Jefferson*, 31 vols. (Princeton, N.J., 1950–?), 19:275–80.

4. Ibid.

5. "Opinion on the Constitutionality of an Act to Establish a Bank," in Harold C. Syrett (ed.), *The Papers of Alexander Hamilton*, 27 vols. (New York, 1961–87), 8:97–134.

6. Hammond, *Banks and Politics in America*, 197–226.

7. Ibid., 144–96. The growth and problems involved with the development of state banking in the early nineteenth century are examined in Davis R. Dewey, *State Banking before the Civil War* (Washington, D.C., 1910);

J. Van Fenstermaker, *The Development of American Commercial Banking: 1782–1837* (Kent, Ohio, 1965); Howard Bodenhorn, *State Banking in Early America: A New Economic History* (New York, 1993), and Bodenhorn, *A History of Banking in Antebellum America: Financial Markets and Economic Development in an Age of Nation Building* (New York, 2000). Although these works are of high quality, they do not really explore the interactions between the first or second national banks and the state banks. J. Van Fenstermaker and John E. Filer, "Impact of the First and Second Banks of the United States and the Suffolk System on New England Bank Money," *Journal of Money, Credit, and Banking* 18 (February 1986), 28–40, is an important exception.

8. Edward J. Perkins, *American Public Finance and Financial Services, 1700–1815* (Columbus, Ohio, 1994), 324–48; John Denis Haeger, *John Jacob Astor: Business and Finance in the Early Republic* (Detroit, Mich., 1991), 138–69; Kenneth Wiggins Porter, *John Jacob Astor: Businessman*, 2 vols. (Cambridge, Mass., 1931), 2:955–71; John Bach McMaster, *Life and Times of Stephen Girard*, 2 vols. (Philadelphia, 1918), 2:286–92, 308–17, 345–53.

9. *American State Papers: Finance*, 38 vols. (Washington, D.C., 1832–1861), 2:866–67; Alexander Dallas to William Jones, 8 April 1814, Jones Papers, Historical Society of Pennsylvania (HSP); Dallas to James Monroe, 8 September 1814, Monroe Papers, New York Public Library; Dallas to Jones, 18, 26, 30 September, 2 October 1814, Jones Papers, HSP; Raymond Walters, Jr., *Alexander James Dallas: Lawyer, Politician, Financier* (Philadelphia, 1943), 189–217; Raymond Walters, Jr., "Origins of the Second Bank of the United States," *Journal of Political Economy* 53 (1945), 115–31; Robert Williams Keyes III, "The Formation of the Second Bank of the United States, 1811–1817" (Ph.D. diss., University of Delaware, 1975).

10. Dallas to Jones, 8 April 1814, Jones Papers, HSP.

11. *American State Papers: Finance*, 2:868–69.

12. Ibid., 867–68.

13. Walters, "Origins of the Second Bank of the United States," 124–25; Walters, *Dallas*, 194–95; Keyes, "The Formation of the Second Bank of the United States," 35–60.

14. Dallas to Jones, 29 January 1815, Jones Papers, HSP.

15. "Veto Message," 30 January 1815, in James F. Richardson (ed.), *A Compilation of the Messages and Papers of the Presidents, 1789–1897*, 10 vols. (Washington, D.C., 1900), 1:555–57.

16. Albert Gallatin to Thomas Jefferson, 27 November 1815, Gallatin Papers, New York Historical Society (NYHS); Albert Gallatin, *Considerations on the Currency and Banking System of the United States* (1831; 1968 reprint edition), 80–81; Raymond Walters, Jr., *Albert Gallatin: Jeffersonian Financier and Diplomat* (New York, 1957), 296–97.

17. Richardson (ed.), *Messages and Papers of the Presidents*, 1:566; *Debates and Proceedings in the Congress of the United States, 1789–1824*, 42 vols. (Washington, D.C., 1834–1856), 14:1, 281, 1219 (hereafter, *Annals of Congress*).

18. *Statutes at Large of the United States of America, 1789–1873*, 17 vols. (Washington, D.C., 1850–1873), 3:266–77. The charter is also conveniently reprinted in Ralph C. H. Catterall, *The Second Bank of the United States* (Chicago, 1902), 47–87; M. St. Clair Clarke and D. A. Hall (eds.), *Legislative and Documentary History of the Bank of the United States . . .* (Washington, D.C., 1832; reprint edition, 1967).

19. *Historical Statistics of the United States: Colonial Times to 1957* (Washington, D.C., 1961), 623; Stuart Bruchey, "Alexander Hamilton and the State Banks, 1789 to 1795," *William and Mary Quarterly* 27 (1970), 347–78.

20. J. Mauldin Lesesne, *The Bank of South Carolina* (Columbia, S.C., 1970), 140–41. See also Arthur Smith to C. W. Gooch, 19 November 1819, Gooch Family Papers, University of Virginia; W. C. Nicholas to William Jones, 16 October 1818, Jones Papers, HSP.

21. Louis McLane to [George Read], 24 March 1816, Read Papers, HSP; Lesesne, *Bank of South Carolina*, 140–41.

22. Richard Sylla et al., "Banks and State Public Finance in the New Republic: The United States, 1790–1860," *Journal of Economic History* 47 (1987), 391–403; Fenstermaker, *Development of American Commercial Banking*, 15–21; John Anthony Muscalus, *The Use of Banking Enterprises in the Financing of Public Education, 1796–1866* (Philadelphia, 1945); Robert C. Weems, "Mississippi's First Banking System," *Journal of Mississippi History* 29 (1967), 386–409.

23. *Harrisburg Chronicle*, 16 March 1818.

24. Charles G. Sellers, Jr., "Banking and Politics in Jackson's Tennessee, 1817–1827," *Mississippi Valley Historical Review* 41 (1954), 61–84; Jonathan Roberts to William Jones, 27 January 1818, Jones Papers, HSP; *Nashville Whig and Public Advertiser*, 1, 15 December 1817; 31 January 1818; 7, 28 February 1818; 24 October 1818.

25. The problems created by this policy are a central focus of Marion Alice Brown, *The Second Bank of the United States and Ohio (1803–1860):*

A Collision of Interests (Lewiston, N.Y., 1998), chapters 2 and 3. See also Marilynn Melton Larew, "The Cincinnati Branch of the Second Bank of the United States and Its Effect on the Local Economy, 1817–1836" (Ph.D. diss., University of Maryland, 1978), chapters 1–5.

26. *Annals of Congress*, 14:1, 440, 919; Chase, *Statutes*, 3:342; Catterall, *Second Bank of the United States*, 23.

27. Catterall, *Second Bank of the United States*, 22–50; Davis R. Dewey, *The Second United States Bank* (Washington, D.C., 1910), 157–63; Walter B. Smith, *Economic Aspects of the Second Bank of the United States* (Cambridge, 1953), 99–116; Leon M. Schur, "The Second Bank of the United States and the Inflation after the War of 1812," *Journal of Political Economy* 68 (1960), 118–34.

28. Bez. Wells et al. to William H. Crawford, 15 March 1817, in *American State Papers: Finance*, 4:994; Edward Crouch to William Jones, 5 December 1817, Jones Papers, HSP.

29. Wm. Ward to William H. Crawford, 1 January 1817, in *American State Papers: Finance*, 4:974.

30. William H. Crawford to William Jones et al., 3 July 1817, in *American State Papers: Finance*, 4:541; William Jones to James A. Buchanan [Draft], 9 July 1818, Jones Papers, HSP.

31. Quoted in Murray N. Rothbard, *The Panic of 1819* (New York, 1962), 10–11.

32. "Bank of the United States and Other Banks and the Currency: Report Communicated to the House of Representatives," 24 February 1820, in *American State Papers: Finance*, 3:496.

33. Julian P. Boyd, "John Sergeant's Mission," *Pennsylvania Magazine of History and Biography* 58 (1934), 213–31; Smith, *Economic Aspects of the Second Bank of the United States*, 100; Hammond, *Banks and Politics in America*, 254–55; Jonathan Roberts to William Jones, 11 December 1817, Jones Papers, HSP.

34. Kenneth L. Brown, "Stephen Girard, Promoter of the Second Bank of the United States," *Journal of Economic History* 2 (1942), 125–48.

35. Scholars who have studied the 2BUS invariably give Jones and his presidency very low marks. See Catterall, *Second Bank of the United States*, 22–50; Smith, *Economic Aspects of the Second Bank of the United States*, 99–116; Hammond, *Banks and Politics in America*, 251–60; Fritz Redlich, *The Molding of American Banking* (New York, 1947), 104–7; Charles Jared Ingersoll, *Historical Sketch of the Second War between the United States of America and Great Britain*, 2 vols. (Philadelphia, 1846), 2:252. For an

attempt to defend Jones, which is unsuccessful in my opinion, see Sister M. Saint Pierre Corrigan, "William Jones and the Second Bank of the United States: A Reappraisal" (Ph.D. diss., St. Louis University, 1966).

36. Catterall, *Second Bank of the United States*, 39–42; Hammond, *Banks and Politics in America*, 257–62; John Jacob Astor to William Jones, 15 December 1817, Jones Papers, HSP; Jones to Astor, 20 November 1817, ibid.

37. Manuel Eyre to Jonathan Roberts, 22 February 1819, Roberts Papers, HSP.

38. Jas. McCulloch to William H. Crawford, 7 March 1817 [postmarked 7 April 1817], in *American State Papers: Finance*, 4:774.

39. William Jones to William H. Crawford, 20 July 1817, in ibid., 807.

40. Dewey, *The Second United States Bank*, 195, 194–202.

41. Ibid., 194–202; Catterall, *Second Bank of the United States*, 30–35; Hammond, *Banks and Politics in America*; Smith, *Economic Aspects of the Second Bank of the United States*, 104–8.

42. "Second Inaugural Address," 4 March 1805; "Sixth Annual Address," 2 December 1806, both in Richardson (ed.), *Messages and Papers of the Presidents*, 379, 409; Joseph H. Harrison, "Sic et Non: Thomas Jefferson and Internal Improvements," *Journal of the Early Republic* 7 (1987), 335–49.

43. *Statutes*, 2:225–27; John Larson, *Internal Improvements: National Public Works and the Promise of Popular Government in the Early United States* (Chapel Hill, N.C., 2001), 52–63; James Simeon Young, *A Political and Constitutional Study of the Cumberland Road* (Chicago, 1904); Carter Goodrich, "National Planning of Internal Improvements," *Political Science Quarterly* 63 (1948), 16–44; Albert Gallatin, "Report of the Secretary of the Treasury on the Subject of Public Roads and Canals," in *American State Papers: Miscellaneous*, 1:753–921.

44. "Sixth Annual Address," in Richardson (ed.), *Messages and Papers of the Presidents*, 1:410.

45. "Seventh Annual Message," 5 December 1815, in ibid., 567–68.

46. *Annals of Congress*, 14:1, 516–17; Robert L. Meriwether (ed.), *Papers of John C. Calhoun*, 28 vols. to date (Columbia, S.C., 1959–), 1:314–15.

47. *Annals of Congress*, 14:2, 866–68, 870; Meriwether (ed.), *Papers of John C. Calhoun*, 1:372, 398–409, quote on p. 403.

48. Hopkins (ed.), *Papers of Henry Clay*, 1:309; *Annals of Congress*, 14:2, 866–68.

49. "Veto Message of 3 March, 1817," in Richardson (ed.), *Messages and Papers of the Presidents*, 1:584–85; Drew McCoy, *The Last of the Fathers: James Madison and the Republican Legacy* (New York, 1989), 92–103.

50. "First Annual Message," 6 December 1825, in Richardson (ed.), *Messages and Papers of the Presidents*, 2:306–17.

51. C. Edward Skeen, "'Vox Populi, Vox Dei': The Compensation Act of 1816 and the Rise of Popular Politics," *Journal of the Early Republic* 6 (1986), 253–74; Skeen, *1816: America Rising* (Lexington, Ky., 2003), 77–96; George T. Blakey, "Rendezvous with Republicanism: John Pope vs. Henry Clay in 1816," *Indiana Magazine of History* 62 (1966), 233–50; Adams, *History of the United States*, 2:1263–65, 1273–76, 1280–81; William T. Bianco et al., "The Electoral Connection in the Early Congress: The Case of the Compensation Act of 1816," *American Journal of Political Science* 40 (1996), 145–71.

52. *Annals of Congress*, 14:2, 234, 257, 258, 1063–64.

53. Thomas Todd to Henry Clay, 1 June 1817, in Melba Porter Hey (ed.), *The Papers of Henry Clay, Supplement: 1793–1852* (Lexington, Ky., 1992), 61.

54. Jonathan Roberts to William Jones, 21 January 1818, Jones Papers, HSP.

55. John C. Calhoun to Dr. James MacBride, 16 [17?] February 1812, 8 April 1812, in Meriwether (ed.), *Papers of John C. Calhoun*, 1:90, 99–100, 146.

56. *Annals of Congress*, 14:2, 574–82, 653–54; "First and Second Speeches on Amendments to the Compensation Law," 17 and 20 January 1817, in Meriwether (ed.), *Papers of John C. Calhoun*, 1:382–95. Also see William K. Bolt, "Founding Father and Rebellious Son: James Madison, John C. Calhoun, and the Use of Precedents," *American Nineteenth Century History* 5 (2004), 1–27.

57. Henry Clay to James Madison, 3 March 1817, in Hopkins (ed.), *Papers of Henry Clay*, 2:322.

58. "First Annual Address," 2 December 1817, in Richardson (ed.), *Messages and Papers of the Presidents*, 2:8, 18.

59. *Annals of Congress*, 15:1, 1359–79; "Speech on Internal Improvements" [7 March 1818] and "Speech on Internal Improvements" [13 March 1818], in Hopkins (ed.), *Papers of Henry Clay*, 2:448–67; David P. Currie, *The Constitution in Congress: The Jeffersonians, 1801–1829* (Chicago, 2001), 267–71; Maurice G. Baxter, *Henry Clay and the American System* (Lexington, Ky., 1995), 46–49.

60. *Annals of Congress*, 15:1, 451–60; Currie, *The Constitution in Congress: The Jeffersonians*, 271–78; H. Jefferson Powell, *A Community Built on Words: The Constitution in History and Politics* (Chicago, 2002), 137–46.

CHAPTER 3

1. Murray N. Rothbard, *The Panic of 1819* (New York, 1962), 1–23; William E. Folz, "The Financial Crisis of 1819: A Study in Post-War Economic Readjustment" (Ph.D. diss., University of Illinois, 1935); William Buckingham Smith and Arthur Harrison Cole, *Fluctuations in American Business, 1790–1860* (Cambridge, Mass., 1935), 3–33; Walter B. Smith, *Economic Aspects of the Second Bank of the United States* (Cambridge, Mass., 1953), 107–16.

2. For the impact of the Panic of 1819, see Charles Sellers, *The Market Revolution: Jacksonian America, 1815–1846* (New York, 1991), 103–71; George Dangerfield, *The Awakening of American Nationalism, 1815–1828* (New York, 1965), 72–96; Samuel Reznick, "The Depression of 1819–22: A Social History," *American Historical Review* 39 (1933), 28–47; Thomas H. Greer, "Economic and Social Effects of the Depression of 1819 in the Old Northwest," *Indiana Magazine of History* 49 (1948), 227–43; Thomas Senior Berry, *Western Prices before 1861: A Study of the Cincinnati Market* (Cambridge, 1943), 384–400; Daniel S. Dupre, *Transforming the Cotton Frontier: Madison County, Alabama, 1800–1814* (Baton Rouge, La., 1997), 49–71; J. David Lehman, "Explaining Hard Times: Political Economy and the Panic of 1819 in Philadelphia" (Ph.D. diss., University of California, Los Angeles, 1992); Robert M. Blackson, "The Panic of 1819 in Pennsylvania" (Ph.D. diss., Pennsylvania State University, 1978); Sarah Alice Kidd, "The Search for Moral Order: The Panic of 1819 and the Culture of the Early American Republic" (Ph.D. diss., University of Missouri, Columbia, 2002).

3. O. Spencer et al. to William Jones, 20 August 1818, in *American State Papers: Finance*, 4:859–61; "Report of the Joint Committee of the Planters' Bank and the Bank of the State of Georgia, 21 June 1820, in ibid., 4:1055–56; Thomas P. Govan, "Banking and the Credit System in Georgia, 1810–1860," *Journal of Southern History* 4 (1938), 164–84; Thomas C. McKenney to William Jones, 11 November 1818, Jones Papers, HSP; James A. Buchanan to Langdon Cheves, Cheves Papers, South Carolina Historical Society (SCHS).

4. *Annals of Congress*, 15:2, 317–19, 325–36, 552–80; Clarke and Hall (eds.), *Documentary History of the Bank of the United States*, 714–32.

5. *Annals of Congress*, 15:2, 598–600, 922–25, 1102–3, 1140–42, 1240–1409; John Monroe, *Louis McLane: Federalist and Jacksonian* (New Brunswick, N.J., 1973), 83–90; Carl J. Vipperman, *William Lowndes and*

the Transition of Southern Politics (Chapel Hill, N.C., 1989), 170–80; James McCulloch to William Jones, 7 September 1818, Jones Papers, HSP; Henry Southard to Samuel L. Southard, 24 December 1819, Samuel L. Southard Papers, Princeton University Library.

6. Entry of 8 January 1820, in C. F. Adams (ed.), *Memoirs of John Quincy Adams*, 12 vols. (Philadelphia, 1874–1877), 4:499.

7. George Williams to William Jones, 13 December 1817, Jones Papers, HSP.

8. Thomas Worthington to William Jones, 5 August 1818, in ibid.; Wilson Cary Nicholas to William Jones, 4 August 1816, in ibid.; Daniel D. Tompkins to Langdon Cheves, 6 November 1819, Cannaroe Collection, HSP; James Madison to George Graham, 27 March 1824, in ibid.

9. James C. Fisher to Rufus King, 25, 30 January 1819, in Charles R. King (ed.), *Life and Correspondence of Rufus King*, 10 vols. (New York, 1896), 6:197–98, 200–201; Fritz Redlich, "William Jones' Resignation from the Presidency of the Second Bank of the United States," *Pennsylvania Magazine of History and Biography* 71 (1947), 223–41; Rufus King to Charles King, 29 January 1819, King Papers, NYHS; William H. Crawford to Langdon Cheves, 18 December 1819, Cheves Papers, SCHS; Jonathan Roberts to William Jones, 2 March 1819, Jones Papers, HSP.

10. Archie Vernan Huff, Jr., *Langdon Cheve[s] of South Carolina* (Columbia, S.C., 1977), 96–127.

11. Ralph C. H. Catterall, *The Second Bank of the United States* (Chicago, 1902), 64–65; Lucius Q. C. Lamar, Esq., *Laws of the State of Georgia . . .* (Augusta, Ga., 1821), 889–91, 1206; *Niles' Weekly Register* 15 (9 January 1819), 362–67; William H. Crawford to William Jones, 21 April 1818, Cannaroe Collection, HSP.

12. Catterall, *The Second Bank of the United States*, 64–65.

13. Henry Clay to Martin D. Hardin, 4 January 1819, in Hopkins and Hargreaves (eds.), *Papers of Henry Clay*, 2:623.

14. Ames (ed.), *State Documents on Federal Relations*, 92.

15. The law is reprinted in 4 Wheaton 320–21.

16. *Niles' Weekly Register* (9 January 1819), 362.

17. Davis R. Dewey, *The Second United States Bank* (Washington, D.C., 1910), 199.

18. George Williams to William Jones, 10 December 1817, Jones Papers, HSP.

19. 4 Wheaton 346.

20. *Votes and Proceedings of the Senate of Maryland* (Annapolis, Md., 1818), 40; *Votes and Proceedings of the House of Delegates of the State of Maryland* (Annapolis, Md., 1818), 104–5.

21. *Daily National Intelligencer* (Washington, D.C.), 12 February 1818.

22. *Annals of Congress*, 15:2, 1411–12.

23. Herman V. Ames, *The Proposed Amendments to the Constitution of the United States* (1896; reprint edition, New York, 1970), 256; *Votes and Proceedings of the House of Delegates of the State of Maryland, 1820–21*: 29 January 1821 (Annapolis, Md., 1821), 77 and 118; *Votes and Proceedings of the Senate of Maryland, 1820–21*: 17 February 1821 (Annapolis, Md., 1821), 65–66.

24. 4 Wheaton 346.

25. Robert J. Brugger et al., *Maryland: A Middle Temperament, 1634–1980* (Baltimore, Md., 1999), 179, 196–97, 219–21, 229; Richard McCormick, *The Second American Party System: Party Formation in the Jacksonian Era* (Chapel Hill, N.C., 1966), 154–66; Mark H. Haller, "The Rise of the Jackson Party in Maryland, 1820–1829," *Journal of Southern History* 27 (August 1962), 307–26; Whitman H. Ridgway, *Community Leadership in Maryland, 1790–1840: A Comparative Analysis of Power in Society* (Chapel Hill, N.C., 1979); Max Renzulli, *Maryland: The Federalist Years* (Rutherford, N.J., 1972); L. Steven Demaree, "Maryland during the First Party System: A Roll Call Analysis of the House of Delegates, 1789–1824" (Ph.D. diss., University of Missouri, 1984). See also R. H. Goldsborough to J. Mason, 11 September 1816 and 21 July 1817, Mason Papers, New Hampshire Historical Society.

26. George Williams to William Jones, 10 December 1817, Jones Papers, HSP.

27. The speech may be found in the following newspapers: *Maryland Gazette and Political Intelligencer* (Annapolis), 17 December 1818; *Frederick Town Herald*, 26 December 1818; *Baltimore Patriot and Mercantile Advertiser*, 17 December 1818.

28. *National Messenger* (Georgetown, D.C.), 21 December 1818.

29. "Appellate Case Files of the Supreme Court of the United States, 1782–1831," microfilm reel 49, case 938, frames 2–23, National Archives.

30. "Court of Appeals Docket, Western Shore, June Term 1818, McCulloch v. State and John James," Maryland State Archives, Annapolis; see especially Joseph Story to Nathaniel Williams, 22 February 1815, in W. W. Story (ed.), *Life and Letters of Joseph Story*, 2 vols. (Boston, 1851),

1:254; see also 1:243–49, 255–58, 262–63, 269–70, 279–80; R. Kent
Newmyer, *Supreme Court Justice Joseph Story: Statesman of the Old
Republic* (Chapel Hill, N.C., 1985), chapters 3–5.

31. E. W. duVal to William Jones, 18, 22, 23 January, 1, 20, 23, 24, 25
February, 4 March 1819, Jones Papers, HSP.

32. William Pinkney, *The Life of William Pinkney* (New York, 1853); Robert M.
Ireland, *The Legal Career of William Pinkney, 1764–1822* (New York, 1986).

33. James W. McCulloch to Samuel McCulloch, 17 February 1819, John
Campbell White Papers, Maryland Historical Society; Rufus King to
Edward King, 12 March 1819, King Papers, Cincinnati Historical
Society; Henry Clay to Martin D. Hardin, 4 January 1819, in Hopkins
and Hargreaves (eds.), *Papers of Henry Clay*, 2:623; John Bolton to
Langdon Cheves, 25 March 1819, Cheves Papers, SCHS; Henry
Southard to Samuel L. Southard, 24 February 1819, Southard Papers,
Pierpont Morgan Library (PML).

34. *Niles' Weekly Register* 18 (15 April 1820), 129; *Maryland Gazette
and Political Intelligencer* (Annapolis), 23 December 1819.

35. *Maryland Gazette and Political Intelligencer* (Annapolis), 23 December 1819.

36. William Pinkney to Daniel Webster, 28 December 1818, in Charles
M. Wiltse and Harold D. Moser (eds.), *The Papers of Daniel Webster:
Correspondence*, 16 vols. (Hanover, N.H., 1974–1989), 1:238.

CHAPTER 4

1. Joseph Story to Henry Wheaton, 9 December 1818, Henry Wheaton
Papers, PML.

2. Joseph Story to Stephen White, 3 March 1819, in W. W. Story (ed.), *Life
and Letters of Joseph Story*, 2 vols. (Boston, 1851), 1:325.

3. Melvin I. Urofsky (ed.), *The Supreme Court Justices: A Biographical
Dictionary* (New York, 1994), 153–54, 273–76, 285–86, 479–82, 511–13;
Leon Friedman and Fred L. Israel (eds.), *The Justices of the United States
Supreme Court*, 5 vols. (New York, 1969–1980), 1:243–57, 355–72,
387–98, 407–12, 419–29.

4. *Annals of Congress*, 15:2, 132.

5. *McCulloch v. Maryland* (1819), 4 Wheaton 323.

6. Ibid., 325.

7. Ibid., 325–26.

8. Ibid., 327.

9. Ibid., 327.

10. Ibid., 327–28.

11. Ibid., 330.

12. Daniel Webster to Jeremiah Mason, 23 February 1819, in G. S. Hilliard (ed.), *Memoir and Correspondence of Jeremiah Mason* (Cambridge, 1873), 222; see also E. W. duVal to William Jones, 4 March 1819, Jones Papers, HSP, for another example of confidence that the outcome would favor the 2BUS.

13. *McCulloch v. Maryland* (1819), 4 Wheaton 331.

14. Ibid., 332–33.

15. Ibid., 334.

16. Ibid., 335.

17. Ibid.

18. Ibid., 336–37.

19. Ibid., 337.

20. Ibid., 337–39.

21. Ibid., 340–41.

22. Ibid., 346.

23. Ibid., 347.

24. Ibid.

25. Ibid., 346.

26. Ibid., 349.

27. Ibid., 353.

28. Ibid., 357.

29. Ibid., 361–62.

30. Ibid., 365.

31. Ibid., 365.

32. Ibid., 368.

33. Ibid., 369–72.

34. Paul S. Clarkson and Samuel R. Jett, *Luther Martin of Maryland* (Baltimore, Md., 1970).

35. *McCulloch v. Maryland* (1819), 4 Wheaton 372–73, 374.

36. Ibid., 375–76.

37. Ibid.

38. Ibid., 376–77.

39. G. Edward White (with Gerald Gunther), *The Marshall Court and Cultural Change, 1815–1835* (New York, 1988), 244; Samuel Tyler (ed.), *Memoir of Roger Brooke Taney* (Baltimore, Md., 1872), 71.

40. Joseph Story to Stephen White, 3 March 1819, in Story (ed.), *Life and Letters of Joseph Story*, 1:325. See also E. W. duVal to William Jones,

6 March 1819, Jones Papers, HSP. The board of directors of the 2BUS was so pleased with Pinkney's and Webster's roles in obtaining a favorable decision in the case that it increased their fees. William Pinkney to Langdon Cheves, 4 April 1819, Cannaroe Collection, HSP; Langdon Cheves to Daniel Webster, 2 April 1819, in Charles M. Wiltse and Harold D. Moser (eds.), *The Papers of Daniel Webster: Correspondence*, 16 vols. (Hanover, 1974–1989), 1:254.

41. *McCulloch v. Maryland* (1819), 4 Wheaton 377.
42. Henry Wheaton to Joseph Story, 24 August 1819, Wheaton Papers, PML. Wheaton's notes on the case are to be found in his "Notebooks on the Supreme Court, 1819," in ibid.
43. *McCulloch v. Maryland* (1819), 4 Wheaton 377.
44. Ibid., 378.
45. Ibid., 384, 385.
46. Ibid., 390.
47. Ibid., 390.
48. Ibid., 390, 391.
49. Ibid., 393.
50. Ibid., 400.
51. Ibid., 401.
52. Ibid.
53. Ibid., 403.
54. Ibid., 404–5.
55. Ibid., 405.
56. Ibid., 405–6.
57. Ibid., 406–7.
58. Ibid., 415–16.
59. Ibid., 407–8.
60. Ibid., 420–21.
61. Ibid., 421.
62. Ibid., 424–25.
63. Ibid., 426.
64. Ibid.
65. Ibid., 432.
66. Ibid., 437.
67. *National Intelligencer* (Washington, D.C.), 13 March 1819.
68. William H. Crawford to Thomas Worthington, 13 March 1819, Worthington Papers, Ross County Historical Society (RCHS).

69. James Madison to Spencer Roane, 2 September 1819, in Gaillard Hunt (ed.), *The Writings of James Madison*, 9 vols. (New York, 1900–1910), 8:448.

70. Ibid.

71. John Marshall to James Monroe, 13 June 1822, in Hobson (ed.), *The Papers of John Marshall*, 9:236.

72. Joseph Story to James Monroe, 24 June 1822, Monroe Papers, Library of Congress (LC).

73. William Johnson to James Monroe, undated, in ibid. See also Charles Warren, *The Supreme Court in United States History*, 2 vols. (Boston, 1926), 1:595–97; Donald G. Morgan, *Justice William Johnson*, 122–24.

74. John Marshall to Joseph Story, 24 March 1819, in Hobson (ed.), *The Papers of John Marshall*, 8:280.

75. John Marshall to Bushrod Washington, 27 March [1819], in ibid., 281.

76. John Marshall, *George Washington* (5 vols., reprint, New York, 1983), 4:110–63.

77. 2 Cranch 358.

78. John Marshall to Joseph Story, 27 May 1819, in Hobson (ed.), *Papers of John Marshall*, 8:314.

79. William Crawford to Langdon Cheves, 6 April 1819, Cheves Papers, SCHS.

80. William Gouge, *A Short History of Paper Money and Banking* . . . (Philadelphia, 1833; reprint edition, New York, 1968), part II, 110.

81. "The Sovereignty of the State, Parts I–III," *Niles' Weekly Register* (Baltimore, Md.) 16 (13 March 1819, 3, 24 April 1819), 41–44, 103–7, 145–47.

82. *Niles Weekly' Register* 16 (13 March 1819), 41.

83. *Argus of Western America* (Frankfort, Ky.), 28 May 1819; Donald Cole, *Amos Kendall and the Rise of American Democracy* (Baton Rouge, La., 2004).

84. *Argus of Western America* (Frankfort, Ky.), 18 June 1819.

85. Ibid., 23 July 1819.

86. Ibid., 2 July 1819.

CHAPTER 5

1. Although there is a large body of literature on the Richmond Junto, there is no consensus among scholars about who its members were, how coherent it was, how it operated, how influential and powerful it was, its overall

significance, and even whether it existed at all. See, in particular,
A Virginian: Letters on the Richmond Party (Richmond, Va., 1823); Rex
Beach, "Spencer Roane and the Richmond Party," *William and Mary
Quarterly* 22 (1942), 1–17; Harry Ammon, "The Richmond Junto,
1800–1824," *Virginia Magazine of History and Biography* 61 (1953),
395–418; Joseph H. Harrison, "Oligarchs and Democrats: The Richmond
Junto," *Virginia Magazine of History and Biography* 78 (1970), 184–98;
F. Thornton Miller, "The Richmond Junto: The Secret All-Powerful Club—
or Myth," *Virginia Magazine of History and Biography* 99 (1991), 63–80.

2. G. Gelbach, "Spencer Roane of Virginia, 1776–1822: A Judicial Advocate
   of State Rights" (Ph.D. diss., University of Pittsburgh, 1955); M.
   Horsnell, *Spencer Roane: Judicial Advocate of Jeffersonian Principles* (New
   York, 1986); F. Thornton Miller, "John Marshall versus Spencer Roane:
   A Reinterpretation of *Martin v. Hunter's Lessee*," *Virginia Magazine of
   History and Biography* 96 (1988), 297–314; Timothy S. Huebner, "The
   Consolidation of State Judicial Power: Spencer Roane, Virginia Legal
   Culture, and the Southern Judicial Tradition," *Virginia Magazine of
   History and Biography* 102 (1994), 48–72.

3. Charles A. Ambler, *Thomas Ritchie: A Study in Virginia Politics* (Richmond,
   Va., 1913); Bert M. Mutersbaugh, "Jeffersonian Journalist: Thomas
   Ritchie and the *Richmond Enquirer*, 1804–1820" (Ph.D. diss., University
   of Missouri, 1973).

4. Dennis Golladay, "Wilson Cary Nicholas," in John A. Garraty and Mark
   Carves (eds.), *American National Biography*, 24 vols. (New York, 1999),
   16:378–80; Thomas Perkins Abernathy, "Wilson Cary Nicholas," in
   Dumas Malone (ed.), *Dictionary of American Biography*, 11 vols. (New
   York, 1964), 7:486–87.

5. Information on individual members may be culled from Daniel P. Jordan,
   Political Leadership in Jefferson's Virginia (Charlottesville, Va., 1983);
   Charles D. Lowery, *James Barbour: A Jeffersonian Republican* (University,
   Ala., 1984); John P. Frank, *Justice Daniel Dissenting: A Biography of Peter
   V. Daniel, 1784–1860* (Cambridge, 1964); Dice R. Anderson, *William
   Branch Giles: A Study in the Politics of Virginia and the Nation from
   1790–1830* (Menasha, Wis., 1914); Armistead Gordon, *William Fitzhugh:
   A Virginian of the Old School* (New York, 1909); Francis Fry Wayland,
   Andrew Stevenson: Democrat and Diplomat, 1785–1857 (Philadelphia,
   1949); Robert J. Brugger, *Beverly Tucker: Heart over Head in the Old South*
   (Baltimore, Md., 1978); Robert Seager, *And Tyler Too: A Biography of John
   and Julian Gardner Tyler* (New York, 1963); Douglas R. Egerton, *Charles*

Fenton Mercer and the Trial of National Conservatism (Jackson, Miss., 1989); William G. Shade, *Democratizing the Old Dominion: Virginia and the Second Party System, 1824–1861* (Charlottesville, Va., 1996).

6. Spencer Roane to James Barbour, 4 January 1815 [1816], 12 February 1816, 30 January 1819, "Letters of Spencer Roane," *Bulletin of the New York Public Library* 10 (1906), 160–70, 171–72; P. P. Barbour to W. C. Rives, 9 February 1819, Rives Papers, LC.

7. "Amphictyon," *Richmond Enquirer*, 18 April 1820.

8. George T. Starnes, *Sixty Years of Branch Banking in Virginia* (New York, 1931), 18–44.

9. Carter Goodrich, "The Virginia System of Mixed Enterprise," *Political Science Quarterly* 64 (1949), 355–87; John Larson, *Internal Improvements: National Public Works and the Promise of Popular Government in the Early United States* (Chapel Hill, N.C., 2001), 91–97; Wayland Fuller Dunaway, *History of the James River and Kanawha Company* (New York, 1922): Alexander Crosly Brown, *The Dismal Swamp Canal* (Chesapeake, Md., 1967); Charles Royster, *The Fabulous History of the Dismal Swamp Company: A Story of George Washington's Times* (New York, 1999).

10. Starnes, *Sixty Years of Branch Banking in Virginia*, 25–56; Frank, *Justice Daniel Dissenting*, 35–37.

11. William Gouge, *A Short History of Paper Money and Banking . . .* (Philadelphia, 1833; reprint edition, New York, 1968), part II, 144.

12. Starnes, *Sixty Years of Branch Banking in Virginia*, 56–63.

13. Spencer Roane to James Barbour, 4 January 1815 [1816], "Letters of Spencer Roane," *Bulletin of the New York Public Library* 10 (1906), 169.

14. Spencer Roane to James Barbour, 16 February 1819, in ibid., 172.

15. "Amphictyon," *Richmond Enquirer*, 2 April 1819; Francis Corbin[?] to Wilson Cary Nicholas, 22 February 1817, Nicholas Papers, LC; Joseph Lewis to L. W. Tazewell, 22 January 1818, Tazewell Papers, Virginia State Library.

16. These essays, plus others by Spencer Roane, and Chief Justice John Marshall's responses are conveniently republished in Gerald Gunther (ed.), *John Marshall's Defense of McCulloch v. Maryland* (Stanford, Calif., 1969). Gunther also straightens out the tortured history behind the publication of Marshall's essays. See also Eric Tscheschlok, "Mistaken Identity: Spencer Roane and the 'Amphictyon' Letter of 1819," *Virginia Magazine of History and Biography* 106 (Spring 1998), 201–11. The debate is also analyzed in William E. Dodd, "Chief Justice Marshall and Virginia, 1813–1821," *American Historical Review* 12 (1907), 776–87;

Albert Beveridge, *The Life of John Marshall*, 4 vols. (Boston, 1916–1919), 4:312–23, 787; Charles Warren, *The Supreme Court in United States History*, 2 vols. (Boston, 1926), 1:515–19; anonymous note, "Judge Spencer Roane of Virginia: Champion of State Rights, Foe of John Marshall," *Harvard Law Review* 66 (1953), 1242–59; Horsnell, *Spencer Roane*, 140–67; Charles G. Haines, *The Role of the Supreme Court in American Government and Politics, 1789–1835* (New York, 1960), 357–68; Samuel R. Olken, "John Marshall and Spencer Roane: An Historical Analysis of the Conflict over U.S. Supreme Court Appellate Jurisdiction," *Journal of Supreme Court History* 14 (1990), 125–42; G. Edward White (with Gerald Gunther), *The Marshall Court and Cultural Change, 1815–1835* (New York, 1988), 552–67; Richard E. Ellis, "The Path Not Taken: Virginia and the Supreme Court, 1789–1821," in A. E. Dick Howard and Melvin I. Urofsky (eds.), *Virginia and the Constitution* (Charlottesville, Va., 1992), 24–52.

17. Gunther (ed.), *John Marshall's Defense*, 55.
18. Ibid., 58.
19. Ibid., 64.
20. Ibid.
21. Ibid., 70–71.
22. Ibid., 74–75.
23. Henry Wheaton to Joseph Story, 14 June, 24 August 1819, Wheaton Papers, Morgan Library (ML).
24. Ibid., 14 June 1819.
25. John Marshall to Bushrod Washington, 17 June 1819, in Hobson (ed.), *The Papers of John Marshall*, 8:317.
26. Henry Wheaton to Joseph Story, 14 June 1819, Wheaton Papers, ML.
27. John Marshall to Bushrod Washington, 6 May 1819, in Hobson (ed.), *The Papers of John Marshall*, 8:311.
28. John Marshall to Joseph Story, 27 May 1819, in ibid., 8:314.
29. Ibid., 312n3.
30. Ibid., 91.
31. Ibid., 92.
32. Ibid., 93.
33. Ibid., 99.
34. Ibid., 77.
35. John Marshall to Joseph Story, 27 May 1819, in Hobson (ed.), *The Papers of John Marshall*, 8:314.
36. Gunther (ed.), *John Marshall's Defense*, 83.

37. Ibid., 88, 89.

38. Ibid., 90.

39. Ibid., 96, 97.

40. Ibid., 101.

41. Ibid., 78–79; John Marshall to Bushrod Washington, 27 March 1819, in Hobson (ed.), *The Papers of John Marshall*, 8:281.

42. Gunther (ed.), *John Marshall's Defense*, 103–4.

43. John Marshall to Bushrod Washington, 6 May 1819, in Hobson (ed.), *The Papers of John Marshall*, 8:311.

44. *Richmond Enquirer*, 11 June 1819.

45. Gunther (ed.), *John Marshall's Defense*, 107.

46. Ibid., 110.

47. Ibid., 110–11.

48. Ibid., 130.

49. Ibid., 135–37.

50. Ibid., 146.

51. Ibid., 148.

52. Ibid., 152.

53. John Marshall to Bushrod Washington, 17 June 1819, in Hobson (ed.), *The Papers of John Marshall*, 8:317.

54. John Marshall to Bushrod Washington [ca. 28 June 1819], in ibid., 317.

55. Gunther (ed.), *John Marshall's Defense*, 156–57.

56. Ibid., 155.

57. Ibid.

58. Ibid., 158.

59. Ibid., 206.

60. Ibid.

61. Ibid., 170.

62. Ibid., 203.

63. Ibid., 160.

64. Ibid., 180.

65. Ibid., 214.

66. John Marshall to Joseph Story, 27 May 1819, in Hobson (ed.), *The Papers of John Marshall*, 8:314.

67. *Richmond Enquirer*, 23, 25 December 1819, 12, 15, 29 February 1820; Hobson (ed.), *The Papers of John Marshall*, 8:286–87.

68. W. Ray Luce, *Cohens v. Virginia (1821): The Supreme Court and State Rights* (New York, 1990).

69. *Niles' Weekly Register* 19 (2 September 1820), 3–5.

70. Ibid. (20 January 1821), 340–41, and (24 February 1821), 417–18;
    William H. Gaines, Jr., *Thomas Mann Randolph: Jefferson's Son-in-Law*
    (Baton Rouge, La., 1966), 123–24; Hobson (ed.), *The Papers of John
    Marshall*, 9:106–13; Luce, *Cohens v. Virginia*, 75–111.
71. *Cohens v. Virginia* (1821), 6 Wheaton 290–337.
72. Ibid., 380–81.
73. Ibid., 414.
74. Ibid., 416.
75. Ibid., 405–8.
76. Ibid., 440–47.
77. *Richmond Enquirer*, 25, 29 May, 1, 5, 8 June 1821, reprinted in *John
    P. Branch Historical Papers of Randolph-Macon College* (1906), 2:78–103.
78. *John P. Branch Historical Papers* (1906), 2:79, 80; Haines, *The Role of the
    Supreme Court in American Government and Politics*, 438–43.
79. Robert Shalhope, *John Taylor of Caroline: Pastoral Republican* (Columbia,
    S.C., 1980).
80. *New Views on the Constitution* (Washington, D.C., 1822), quoted in
    Charles Haines, *The Role of the Supreme Court in American Government
    and Politics* (reprint, New York, 1973), 453–54.
81. Ellis, *The Jeffersonian Crisis*, 19–107; Richard Hofstadter, *The Idea of a
    Party System: The Rise of Legitimate Opposition in the United States,
    1780–1840* (Berkeley, Calif., 1969), 170–211.
82. Thomas Jefferson to Spencer Roane, 6 September 1819, in Paul L. Ford
    (ed.), *The Writings of Thomas Jefferson*, 10 vols. (New York, 1892–1899),
    10:140–43.
83. Thomas Jefferson to Thomas Ritchie, 25 December 1820, in ibid., 169–71.
84. Thomas Jefferson to Charles Jarvis, 28 September 1820, in ibid., 160–61;
    Thomas Jefferson to Archibald Thweat, 19 January 1821, in ibid., 184;
    Thomas Jefferson to William Johnson, 27 October 1822, in ibid., 2222–26.
85. John Marshall to Joseph Story, 18 September 1821, in Hobson (ed.), *The
    Papers of John Marshall*, 9:183.
86. John Marshall to Joseph Story, 13 July 1821, in ibid., 179.
87. John Marshall to Joseph Story, 18 September 1821, in ibid., 183–84.
88. John Marshall to Joseph Story, 13 July 1821, in ibid., 179, 180n6.
    According to Hobson, reference is here made to the essays entitled
    "Fletcher of Saltoun," published in the *Richmond Enquirer*, 22, 26 June,
    3, 6 July 1821, and "Somers," published in the *Richmond Enquirer*, 15, 22
    May, 1, 12, 19, 26 June, and 13 July 1821. See Hobson, ed., *The Papers of
    John Marshall*, 9:113nn23, 24, and 180n6.

89. John Marshall to Joseph Story, 13 July 1821, in Hobson (ed.), *The Papers of John Marshall*, 9:179.

90. Gunther (ed.), *John Marshall's Defense*, 77.

91. *Richmond Enquirer*, 25 May 1821, in *John P. Branch Historical Papers* (1906), 2:79.

92. Gunther (ed.), *John Marshall's Defense*, 58.

93. Ibid., 152.

94. 4 Munford 9.

95. William E. Dodd, "Chief Justice Marshall and Virginia, 1813–1821," *American Historical Review* 12 (1907), 776–87.

96. I have explored the implications of this more fully in Richard E. Ellis, *The Union at Risk: Jacksonian Democracy, States' Rights and the Nullification Crisis* (New York, 1987). See also Richard E. Ellis, "The Market Revolution and the Transformation of American Politics, 1801–1837," in Melvyn Stokes and Stephen Conway (eds.), *The Market Revolution in America* (Charlottesville, Va., 1996), 149–76, especially 165–66.

97. The standard work on the Missouri Compromise remains Glover Moore, *The Missouri Controversy, 1819–1821* (Lexington, Ky., 1953).

98. Spencer Roane to James Barbour, 29 December 1819, in "Letters to James Barbour, Senator of Virginia in the Congress of the United States," *William and Mary Quarterly*, 1st ser., 10 (1901–1902), 7–8.

99. Moore, *The Missouri Controversy*, 167.

100. Ibid., 97–98.

101. Taylor, *Construction Construed* (Richmond, 1820).

102. Thomas Jefferson to Nathaniel Macon, 19 August 1821, 20 October 1821, in Ford (ed.), *The Writings of Thomas Jefferson*, 10:192–94; Duma Malone, *Jefferson and His Time: The Sage of Monticello* (Boston, 1981), 328–44, 352–61; Donald N. Mayer, *The Constitutional Thought of Thomas Jefferson* (Charlottesville, Va., 1994), 277–94.

CHAPTER 6

1. The standard works on the subject, all of which are very helpful, are E. L. Bogart, "Taxation of the Second Bank of the United States by Ohio," *American Historical Review* 17 (1912), 312–31; C. C. Huntington, "A History of Banking and Currency in Ohio before the Civil War," *Ohio Archaeological and Historical Society Publications* 24 (1915), 235–539; Joseph Douglas Aiello, "Ohio's War upon the Bank of the United States: 1817–1824" (Ph.D. diss., Ohio State University, 1972); Patricia L. Franz,

"Ohio v. the Bank: An Historical Examination of *Osborn v. the Bank of the United States*," *Journal of Supreme Court History* 23 (1999), 112–37.

2. For the economic, social, and political development of Ohio in the early nineteenth century, see William T. Utter, *The Frontier State: 1803–1825* (Columbus, Ohio, 1942); Andrew R. L. Cayton, *The Frontier Republic: Ideology and Politics in the Ohio Country, 1780–1825* (Kent, Ohio, 1986); Donald J. Ratcliffe, *Party Spirit in a Frontier Republic: Democratic Politics in Ohio, 1793–1821* (Columbus, Ohio, 1998). On the growth of banks, see J. Van Fenstermaker, *The Development of American Commercial Banking: 1782–1837* (Kent, Ohio, 1965), 166–67.

3. Salmon P. Chase (ed.), *The Statutes of Ohio and of the Northwest Territory Adopted or Enacted from 1788 to 1833*, 3 vols. (Cincinnati, 1833), 2:868–69, 904–5, 913–24; Huntington, "A History of Banking and Currency in Ohio," 269–85.

4. *Journal of the House of Representatives of the State of Ohio: Sixteenth General Assembly* (Columbus, Ohio, 1817), 145.

5. Ibid., 146.

6. Ibid.

7. Ibid.

8. Ibid., 146–47.

9. Ibid., 312.

10. Ibid., 313.

11. Ibid., 314.

12. Ibid., 307–15, 318, 359; Aiello, "Ohio's War upon the Bank of the United States," 36.

13. *The Supporter* (Chillicothe), 2 Sept. 1818.

14. W. H. Crawford to Thomas Worthington, 13 March 1819, Worthington Papers, RCHS; Thomas Worthington to William Jones, 5 August 1818, Jones Papers, HSP; Ratcliffe, *Party Spirit in a Frontier Republic*, 223–29; *Niles' Weekly Register* 15 (31 October 1818), 149; Alfred Byron Sears, *Thomas Worthington: Father of Ohio Statehood* (Columbus, Ohio, 1958), 208–9; Cayton, *Frontier Republic*, 129–37.

15. *Journal of the House of Representatives of the State of Ohio: Seventeenth General Assembly* (Columbus, Ohio, 1818), 92–93, 97–98; John Still, "The Life of Ethan Allen Brown" (Ph.D. diss., Ohio State University, 1951).

16. No modern biography of Hammond exists. Some help may be gleaned from Francis Phelps Weisenburger, "A Life of Charles Hammond: The First Great Journalist of the Old Northwest," *Ohio Archaeological and*

Historical Quarterly 42 (1934), 340–427; Wm. Henry Smith, *Charles Hammond and His Relation to Henry Clay and John Quincy Adams . . .* (Chicago, 1885).

17. James Wilson to W. D. Gallagher, 10 October 1840, Charles Hammond Papers, Ohio State Library (OSL).

18. Charles Hammond to Governor Thomas Worthington, 24 March 1817, ibid. See also Charles Hammond et al. to President and Directors of the Bank of the United States, 15 March 1817, ibid.; Charles Hammond et al. to Jonathan Smith, Cashier of the Bank of the United States, 14 April 1817, in *American State Papers: Finance*, 4:788.

19. *Journal of the House of Representatives of the State of Ohio: Seventeenth General Assembly* (Columbus, Ohio, 1818), 393–410.

20. Chase, *Statutes*, 2:1072.

21. *The Supporter* (Chillicothe), 31 March 1819; *Liberty Hall and Gazette* (Cincinnati), 6 April 1819.

22. William Creighton to Langdon Cheves, 22 September 1819, in *American State Papers: Finance*, 4:910.

23. Ethan Allen Brown to Charles Hammond, 29 May 1819, Ethan Allen Brown Papers, OSL. See also Benjamin Tappan to Ethan Allen Brown, 21 July 1819, ibid.

24. *Journal of the House of Representatives of the State of Ohio: Eighteenth General Assembly* (Columbus, Ohio, 1819), 38–44; *Niles' Weekly Register* 17 (January 1820), 310–11; Ralph Osborn, *Communication from the Auditor of Ohio, Accompanied with Documents to Both Houses of the Legislature, at the Commencement of the First Session of the Eighteenth General Assembly*: 8 December 1819 (Columbus, Ohio, 1819).

25. *Journal of the House of Representatives of Ohio: Eighteenth General Assembly*, 44–50.

26. Ibid., 50.

27. A. G. Claypoole to W. H. Crawford, 17 September 1819, in *American State Papers: Finance*, 4:903; Abram G. Claypoole to William H. Crawford, 25 September 1819, in ibid., 904; Abram G. Claypoole to Jon Smith, 17 September 1819, in ibid., 905; William Creighton to Langdon Cheves, 22 September 1819, in ibid., 910.

28. *Journal of the House of Representatives of Ohio: Eighteenth General Assembly*, 50–64.

29. Langdon Cheves to William H. Crawford, 20 September 1819, in *American State Papers: Finance*, 4:905.

30. Henry Wheaton to Joseph Story, 22 October 1819, Wheaton Papers, PML.

31. *National Intelligencer* (Washington, D.C.), 6 November 1819.

32. *Niles' Weekly Register* 17 (2 October 1819), 65; (30 October 1819), 133.

33. Gorham A. Worth to Thomas Sloo, Jr. (15 December 1819), in Isaac Joslin Cox (ed.), "Selections from the Torrence Papers," *Quarterly Publications of the Historical and Philosophical Society of Ohio* 6 (1911), 23.

34. *Supporter* (Chillicothe), 22 September 1819; *Niles' Weekly Register* 17 (9 October 1819), 87; Marie Dickorie, *General Joseph Kerr of Chillicothe, Ohio: Ohio's Lost Senator* (Oxford, Miss., 1941), 34–36.

35. *Niles' Weekly Register* 17 (30 October 1819), 139.

36. Ibid.; Dorothy Burne Goebel, *William Henry Harrison: A Political Biography* (Indianapolis, Ind., 1926), 227–28.

37. Thomas Worthington to Langdon Cheves, 17 September 1819, Cheves Papers, SCHS; an extract of this letter is printed in *American State Papers: Finance*, 4:905–6.

38. Thomas Worthington to Langdon Cheves, 22 November, 2, 11 December 1819, Cheves Papers, SCHS. Copies of these letters may also be found in the Worthington Papers, RCHS.

39. Henry Clay to Langdon Cheves, 14 November 1819, in Hopkins (ed.), *Papers of Henry Clay*, 2:721.

40. Francis P. Weisenburger, "The Middle Western Antecedents of Woodrow Wilson," *Mississippi Valley Historical Review* 23 (1936), 375–76; Cayton, *Frontier Republic*, 132; Ratcliffe, *Party Spirit in a Frontier Republic*, 185, 212, 215; Utter, *The Frontier State*, 300–305.

41. *Niles' Weekly Register* 17 (30 October 1819), 149–53; Charles Hammond to Ethan Allen Brown, 4 November 1819, Hammond Papers, OSL.

42. Ibid.

43. Ibid.

44. Ibid.

45. Ibid.

46. Ibid.

47. Ibid.

48. Ibid.

49. Ibid. (December 1819), 227–29.

50. Ibid. (January 1820), 361.

51. Ibid., 294–96.

52. Charles Hammond, Jr., to John C. Wright, 27 October 1819, Hammond Papers, OSL. For more on this problem, see John C. Wright to Elisha

Whittlesey, 5 June 1823, Whittlesey Papers, Western Reserve Historical Society (WRHS).

53. *Niles' Weekly Register* 15 (17 October 1818), 1.

54. Ibid., 17 (26 February 1820), 449–50.

55. Ibid., 19 (7 October 1820), 82–84; *Cleveland Herald*, 26 September 1820; *The Supporter* (Chillicothe), 26 September 1820.

56. The report is reprinted in *Annals of Congress*, 16:2, Appendix, 1685–1714. The citations that follow are from this version because it is the most accessible. The original version may be found in *Journal of the House of Representatives of the State of Ohio: Nineteenth General Assembly* (Columbus, Ohio, 1820), 99–132; an edited version is also to be found in Ames (ed.), *State Documents on Federal Relations*, 94–101.

57. *Annals of Congress*, 16:1, 1694, 1714.

58. Ibid., 1696.

59. Ibid., 1696–97.

60. Ibid., 1697.

61. Ibid., 1702.

62. Ibid., 1698.

63. Ibid., 1707–8.

64. Ibid., 1704, 1708.

65. Ibid., 1712–13.

66. Ibid., 1714.

67. Chase, *Statutes*, 2:1185–86, 1198–99.

68. Henry Clay to Langdon Cheves, 15 February 1821, in Hopkins (ed.), *Papers of Henry Clay*, 3:41.

69. "United States Circuit Court, Ohio, Transcript of the Case, 1819–1821 of the Bank of the United States vs. Ralph Osborn," Ohio Historical Center Library, Columbus, Ohio.

70. Bogart, "Taxation of the Second Bank of the United States by Ohio," 325; Aiello, "Ohio's War upon the Bank of the United States," 102–3; Franz, "Ohio v. the Bank," 126–27.

CHAPTER 7

1. Donald Roper, *Mr. Justice Thompson and the Constitution* (New York, 1987); Gerald T. Dunne, "Smith Thompson," in Leon Friedman and Fred L. Israel (eds.), *The Justices of the United States Supreme Court*, 5 vols. (New York, 1969–1980), 1:475–92; David B. Roe and Russell K. Osgood, "United States Supreme Court: February Term 1824," *Yale Law Journal* 84 (1974–1975), 770–808.

2. *Osborn et al. v. Bank of the United States* (1824), 9 Wheaton 765.

3. Ibid., 766.

4. Ibid., 766–67.

5. Ibid., 775.

6. Ibid., 775–76.

7. Ibid., 776–77.

8. Ibid., 777–82.

9. Ibid., 785.

10. Ibid., 786–87.

11. Ibid., 787.

12. Ibid.

13. Ibid., 788.

14. Ibid.

15. Ibid.

16. Ibid., 788–89.

17. Ibid., 794–95.

18. Ibid., 795–96. On Clay's role, see also Maurice G. Baxter, *Henry Clay: The Lawyer* (Lexington, Ky., 2000), 59–70.

19. 9 Wheaton 795–96.

20. Ibid., 796–97.

21. Ibid., 798–800.

22. Ibid., 804. See also Charles Hammond to Elisha Whittlesey, 2 February 1824, Whittlesey Collection, WRHS.

23. 9 Wheaton 805–6.

24. Ibid., 806–9.

25. Ibid., 810–11.

26. Ibid.

27. Ibid., 811.

28. Ibid., 815.

29. Ibid., 816.

30. Ibid., 817.

31. Ibid., 818.

32. Ibid., 828–46.

33. Ibid., 847–59.

34. Charles Hammond, *State of the Case and Argument from the Appellants in the Case of the United States, versus the Auditor for and Treasurer of the State of Ohio in the Supreme Court of the United States* (Cincinnati, Ohio, 1823); John Marshall to Charles Hammond, 28 December 1823, in Hobson (ed.), *The Papers of John Marshall*, 9:317.

35. *Osborn et al. v. Bank of the United States* (1824), 9 Wheaton 868. One scholar has described the decision as revealing "Marshall at his most dogmatic and impervious to argument." Currie, *The Constitution in the Supreme Court, 1789–1888* (Chicago, 1985), 107.

36. 9 Wheaton 871.

37. Ibid., 872–74.

38. Ibid., 896. The jurisdiction issue is examined at length in G. Edward White (with Gerald Gunther), *The Marshall Court and Cultural Change, 1815–1835* (New York, 1988), 486–87, 528–29, 531–32, 534–35. See also G. Edward White, "Recovering Conterminous Power Theory: The Lost Dimension of Marshall Court Sovereignty Cases," in Maeva Marcus (ed.), *Origins of the Federal Judiciary: Essays on the Judiciary Act of 1789* (New York, 1992), 66–105.

39. Henry Clay to Langdon Cheves, 8 September 1821, in Hopkins (ed.), *Papers of Henry Clay*, 3:111–13.

40. *Journal of the House of Representatives of the State of Ohio: Nineteenth General Assembly* (Columbus, Ohio, 1820), 336–43.

41. *Niles' Weekly Register* 21 (22 February 1822), 404.

42. Elisha Whittlesey to Ethan A. Brown, 25 February 1822, Brown Papers, OSL; Ethan A. Brown to General A. Dayton, 4 February 1821, ibid.

43. Charles Hammond to J. C. Wright, 26 March 1824, Hammond Papers, OSL.

44. J. C. Wright to Charles Hammond, 22 March 1824, ibid.

45. *Chisholm v. Georgia* (1793), 2 Dallas 419; *Fletcher v. Peck* (1810), 6 Cranch 129.

46. Warren, *The Supreme Court in United States History*, 1:391–92.

47. William Jones to Jonathan Roberts, 23 January 1818, Roberts Papers, HSP.

48. *Niles' Weekly Register* 14 (7 March 1818), 23; Warren, *The Supreme Court in United States History*, 1:391–92; Currie, *The Constitution in the Supreme Court, 1789–1888*, 85–88.

49. *Georgia Journal* (Milledgeville), 4 May 1819.

50. Letter of "Editor of the *Savannah Republic*" in *American Beacon* (Norfolk, Va.), 16 December 1819.

51. *Pennsylvania Archives*, 4th ser. (Harrisburg, 1901–1902), 4:445.

52. *Journal of the Senate of the State of Georgia in 1821* (Milledgeville, Ga.), 99–100; *Niles' Weekly Register* 21 (5 January 1822), 296.

53. Ulrich B. Phillips, *Georgia and State Rights* (Washington, D.C., 1902), chapter 4.

54. Milton Heath, *Constructive Liberalism: The Role of the State in Economic Development in Georgia to 1860* (Cambridge, 1954), 174–75, 180.

55. *Journal of the Senate of the State of Georgia in 1820* (Milledgeville, Ga.), 24–25; William C. Dawson (ed.), *Compilation of the Laws of the State of Georgia . . . 1819 to 1829* (Milledgeville, Ga., 1831), 70–71.

56. Thomas Payne Govan, *Banking and the Credit System in Georgia, 1810–1860* (New York, 1978), 50–75; Govan, "Banking and the Credit System in Georgia, 1810–1860," *Journal of Southern History* 4 (1938), 164–84; Heath, *Constructive Liberalism*, 180–83.

57. *The Bank of the United States v. the Planters Bank of Georgia* (1824), 9 Wheaton 910–14; Warren, *The Supreme Court in United States History*, 1:629–30.

58. 9 Wheaton 904–7.

59. Ibid., 907–8.

60. Dawson (ed.), *Compilation of the Laws of the State of Georgia*, 71.

CHAPTER 8

1. John Haywood to James A. Cameron, 1 October 1819, and James Cameron to John Haywood, 6 October 1819, North Carolina General Assembly, Session Records, November–December 1819, Miscellaneous Correspondence, North Carolina State Archives. See also William H. Crawford to William Jones, 21 April 1818, Cannaroe Collection, HSP.

2. A. D. Murphey to William Polk, 24 July 1821, in William H. Hoyt (ed.), *The Papers of Archibald D. Murphey*, 2 vols. (Raleigh, N.C., 1914), 1:217.

3. *Journal of the North Carolina Senate*: 18 December 1820 (Raleigh, N.C., 1821), 55–56.

4. *Journal of the North Carolina Senate*: 18 December 1821 (Raleigh, N.C., 1822), 56.

5. Steven Russell, "Inconvertible Banking in Early Nineteenth Century North Carolina" (Ph.D. diss., University of Minnesota, 1995), 127–36; Harry L. Watson, *Jacksonian Politics and Community Conflict: The Emergence of the Second American Party System in Cumberland County, North Carolina* (Baton Rouge, La., 1981).

6. Russell J. Ferguson, *Early Western Pennsylvania Politics* (Pittsburgh, Pa., 1938), 231–59; James A. Kehl, *Ill Feeling in the Era of Good Feelings: Western Pennsylvania Political Battles, 1815–1825* (Pittsburgh, Pa., 1956), 82–84, 113–14; Kim T. Phillips, "Democrats of the Old School in the Era of Good Feeling," *Pennsylvania Magazine of History and Biography* 95

(1971), 363–82; Kim Tousley Phillips, *William Duane, Radical Journalist in the Age of Jefferson* (New York, 1989), 443–92; Jamie Karmel, "The Market Moment: Banking and Politics in Jeffersonian Pennsylvania, 1810–1815," *Pennsylvania History* 70 (2003), 55–80; Robert M. Blackson, "Pennsylvania Banks and the Panic of 1819: A Reinterpretation," *Journal of the Early Republic* 9 (1989), 335–58; J. David Lehman, "Explaining Hard Times: Political Economy and the Panic of 1819 in Philadelphia" (Ph.D. diss., University of California, Los Angeles, 1992), 204–49; "Memorandum" by William Jones, 30 May 1818, Jones Papers, HSP.

7. *Niles' Weekly Register* 14 (21 March 1818), 64.

8. *Journal of the House of Representatives of Pennsylvania* (Harrisburg, Pa., 1818), 58 (7 December 1818), 321 (3 March 1819).

9. Ibid., 691–92 (23 March 1819), 767 (29 March 1819); *Pennsylvania Archives*, 5:206–10, 234–37, 276–77, 410–11.

10. "Bank of the United States, No. X," *Franklin Gazette* (Philadelphia), 15 March 1819; see also *Pittsburgh Gazette*, 30 March 1819.

11. Joseph Hamilton to Thomas Wilson, 7 September 1818, Russ. KY Letter B, Bank of Kentucky Correspondence, Kentucky Department of Archives and History.

12. Henry Clay to William Jones, 3 March 1818, in Hopkins (ed.), *Papers of Henry Clay*, 2:442; Henry Clay to Edmund W. Rootes, 24 November 1818, in ibid., 604–5; Dale M. Royalty, "Banking, Politics, and the Commonwealth of Kentucky, 1800–1825" (Ph.D. diss., University of Kentucky, 1972), 218–31.

13. *The Commonwealth v. Morrison & e. converso*, 9 Kentucky Reports (A. K. Marshall, II), 100.

14. Ibid., 100–101. On Rowan, see Stephen W. Fackler, "John Rowan and the Demise of Jeffersonian Republicanism in Kentucky, 1819–1831," *Register: Kentucky Historical Society* 78 (1980), 1–26.

15. *Journal of the Senate of Kentucky, 1819–20* (Frankfort, Ky., 1819), 20–22 (7 December 1819).

16. *The Bank of the United States v. Norton et al.*, 10 Kentucky Reports (A. K. Marshall, III), 422–29; Sandra F. Van Burkleo, "The Power of Banks: The Origins and Significance of Kentucky's Decision to Tax Federal Bankers, 1818–1820," *Journal of the Early Republic* 9 (1989), 457–87.

17. Royalty, "Banking, Politics, and the Commonwealth of Kentucky," 227–28.

18. Worden Pope to James Monroe, 1 March 1819, in Daniel Preston (ed.), *The Papers of James Monroe: A Documentary History of the Presidential Tours of James Monroe, 1817, 1818, 1819* (Westport, Conn., 2000), 556.

19. *Green v. Biddle* (1821), 8 Wheaton 1 (1823); Paul Gates, "Tenants of the Log Cabin," *Mississippi Valley Historical Review* 49 (June 1962), 3–31; Dwight Wiley Jessup, *Reaction and Accommodation: The Supreme Court and Political Conflict, 1809–1835* (New York, 1987), 213–31; Maurice G. Baxter, *Henry Clay: The Lawyer* (Lexington, Ky., 2000), 38–48. The case of *Green v. Biddle* was decided in Virginia's favor, but the decision proved unenforceable, and the Supreme Court eventually reversed itself in *Hawkins v. Barney's Lessee*, 5 Peters 457 (1831).

20. William Jones to E. W. DuVal, 7 March 1819, Jones Papers, HSP.

21. Charles Warren, "Legislative and Judicial Attacks on the Supreme Court of the United States: A History of the Twenty-Fifth Section of the Judiciary Act," *American Law Review* 47 (January–February 1913), 1–34 and 161–89; Charles Warren, *The Supreme Court in United States History*, 2 vols. (Boston, 1926), 1:633–87; Charles G. Haines, *The Role of the Supreme Court in American Government and Politics, 1789–1835* (New York, 1960), 427–535.

22. Thomas Ritchie to Littleton Waller Tazewell, 28 February 1827, Tazewell Papers, Virginia State Library. See also Francis P. Blair to Henry Clay, 3 October 1827, in Hargreaves and Hopkins (eds.), *Papers of Henry Clay*, 6:1106–7; Amos Kendall to Francis P. Blair, 9 January 1829, Blair-Lee Papers, Princeton University Library.

23. Ellis, *The Union at Risk: Jacksonian Democracy, States' Rights and the Nullification Crisis* (New York, 1987), 13–40, 48–51, 186–87.

24. Andrew Jackson to James K. Polk, 23 December 1833, in John Spencer Bassett (ed.), *Correspondence of Andrew Jackson*, 7 vols. (Washington, D.C., 1926–1935).

25. Amos Kendall to Francis Preston Blair, 22 November 1829, Blair-Lee Papers, Princeton University Library; Andrew Jackson to John Overton, 8 June 1829, Jacob M. Dickinson Papers, Tennessee State Library.

26. Samuel Ingham to Andrew Jackson, 26, 27 November 1829, in Bassett (ed.), *Correspondence of Andrew Jackson*, 4:92–94; John Berrien to Andrew Jackson, 27 November 1829, in ibid., 94–95; James A. Hamilton, *Reminiscences of Men and Events* (New York, 1869), 150; William B. Lewis to James Hamilton, 1 January 1832, in ibid., 235–36; William B. Lewis to Nicholas Biddle, 16 October 1829, Biddle Papers, LC.

27. "First Annual Address," 8 December 1829, in Richardson (ed.), *Messages and Papers of the Presidents*, 2:462; Hamilton, *Reminiscences*, 149–50.

28. "Biddle's Memorandum of a Conversation with Andrew Jackson," N. D. Biddle Papers, LC; "Opinion on Bank" [January 1832], in Bassett (ed.), *Correspondence of Andrew Jackson*, 4:289–90.

29. Andrew Jackson to Moses Dawson, 17 July 1830, in Bassett (ed.), *Correspondence of Andrew Jackson*, 4:161–62; Andrew Jackson to James A. Hamilton, 19 December, 3 June 1830, in Hamilton, *Reminiscences*, 151–52, 167–68; Amos Kendall to Francis P. Blair, 22 November 1829, Blair-Lee Papers, Princeton University Library; Felix Grundy to Andrew Jackson, 22 October 1829, in Bassett (ed.), *Correspondence of Andrew Jackson*, 4:83; Samuel Ingham to Andrew Jackson, 26, 27 November 1829, in ibid., 92–94.

30. "Second Annual Message," 6 December 1830, in Richardson (ed.), *Messages and Papers of the Presidents*, 2:528–29.

31. Ibid., 529.

32. Nicholas Biddle to R. M. Gobbes, 13 December 1831, Biddle Papers, LC; Andrew Jackson to John Randolph, 22 December 1831, in Bassett (ed.), *Correspondence of Andrew Jackson*, 4:387; Andrew Jackson to James A. Hamilton, 12 December 1831, in Hamilton, *Reminiscences*, 234; "Opinion on the Bank" [January 1832], in Bassett (ed.), *Correspondence of Andrew Jackson*, 4:389–90.

33. Thomas Payne Govan, *Nicholas Biddle* (Chicago, 1959), 171–80; Remini, *Andrew Jackson and the Bank War* (New York, 1967), 75–77.

34. "Veto Message," 10 July 1832, in Richardson (ed.), *Messages and Papers of the Presidents*, 2:577, 578.

35. Ibid., 576.

36. Ibid., 581–82.

37. Andrew C. Lenner in his *The Federal Principle in American Politics, 1793–1833* (Lanham, Md., 2001), 193–94, has taken sharp issue with this interpretation of Jackson's relationship with the Supreme Court. In particular, he has singled out my espousal of it in *The Union at Risk*, 39. He argues that I took this passage "entirely out of context," and strongly implies that I purposefully omitted the concluding sentence in which Jackson argues, "the authority of the Supreme Court must not, therefore, be permitted to control the Congress or the Executive when acting in their *legislative capacities but to have only such influence as the force of their reasoning may deserve*" (emphasis added). To begin with, this is absolutely untrue, as

I do include this concluding sentence in my use of Jackson's quote. What I do not do is put on this sentence the stress that Lenner does. Nor do I accept his claim that Jackson "never maintained that the President had a right to ignore the judgments of the Supreme Court simply because he disagreed with them"; Lenner, *The Federal Principle in American Politics*, 194. Lenner provides absolutely no evidence that Jackson, even after he left office, ever fully articulated his views on the relationship of the Supreme Court to the other branches of the government, especially on constitutional issues. As a consequence, Jackson's full views on this question are something of a mystery and in many ways unclear.

To make his case that Jackson really did believe that the president was duty-bound to enforce the decisions of the Supreme Court, Lenner looks at two issues that developed during Jackson's presidency. The first is Jackson's unwillingness to endorse the attempt to repeal section 25 of the Judiciary Act of 1789, which took place early in his first administration. Ibid., 192–93. Here, it is important to point out that Jackson did not actually oppose the measure but simply remained silent. He never indicated a belief that section 25 was either good or necessary. A much more likely explanation for Jackson's silence can be found in the fact that the attempt to repeal section 25 was mainly a nullifier-sponsored measure, and Jackson at this point was purging the nullifiers from his administration: he refused to appoint them to political office; he replaced Duff Green and the *United States Telegraph* as his administration's semi-official representative because of their ties to John C. Calhoun; he openly broke with Calhoun, who was his vice president; and he made clear his belief that a protective tariff was constitutional.

Lenner's second example has to do with the Supreme Court's decision in *Worcester v. Georgia* (1832) where he claims that "the weight of the evidence suggests that Jackson had no intention of challenging the court's authority." Ibid., 190. This also is doubtful. Jackson did nothing during the nine months following the High Court's decision because he was not required to do anything since it had adjourned without having taken any action to actually enforce its decision, like issuing a writ of habeas corpus or a writ of mandamus, which would have required some sort of response on Jackson's part. There were also technical problems since the Judiciary Act of 1789 was flawed in that it had no clear-cut provision requiring a state to officially inform the U.S. Supreme Court what it intended to do in regard to a decision that had been handed down. These issues are well treated in Joseph C. Burke, "The Cherokee

Cases: A Study in Law, Politics, and Morality," *Stanford Law Review* 21 (1969), 500–531; and Hobson (ed.), *The Papers of John Marshall*, 12:150–58. It is for this reason that Jackson referred to *Worcester v. Georgia* as "stillborn" and essentially nonenforceable. Still, the Supreme Court might have tried to issue some kind of writ that would have put Jackson to the test. But this did not occur because the Jackson administration and its loyalists in Georgia, concerned about keeping South Carolina isolated during the nullification crisis, worked out a compromise whereby the imprisoned missionaries agreed to abandon their cause and the Cherokee, accepted a pardon from the governor of Georgia, and agreed to leave the state, thereby leaving the Supreme Court with nothing to do. On this point, see Edwin A. Miles, "After John Marshall's Decision: Worcester v. Georgia and the Nullification Crisis," *Journal of Southern History* 39 (November 1973), 519–44; and Ellis, *The Union at Risk*, 115–20. A similar compromise was arrived at in a boundary dispute between New York and New Jersey, which also might have led to a controversial decision by the Supreme Court and thereby raised enforcement problems. This is well treated in Michael J. Birkner, "The New York–New Jersey Boundary Controversy, John Marshall and the Nullification Crisis," *Journal of the Early Republic* 12 (Summer 1992), 195–212.

If Jackson were inclined to enforce the nationalist decisions of the U.S. Supreme Court in the area of federal-state relations, neither Joseph Story nor John Marshall were aware of it. At the time the High Court handed down its decision in *Worcester v. Georgia*, Story wrote that it

> reversed the decisions of the State Court of Georgia, and declared her laws unconstitutional. . . . Georgia is full of anger and violence. What she will do, it is difficult to say. Probably she will resist the execution of our judgment, and if she does, I do not believe the President will interfere, unless public opinion among the religious of the Eastern and Western and Middle States, should be brought to bear strong upon him. The rumor is, that he has told the Georgians he will do nothing. (Joseph Story to George Ticknor, 8 March 1832, in W. W. Story [ed.], Life and Letters of Joseph Story, 2 vols. [Boston, 1851], 2:83)

This, of course, raises the distinct possibility that the Supreme Court handed down the *Worcester* decision in part to provide ammunition to Jackson's opponents in the forthcoming presidential election of 1832.

Moreover, Story's concerns about what role Jackson would play in the enforcement of the decision were well founded for, in a message to the U.S. Senate on 22 February 1831, the president had made clear he supported the right of the states to extend their laws over the Indians and indicated, "it would not be in the power of the federal government to prevent it." Richardson (ed.), *Messages and Papers of the Presidents*, 2:541.

Jackson's decisive victory in the election of 1832 made it clear that a real confrontation between the president and the High Court would probably occur when the latter reconvened in January 1833. For his part, Marshall, writing before the matter was resolved, was extremely concerned about what was likely to happen. He wrote, "I look with infinite apprehension at the approaching term of the Supreme Court. It will bring with it much that is peculiarly unpleasant." John Marshall to Richard Peters, 3 December 1832, in Hobson (ed.), *The Papers of John Marshall*, 12:242.

Lenner's argument attempts to bring clarity to an issue that is simply unclear. We do not know exactly what role Jackson believed the U.S. Supreme Court had to play in a federal system of government because he never fully articulated it or acted on it. All we do know is that he rejected the High Court's decision in *McCulloch v. Maryland* on strong constitutional grounds and that he was a strong advocate of states' rights while the Marshall Court was much more inclined to be a proponent of nationalism, although it tended to move away from this position somewhat in the late 1820s and 1830s. Most of Jackson's positions on issues involving the High Court, with the exception of his bank veto message, tended to be politically motivated. He probably also had a high personal regard for Marshall, who was a fellow member of the revolutionary generation and whom, despite the fact that they disagreed, he respected. Jean Edward Smith, *John Marshall: Definer of a Nation* (New York, 1996), 524. Entangled in one controversy after another during his two administrations, Jackson was not inclined to go out of his way to get into a fight with the U.S. Supreme Court or with Marshall. He preferred instead to wait out Marshall and the Supreme Court; he appointed five justices, which eventually brought the Court under Jackson's control.

38. Ibid., 585, 586–89.
39. Ibid., 590.
40. Ibid.
41. Ralph C. H. Catterall, *The Second Bank of the United States* (Chicago, 1902), 359–75; Smith, *Economic Aspects of the Second Bank of the United*

States, 178–230; Bray Hammond, *Banks and Politics in America from the Revolution to the Civil War* (Princeton, N.J., 1957), 500–548.

42. Quote in Walter F. Murphy et al., *American Constitutional Interpretation* (New York, 1986), 425; Robert G. McCloskey *The American Supreme Court*, revised by Sanford Levinson (Chicago, 1994), 43–45.

43. Quoted in Merrill Jensen, *The Articles of Confederation: An Interpretation of the Social-Constitutional History of the American Revolution* (Madison, Wis., 1940), 245.

INDEX